ADVANCE PRAISE FOR

The Bottom-Up Revolution:

MASTERING THE EMERGING WORLD

OF CONNECTIVITY

"Kall's well-researched book integrates knowledge from philosophy to economics and ecology. He shows us how, all over the world and across many fields of endeavor, we humans are organizing new and rewarding ways of acting for the common good. His book is both idealistic and realistic and gives us a vision of what we all most need—hope for the future."

—MARY PIPHER, PSYCHOLOGIST, AND #1 *NEW YORK TIMES* BEST-SELLING AUTHOR OF *REVIVING OPHELIA* AND *WRITING TO CHANGE THE WORLD*

"The bottom-up revolution is fueling tremendous change in politics, commerce, and how people relate to each other. Rob Kall's book *The Bottom-Up Revolution* provides a powerful guide to how organizations can understand and tap bottom-up's power."

—CRAIG NEWMARK, FOUNDER OF CRAIGSLIST

"At 350.org we've always wanted to work from the bottom up, and it's good to see people assembling a theoretical framework for understanding this decentralized approach!"

—BILL MCKIBBEN, FOUNDER 350.ORG, AUTHOR OF *THE END OF NATURE*

"Putting real power into the hands of voters and consumers has made bottom-up approaches massively disruptive for politics and brands. It's the present and future of politics and business. Rob Kall pulls together the wisdom and experience of some of the leading thinkers who have brought the bottom-up revolution to full bloom."

—JOE TRIPPI, PIONEERING INTERNET CAMPAIGN MANAGER OF HOWARD DEAN, DIGITAL CAMPAIGN CONSULTANT

"Rob Kall shows us that the high-tech information revolution set the stage for a political and social evolution, the connectivity of which has the capacity to transform everything, everywhere. We have only to say 'yes' to tap [into] the power of this interconnection, participating in it from where we stand."

—DENNIS KUCINICH, FORMER U.S. REPRESENTATIVE (D-OH) AND 2004 AND 2008 DEMOCRATIC PRESIDENTIAL PRIMARY CANDIDATE

"Just as *The Tipping Point* provides an explanation for big changes, Rob Kall offers a unified explanation for the magic behind the success of the biggest tech companies, the Arab Spring, Occupy, and the social media revolution... An important, big picture, visionary approach weaving together technology, economics, evolution, science, and personal relationships—even happiness— to describe a wave of change as significant as the invention of the printing press that is well under way—a wave that could rescue the planet from the top-down system that afflicts the planet."

—THOM HARTMANN, HOST OF NATIONALLY SYNDICATED RADIO SHOW, *THE THOM HARTMANN PROGRAM*, SINCE 2003 AND A NIGHTLY TELEVISION SHOW, *THE BIG PICTURE*, SINCE 2008

"Rob Kall's book offers valuable ways of seeing and powerful tools for enabling new power and connectivity to work to change the hope and promise for the future."

—JEREMY HEIMANS, CEO & CO-FOUNDER OF PURPOSE AND CO-AUTHOR OF *NEW POWER*

"We're at a paradigm-shift moment in history, where we will look back at it and realize that a particular model of how we govern our affairs together became outdated. Kall offers great alternatives and solutions that are not found in conventional governing models."

—CARNE ROSS, FORMER BRITISH DIPLOMAT, STRATEGY COORDINATOR FOR THE UN, AND AUTHOR OF THE BOOK, *THE LEADERLESS REVOLUTION*

"Ever growing inequality and intense and growing political distortions have radically aggravated the top-down imbalance of power, undermining democracy. Rob Kall's book is a guide to taking back humanity's shared legacy of shared responsibility. A stimulating read and an important contribution!"

—GAR ALPEROVITZ, AUTHOR OF *WHAT THEN MUST WE DO? STRAIGHT TALK ABOUT THE NEXT AMERICAN REVOLUTION*

"Rob Kall is a social media force of nature. Accessible, insightful, and forward thinking. *The Bottom-Up Revolution* provides the kind of cutting-edge and savvy thinking that will move anyone's business forward at an accelerating pace. Highly recommended."

—JONATHAN MABERRY, *NEW YORK TIMES* BEST-SELLING AUTHOR, EDITOR, AND LECTURER

"Bringing Rob Kall in as a consultant on making my business and its website more bottom-up was incredibly valuable. Rob's out-of-the-box member registration system suggestions led to a multi-leveled engagement process designed to maximally connect clients with the company, which took the company and the website to the next level. Rob's coaching in bottom-up thinking played a strong role in enabling me to sell my company for over a million dollars."

"Rob Kall's writings on the 'bottom-up' revolution have real potential to show people that they can hold power accountable and improve justice. A book on this subject could help to repair the economic, legal, social, and political fabric of the United States."

"Rob Kall's *The Bottom-Up Revolution* is a revaluation of values, not the empty mouthing of the word 'democracy' that is so common, but the application of belief in popular wisdom to every aspect of life. Actually believing that the views of more people is better, means a new way of thinking about the world that is democratic, feminist, localist, populist, and radically richer than the elitist perspectives that are more common even in the parts of the world that shout the word 'democracy' the most. Here we come to understand both the power of small groups and the upsides to internet crowd sourcing, the potential of nonviolent movements and ways in which the past has not been what we supposed. Don't just read this book; get lots of people to read and talk about it."

"Rob's bottom-up consulting for Thought Technology over the years to help us incorporate bottom-up thinking in our business and product development has been very valuable. It is a truly disruptive technique, well worth considering, which is well explained in his book."

—HAL MYERS, PHD, PRESIDENT, THOUGHT TECHNOLOGY, LTD., MEMBER OF THE BOARD OF DIRECTORS FOR THE TEN TO THE NINTH FOUNDATION (FORMERLY SINGULARITY UNIVERSITY)

"Rob Kall is tapping in, exploring, assessing, and clarifying this important new way of thinking that has been influenced by the civil rights movement; women's movement; and new, more effective ways of doing business. This will be an important book that can make changes in our world."

—DR. LINDA SEGER, AUTHOR OF TWELVE BOOKS, INCLUDING THE BEST-SELLING *MAKING A GOOD SCRIPT GREAT*, *SPIRITUAL STEPS ON THE ROAD TO SUCCESS* AND *THE BETTER WAY TO WIN*

"Rob Kall's book, *The Bottom-Up Revolution*, offers a compelling vision of a way of being in the world, bringing insights from different cultures and fields together while offering concrete steps to make the vision a reality. This is one of the rare books that, once you read it, will change the way you see the world and your relationships."

—HELENA NORBERG-HODGE, AUTHOR OF *ANCIENT FUTURES*, PRODUCER AND CO-DIRECTOR OF THE FILM *THE ECONOMICS OF HAPPINESS*, FOUNDER OF LOCAL FUTURES AND CO-FOUNDER OF THE INTERNATIONAL FORUM ON GLOBALIZATION

"Rob Kall's book is amazing. He's created a real breakthrough, visionary how-to for a sustainable, quality future. Like Saul Alinski's *Rules for Radicals*, this book is destined to become a classic must-read for all those concerned with social, economic, and environmental justice in today's interconnected world. Story shapes the world and our world needs new stories if we are to survive and thrive. The story of the bottom-up evolution and revolution is one that can change individuals, groups, businesses, religions, and governments for the positive as it shows how bottom-up inclusiveness, connectedness, collaboration, empathy, innovation, and freeform creativity can help unleash the great potentials for good inherent in our very nature. If you want to improve things in your world and the world, first read this book, then apply the suggestions. Change is sure to come."

—PAMELA JAYE SMITH, MYTHOLOGIST AND AUTHOR OF *INNERDRIVES*,
POWER OF THE DARK SIDE, SYMBOLS* IMAGES* CODES*
AND AWARD-WINNING WRITER-PRODUCER-DIRECTOR

"Rob Kall has certainly acquired the firsthand experiences and knowledge gained through interviews to deliver some interesting insights about the 'bottom-up' information revolution. Whereas the old 'top-down' systems created stove-pipes and excessive secrecy that blocked information sharing and led to the 'failure to connect the dots' before 9-11, the bottom-up approach should be the main fix. Kall's concept would seem to interface equally well with the founding fathers' idealism in setting forth their democratic theory of governance as with the realism that makes the multi-sourced, bottom-up Wikipedia work. As someone who shares my support of both government and corporate whistleblowing—which is nothing more than encouraging greater horizontal sharing of information, I commend Rob Kall's important work on this topic."

—COLEEN ROWLEY, FORMER FBI SPECIAL AGENT
AND NAMED ONE OF *TIME MAGAZINE'S* "PERSONS OF THE YEAR" IN 2002

"In his new book, Rob Kall's exploration of top-down and bottom-up forces in our culture, our brains, and our planet provides a deep insight into the challenges we face. He offers pathways we can use to create the changes we need to break free of the war economy and build local peace economies."

—JODIE EVANS, CO-FOUNDER OF CODE PINK
AND CHAIR OF THE WOMEN'S MEDIA CENTER

"Humans have spent 99 percent of our developmental time in the wild kingdom, which tutored us in what Rob Kall calls bottom-up values—small, local, interdependent, respectful, egalitarian and decentralized—and which the world desperately needs in order to balance out some of the darker impulses of top-down values. His faith that bottom-up values represent a critical rebalancing act for humanity, if not an outright better mousetrap, is compelling and hard-won, and I offer him a high-five for his courageous inquiry into the deep wisdom inherent in our age-old intimacy with natural rhythms, native intelligences, and interconnectedness."

—GREGG LEVOY, AUTHOR OF *CALLINGS* AND *VITAL SIGNS*

"The book is very well written...very important in this individualized capitalistic illusory world that enslaves us all within its tentacles and forces us to believe that we are atomized and disconnected beings. Indigenous Lakota people end prayers with '*Mitakuye Oyasin*...all my relations...' An ancient African proverb states, 'A person is a person only because of and with others...' This instructive text is very useful for us living in what we are always told is the modern world, because it reconnects us all and reminds us that ultimately, the endless circle of the Universe binds and connects us all and the Earth is Mother to us with no hierarchy...the ones at the bottom matter the most...like the ants who build mounds and hills, all working in unison and harmony...the book teaches that we were created for community and our destiny is organic community...anything else is doomed..."

—JULIAN KUNNIE, PROFESSOR OF RELIGIOUS STUDIES/CLASSICS AT THE UNIVERSITY OF ARIZONA AND AUTHOR OF *THE COST OF GLOBALIZATION: DANGERS TO THE EARTH AND ITS PEOPLE*

"Rob explores the difference between a natural, organic, bottom-up connection consciousness and our corporately imposed top-down hierarchical collective consciousness. What Rob is speaking about is the difference between an artificial and ultimately stagnate way of organizing the world and a natural, organic growth, which starts with a seed, sends downs roots and sends up shoots which blossom. By returning to a Nature-based theory of connection, the Bottom-Up revolution brings us back into alignment with Earth's laws, returning humanity to its place in creation. Like a good gardener, Rob works into the soil of his thesis different voices that exemplify how this Bottom-Up revolution is expanding in politics, business, religion, personal self-awareness and story. And he places technology where it belongs—as a tool to further our connection consciousness, not an end in itself. The bottom-up revolution is about democracy finally living up to its original ideals, where we the people decide what we need from our society."

—CATHY PAGANO, AUTHOR OF *WISDOM'S DAUGHTERS: HOW WOMEN CAN CHANGE THE WORLD*

"In this book, Rob Kall is fueling a discussion that is long overdue, one that can perhaps shake us out of our current herd mentality, back to true community and intertwined purpose. His bottom-up discourse may serve to turn us all upside down just long enough to view our current politic from a different perspective."

—DR. MARI K. SWINGLE, AUTHOR OF *I-MINDS: HOW CELL PHONES, COMPUTERS, GAMING, AND SOCIAL MEDIA ARE CHANGING OUR BRAINS, OUR BEHAVIOR, AND THE EVOLUTION OF OUR SPECIES*

"Yes, the Internet can be used for something other than extracting value and data from human beings. Rob Kall is here to show us how to leverage the power of networks to actually network."

—DOUGLAS RUSHKOFF, DIGITAL THOUGHT LEADER, AUTHOR OF *PRESENT SHOCK*

"Rob Kall's book *The Bottom-Up Revolution* is both a welcomed manifesto and a guide for rethinking the power of human agency, understanding the connections that both make us human and legitimate human planetary relations. Moreover it is a powerful call for providing the ideas, social practices, and relations that make human connections possible, enable them to work together from the bottom up, and to transform such connections into a powerful movement in which people take control of their lives and create a better future for everyone."

—**HENRY GIROUX**, DIRECTOR OF THE MCMASTER CENTRE FOR RESEARCH IN THE PUBLIC INTEREST, AUTHOR OF *ZOMBIE POLITICS AND CULTURE IN THE AGE OF CASINO CAPITALISM, AMERICA'S EDUCATION DEFICIT* AND *THE WAR ON YOUTH*, AND DOZENS MORE.

"*The Bottom-Up Revolution* is a direct and logical look at how we live our lives, conduct our business, manage our societies, and, most importantly, communicate with each other. Author Rob Kall explains it all in plain English. But don't let the readability of this book fool you into thinking that it's not important. Kall cuts to the heart of the most critical issues in communication today. This book is as important as game theory. And people will take notice."

—**JOHN KIRIAKOU**, FORMER CIA OFFICER AND AUTHOR OF *THE RELUCTANT SPY* AND *DOING TIME LIKE A SPY*

"Human survival depends on learning to organize the way all successful living communities organize as they adapt to ever changing local conditions—from the *Bottom-Up*. A timely contribution to confronting the transformation imperative confronting humanity."

—**DAVID KORTEN**, AUTHOR OF *WHEN CORPORATIONS RULE THE WORLD, THE GREAT TURNIN*, AND *CHANGE THE STORY, CHANGE THE FUTURE*

"Rob Kall's book weaves together the many strands of new thinking about how to use decentralized, non-hierarchical approaches to solve crucial social and economic problems. *The Bottom-Up Revolution* presents a tapestry of ideas and examples that can inspire and guide readers."

—PETER PLASTRIK, CO-AUTHOR OF *CONNECTING TO CHANGE THE WORLD: HARNESSING THE POWER OF NETWORKS FOR SOCIAL IMPACT*

"In his groundbreaking new book *The Bottom Up Revolution: Mastering the Emerging World of Connectivity*, Rob Kall invites and eases us into in a much-needed meta-level shift—a truly basic paradigmatic shift from top-down to bottom-up. He capably and imaginatively explores the differences between these ways of approaching life, clearly demonstrating that bottom-up allows us to flourish. His vision and his book are enriched by telling references to interviews which he has engaged in over the years with bottom-up researchers, theorists, activists, and dreamers in a variety of areas. Think about Rob's interviews. Read this revolutionary book. And take one step further into the bottom-up universe yourself. You will not regret it."

—BONNIE BURSTOW, MD, *AUTHOR OF PSYCHIATRY AND THE BUSINESS OF MADNESS AND RADICAL FEMINIST THERAPY*, ASSOCIATE PROFESSOR AT THE UNIVERSITY OF TORONTO

"Rob Kall has been the center of a vast, decentralized conversation for years, letting us hear in interviewees' own words the power of connection in every realm. His new book brings it all together, showing us that the old order is broken and fast being replaced from the bottom up. The old power elite may not know it yet, but millions of us—organizers, artists, thinkers and doers— have gotten the message. So should you, by reading *The Bottom-Up Revolution*."

—ARLENE GOLDBARD, *AUTHOR OF THE CULTURE OF POSSIBILITY: ART, ARTISTS & THE FUTURE*

"Fascinating, eye-opening, and extraordinary, Rob Kall's *The Bottom Up Revolution* explores the emerging paradigm of our age—bottom-up thinking—connecting an enormous range of disciplines and topics from systems, chaos, and complexity theories to the evolving role of technology in our lives. Not merely a cogent exposition of contemporary thinking, however, *Bottom Up* extrapolates from abstract ideas to derive practical, everyday steps we can take to improve our chances of global survival, peace, and prosperity. Following Rob's lead, we can change habits as individuals to deepen our connection with others across the planet."

—WENDELL POTTER, FORMER HEALTH INSURANCE EXECUTIVE, CO-AUTHOR OF *NATION ON THE TAKE: HOW BIG MONEY CORRUPTS OUR DEMOCRACY AND WHAT WE CAN DO ABOUT IT,* AND FOUNDER OF TARBELL.ORG

"Wonderful work! An insightful, integrative adventure into what makes humans flourish. Rob Kall shows us that we know how to do this, that most of human history was about connection and that there are ways to make it happen again. He offers real solutions and practical suggestions for taking back the world for community, connection and well-being—away from hierarchy, exclusion, and destruction. A new handbook for the necessary revolution!"

—DARCIA NARVAEZ, PROFESSOR OF PSYCHOLOGY, NOTRE DAME, UNIVERSITY, AUTHOR OF *NEUROBIOLOGY AND THE DEVELOPMENT OF HUMAN MORALITY: EVOLUTION, CULTURE AND WISDOM*

"Rob Kall's *The Bottom-Up Revolution* takes a very holistic view of bottom-up thinking and action, from changes in our psychology to our systems of work, living and governance. As someone who's been working to make bottom-up economics a reality for over 30 years, this book reinforces the need for and potential of redirecting our priorities—and resources—from the few at the top to the many at the bottom."

—ANTHONY FLACCAVENTO, AUTHOR OF *BUILDING A HEALTHY ECONOMY FROM THE BOTTOM UP*

"There's no dispute that we now live in a hyper-connected, globalized world—but plenty of argument over the type of globalization that's best for our collective future. In this timely work, Rob Kall makes a persuasive case for 'trickle-up' globalization from below and that the truest, best, and most long-lasting fundamental change always comes from the bottom up. Read this book—then act on it!"

—RORY O'CONNOR, AWARD-WINNING FILMMAKER AND AUTHOR OF *FRIENDS, FOLLOWERS, AND THE FUTURE: HOW SOCIAL MEDIA ARE CHANGING POLITICS, THREATENING BIG BRANDS, AND KILLING TRADITIONAL MEDIA*

"You have something special and important here. Somehow you manage to teach and suggest and introduce the reader to concepts in a way that feels inclusive. Like, we're thinking about it together. Partly it might be because the subject, bottom-up, is innately understood by all of us and so it feels like you're stirring up stuff we already know. But also I think it's because you truly are practiced at connection consciousness and so it's natural for you (I'm guessing) to write about it with a desire to include us. As a reader I was learning more because it feels like you're inviting me to think with you."

—TSARA SHELTON, AUTHOR

"The world is seemingly full of disconnected crises, but Rob Kall begs to differ. An exceptional pattern thinker, he connects a range of contemporary challenges through a framework of bottom-up solutions in a world dominated by top-down thinking. Mining extensive interviews with thought leaders and exploring an eclectic mix of leading-edge ideas, *The Bottom-Up Revolution* describes a variety of latent and emergent characteristics of an evolutionary paradigm shift that's changing the world. Whether your focus is in business, leadership, activism, or organizations, Kall offers a practical conceptual map and toolset to engage the planetary evolution taking place all around us. If you want to make a difference and need inspiration for how to participate in this global transformation, there is plenty in this book to draw from."

—ANTONIO LOPEZ, AUTHOR OF *THE MEDIA ECOSYSTEM*

"Stressed? Oppressed? Isolated? Kall's *The Bottom-Up Revolution* offers a lifeline for connecting with yourself, with others, and with your whole community or organization so that everyone thrives. He offers compelling science, stories, and insights from business, government, the arts, and more to make visible an unabashedly hopeful bottom-up revolution towards cooperation, compassion, and meaning. Join him."

"In *The Bottom-Up Revolution,* Rob Kall offers a blueprint for human surviving and thriving that everyone can follow. Using personal stories from his many famous contacts (from Capra to Quinn), he shows how in every aspect of life we can reconnect with that which is in our DNA by replacing our artificial and oppressive hierarchical priorities via a return to a consciousness based on the kind of egalitarian relationships that we honored for most of human history."

"Rob Kall's book, *The Bottom-Up Revolution* has really caused me to relook and reframe many of my thoughts on where our connectedness using social media tools like LinkedIn is headed, and not just for career trajectory but for life. If you are looking for a new perspective on our sometimes zany digital world we live in, this book will keep you reading and may ultimately revise but for sure challenge your current paradigm."

"Rob Kall's must-read book offers a VIP look at today's many 'connection revolutions,' plus key suggestions for bottom-up leadership in each one."

"Rob Kall gives readers an important wake up call to the bottom-up power that they have to protect their rights, powers, and freedoms. His advice applies to all aspects of life, including politics, economics, journalism, entertainment, and psychology and wellness. Kall's book explains the differences between the top-down leadership approach of dominating, fear based, disconnected authoritarianism and the bottom-up connection consciousness that emphasizes values, justice, fairness, equity, and kindness. This book helps readers see the whole elephant as opposed to the disconnected parts. Kall gives great advice as to intensifying, expanding, prolonging, and deepening connections.

With his professional background, Rob Kall is the perfect person to write this book. This is a very well-researched book that includes dozens of insightful interviews with top-notch experts. Kall shows how bottom-up small acts can produce massive results. He emphasizes that since we can't avoid this emerging bottom-up connection revolution, we need to learn how to navigate and embrace it. This bottom-up leadership will result in power to the people. This is a fascinating and insightful book, especially in this new era of digital hunting and gathering."

"Rob Kall already had a serious understanding of the internet and its implications for media and democracy while I was still figuring out how to use email. Some see internet connectivity solely as a means toward power and profit; Rob's book, *The Bottom-Up Revolution*, sees and offers it as a vehicle for bettering society and ourselves."

"In *The Bottom-Up Revolution*, Rob Kall offers important insights on why our society is in such disarray and what we must do to change it. He demonstrates how 'top down' thinking is what has produced our current mess, and how bottom-up thinking is much more efficient for solving problems and producing change. Rob shows how lasting change must come from the people themselves and not from the leaders. This was as true in the days of the Magna Carta as it was for the Bill of Rights as it was for the Union movement that first gave workers' rights and protection in this country, as it is today. Indigenous elders have told me, 'if you want to change the world, start talking and keep talking.' Rob is doing this with this book and with his OpEdNews, and he is making a difference. I recommend this book to all who wish to see lasting, human-friendly, compassionate change that will sustain humanity is this crazy world of today."

—**LEWIS MEHL-MADRONA, MD**, AUTHOR OF THE COYOTE TRILOGY THAT DISCUSSES HEALING PRACTICES FROM LAKOTA, CHEROKEE, AND CREE TRADITIONS AND HOW THEY INTERSECT WITH CONVENTIONAL MEDICINE

"We are in the midst of a profound change of paradigms: from seeing the world as a machine to understanding it as a network. Rob Kall has interviewed many of the leaders, both thinkers and activists, of this global cultural transformation. In this eminently readable book he weaves their statements, values, and ideas into a coherent and inspiring whole. *The Bottom-Up Revolution* is a joy to read!"

—**FRITJOF CAPRA**, AUTHOR OF *THE WEB OF LIFE* AND *THE HIDDEN CONNECTIONS*, CO-AUTHOR OF *THE SYSTEMS VIEW OF LIFE*

"One of the primary means of human communication, internal and external, is storytelling. Here, in *The Bottom-Up Revolution*, Rob Kall is challenging humanity to tell itself a new story, one designed to free us from hierarchicalism to a more egalitarian, interconnected web of meaning."

—**STEVEN BARNES**, TELEVISION WRITER (*TWILIGHT ZONE, OUTER LIMITS, STARGATE*) AND AUTHOR OF *LION'S BLOOD*

"Rob Kall's book points the way to a more caring and connected world. This stimulating book combines realistic facts with idealistic optimism at a time when both are so urgently needed."

"Kall's *The Bottom-Up Revolution* explores refreshing yet timeless ways of seeing and ways of thinking about economics, knowledge and wisdom. He presents his message, that decentralized, local and small are both good and healthy in business and economics, in a model that makes sense and offers practical solutions."

"The most effective ways to create a more inclusive, fair-for-all future will be from the bottom up. Rob Kall's book lays out how that would look with a hopeful, pragmatic vision that will change the way you see the world."

THE BOTTOM-UP REVOLUTION

MASTERING THE EMERGING WORLD OF CONNECTIVITY

ROB KALL

BEAUFORT BOOKS

Library of Congress Cataloging-in-Publication Data
Names: Kall, Rob (Robert Alan), author.
Title: The bottom-up revolution : mastering the emerging world of
  connectivity / Rob Kall.
Description: First edition. | New York, NY : Beaufort Books, [2019] |
  Identifiers: LCCN 2019003830 (print) | LCCN 2019006157 (ebook) | ISBN
  9780825308055 (e-book) | ISBN 9780825308956 (pbk. : alk. paper)
Subjects: LCSH: Organizational sociology. | Social interaction. | Social
  stratification. | Interpersonal relations.
Classification: LCC HM786 (ebook) | LCC HM786 .K3638 2018 (print) | DDC
  302.3/5--dc23

LC record available at lccn.loc.gov/2019003830

For inquiries about volume orders, please contact:
Beaufort Books
27 West 20th Street, Suite 1102
New York, NY 10011
sales@beaufortbooks.com

Published in the United States by Beaufort Books
www.beaufortbooks.com

Distributed by Midpoint Trade Books,
a division of Independent Publishers Group
www.midpointtrade.com
www.ipgbook.com

Book designed by Mark Karis

Printed in the United States of America

CONTENTS

Bottom-Up

MASTERING THE EMERGING WORLD

OF CONNECTIVITY

From little acorns, the saying goes, grow big trees. It's that way for pretty much everything in organic systems: bottom-up is the way of nature. Plants grow from seeds, mushrooms from spores, animals from egg and sperm, and even a nasty viral or bacterial infection starts with just one or a few individual bugs. Even seemingly top-down things, like a colony of ants or termites all "serving" the queen turns out to grow from the bottom up, from the queen producing the first helper insects.

Rob Kall has brilliantly taken a variation on this basic concept of nature and applied it to a whole range of things, particularly to social and political systems. It's a stark contrast to the most widely seen sort of history we learn through our school years, which is that "history" is the story of the leaders and kings or queens. The reality is that without bottom-up movements, even ones that are ultimately destructive (think Germany, Italy, and Spain in the 1930s), there wouldn't be most "leaders."

Rob introduces us to an entirely new way of looking at a broad range of disciplines, and even cross-disciplinary strategies, studies, and techniques. It all begins from the beginning, from the bottom up.

With this new set of roadmaps and insights, you'll find yourself taking the core concepts in this book multiple steps forward, from ways that bottom-up thinking and understanding can positively affect your own life to ways we can transform governance and even business structures.

Additionally, you'll get a clearer picture of how—and, more important, *why*—top-down structures (like billionaires funding political campaigns causing the loss of consideration for the needs of average people) are so often so toxic and ultimately self-destructive.

As a serial entrepreneur (I've started 7 successful businesses over the past 50 years, and a few that didn't work out so well) I've learned well—although I couldn't have articulated them as well as Rob did here before reading his book—how this all applies to business. If you want a company, from a few employees to a multinational, to work at optimal efficiency and flexibility, bottom-up is the way to go!

In *The Bottom-Up Revolution*, you'll discover entirely new stories about how the world has always worked, works now, and can work better for all life on our planet. Rob tells these stories with elegance, grace, wit, and beautiful examples.

Get ready for a really fascinating ride into a whole new understanding of, essentially, *everything*. Enjoy!

—THOM HARTMANN, PORTLAND, OREGON 2018

Preface

I believe that understanding the bottom-up connection revolution can help people in many aspects of their lives, and that getting people and organizations to think and behave in bottom-up ways will make the world a better, happier place. You can use the information in this book to become more effective in business, politics, power or diplomacy, if those are your interests. You may also find that by using bottom-up approaches for business or professional reasons, you can make positive changes in your personal life—in the way that you see the world and relate to others.

I believe this book can benefit many categories of readers. Every reader can benefit from reading the Introduction and chapters 1–3. Listed below are categories of readers and the chapters I think will be valuable to them specifically.

THOSE WHO WORK IN BUSINESS: Bottom-up ways of leading, communicating, branding, marketing, managing, connecting, investing, seeing customers, employees, products, services, features and functions, platform development, community are discussed in the Introduction, Chapters 1, 2, 3, 4, 6, 7, 8, and the Epilogue.

SOCIAL MEDIA AND SOFTWARE PROFESSIONALS: There are bottom-up ways to think about using the internet and social media. And it's hard to imagine effectively using, designing, and creating software, websites, and apps without a deep understanding of all aspects of bottom-up and top-down approaches. See the Introduction and Chapters 1, 2, 3, 4, 6, and 8.

THOSE INVOLVED OR INTERESTED IN DIPLOMACY, ACTIVISM, GOVERNMENT, POWER, CIVIC PLANNING, AND ORGANIZING: The bottom-up revolution has shaken the world because it has changed the power-balance, what America's first-ranked expert on diplomacy, Joseph Nye, describes in chapter 5 as power diffusion. Bottom-up changes have led to revolutions, totally changed elections, and the way the processes of activism, diplomacy, and war are thought about and done. You can read about these in the Introduction, Chapters 1, 2, 3, 4, 5, 6, 7, and Epilogue.

THOSE INTERESTED IN SELF-HELP/PERSONAL GROWTH/HAPPINESS: In learning how to see life from the viewpoint of bottom-up, you can find the means to achieve personal success; deeper, more connected relationships; and greater happiness in many dimensions of your life. This is discussed in the Introduction, Chapters 1, 2, 3, 9, and Epilogue.

READERS WHO ARE WRITERS, ARTISTS, AND CREATORS: If you are a creator or engage in the art or business side of creation—writing, music, performance—an understanding of how bottom-up touches your work, business, and life will make a huge difference, perhaps even in how you apply your creativity. The Introduction and Chapters 1, 2, 3, 4, 6, 9 should be of special interest to you.

Acknowledgments

AND THANKS TO THE FOLLOWING:

My children, Elissa, Ben, and Noah, for their support, but also for their help thinking about and discussing ideas this book explores, and reading parts of the book. My four-year-old granddaughter, Nancy, for helping me to see through a child's eyes.

Margo Rush, for reading every chapter of the book as I wrote them and for routinely seeing bottom-up manifestations and sharing them with me.

Meryl Ann Butler and Robert Anschuetz for exceptional help with editing.

Eric Kampmann, my publisher and Megan Trank, my editor at Beaufort Books.

Bill Gladstone, my literary agent, for advice, counsel, and helping to make this book become a reality.

Nancy Sugihara, my editor, for helping to make the book more readable and reader-friendly, while selectively bearing with my use of words that are not in the dictionary.

For feedback, being sounding boards, and offering suggestions: Scott Baker, Joan Brunwasser, Daniel Geery, Thom Hartmann, Stu Herman, Dave Rudick, Josh Mitteldorf, Sheila Samples, Les Toll, Tsara Shelton, Stephen Fox, Melody Laurel, Kevin Tully, Jay Farrington, Paula Sayles, Rhonda Greenberg, Linda Milazzo, Cheryl Biren, Chuck Pennachio, Deena Stryker, Robert Becker, and the many people I cite in the book.

Elmer Green, Siegfried Othmer, Thom Budzynski, Karl Pribram, Thom Hartmann, Jonathan Maberry, Don Lafferty, Don Smith, Ray McGovern, Wendell Potter, Cathy Pagano, Coleen Rowley, Jodie Evans, Don Brown, and Dennis Kucinich.

Special thanks to Micah Sifry and Andrew Rasiej of Personal Democracy Forum for giving me access, through attending their conference, to the best collection of bottom-up thinkers and innovators to be found anywhere.

The editors, writers, commenters and readers at OpEdNews.com, my readers at HuffPost, my *Rob Kall Bottom-Up Radio Show* listeners, and the hundreds of great thinkers, researchers, visionaries, change makers, and creators I've interviewed on my radio show.

Bottom-Up and Top-Down Basics

CONNECTION CONSCIOUSNESS AND

WHY YOU SHOULD CARE ABOUT IT

"We are at the threshold of an era, if we can break through the thinking that basically encapsulates our world right now, where people all over are going to come together, where the impulse toward human unity will actually be realized."

—DENNIS KUCINICH

The biggest, most powerful cultural shift, not in human history, but in human existence, explosively re-emerged about twenty years ago. It has disrupted or even destroyed older industries and business models. It has taken down dictatorships, elected presidents, and has created trillions of dollars in new industries and opportunities. It has virtually altered the brain functioning of people born after 1980, and yet most people are clueless about what it is.

The phenomenon is what I call "the bottom-up connection consciousness revolution."

This deeply affects every person, every relationship, every business and every government. It is changing the way people communicate, the way history is taught and the way power is exercised. It's affecting you, your parents, and your children—all your relationships and communities. You absolutely cannot avoid it, because the long dormant seeds of "bottom-up" culture, evolutionarily baked deeply into our DNA and our neurophysiological systems, are vibrantly reawakening. Craigslist founder Craig Newmark told me, "We are going to see a bottom-up change in tremendous amounts—in politics, commerce, and just people socializing."

For those unfamiliar with bottom-up concepts, here are some common definitions for bottom-up:

The Merriam-Webster dictionary defines "bottom-up" as "progressing upward from the lowest levels (as of a stratified organization or system.)" It defines "top-down" as

"1: controlled, directed, or instituted from the top level" and "2: proceeding by breaking large general aspects (as of a problem) into smaller more detailed constituents: working from the general to the specific."

Dictionary.com defines "bottom-up" as "of, pertaining to, or originating with the common people, nonprofessionals, or the lower ranks of an organization."

But these simple definitions don't go deep enough. Bottom-up and top-down concepts are used in economics, politics, marketing, diplomacy, many fields of science, and in programming and civic development. Just as far-north indigenous peoples use over fifty words for snow, understanding the bottom-up connection revolution requires a comparable, nuanced vocabulary. This book will build your bottom-up vocabulary.

Most people, when they think of bottom-up, cite grassroots activism, crowdsourcing and crowdfunding, the reviews on Amazon and Yelp, the revolts of the Arab Spring, and social media. But we need to understand that a bottom-up culture and a bottom-up organization of people is the way humans lived for millions of years—cooperating, being interdependent, and caring about each other and the environment—before top-down civilization massively repressed our bottom-up natures.

So when people like Twitter's Jack Dorsey, Google's Sergei Brin, and Facebook's Mark Zuckerberg came up with their breakthrough ideas, they were building bottom-up tools that stimulated the re-awakening Their brilliant ideas were an expression of our long dormant and repressed bottom-up epigenetic potentials.

This tsunami of bottom-up thinking and behavior is causing a bigger paradigm shift than the inventions of writing or Gutenberg's printing press because we're already genetically primed for this by our millions of years of human evolution. That's why we are so explosively re-awakening our "bottom-up-ness" and the "new" consciousness that is its hallmark. These disruptive shifts signify a worldwide transition from a predominantly top-down world back to the more bottom-up way of our predecessors.

Bernie Sanders, Barack Obama, Hillary Clinton, and George W. Bush have all said that *change happens from the bottom up*. In fact, the bottom-up approach has become one of the most powerful memes of the century. But what does it mean, and how do you do bottom-up thinking and actions better and smarter?

My purpose is to demonstrate how what I call a "bottom-up connection consciousness" is a revolutionary way of seeing, being, and relating to others, and that it affects how we behave in our community and all our other activities, including our "activism," child rearing, religious practice, and, of course, doing business. It enhances our ability to be cooperative, interdependent, sharing, caring, empathic, egalitarian, and transparent, and although often small, it can be incredibly powerful.

The Bottom-Up Revolution: Mastering the Emerging World of Connectivity is a how-to book for businesses, leaders, organizations, activists, and individuals to crack wide open the possibilities of humankind's biggest cultural shift in seven million years. By understanding the roots and implications of bottom-up and top-down concepts you'll be better able to tap the incredible power of this trend, as the billionaire founders of Google, Facebook, Craigslist, and Twitter have done.

An example of how effective this way of thinking can be in daily life is an experience I had a few years ago. I wrote an article about a US senator, hoping to put pressure on him to take a stand on an issue.

Within two hours, one of his aides contacted me, assuring me the senator would be acting shortly. I had used my knowledge of how legislative staffers use bottom-up media tracking to get a response. It's a bottom-up technique for getting past phone call and email screeners that not many people, not even media-savvy people, know about.

In the movie *Lucy*, a drug increases Scarlett Johansson's brain efficiency from 10 percent to 100 percent, giving her extraordinary abilities. Imagine something momentous happening that dumbs down a key dimension of intelligence, diminishing some of the best aspects of being human. Then imagine another development comes along and raises it back up. We are living that reality today. Yet knowledge of this revolution is a huge blind spot for most people and businesses, even in those making billions from it. Many of the most successful bottom-up visionaries are like fish that live their lives without awareness of the existence of water.

OUR BOTTOM-UP CONNECTION CONSCIOUSNESS IS ENCODED IN OUR DNA.

Humans and our predecessors evolved for millions of years during their lives in hunter-gatherer bands. For 99 percent of the five to seven million years hominids existed, we lived bottom-up lives in sustainable bottom-up cultures, raising bottom-up children to have bottom-up brains. We enjoyed high levels of bottom-up intelligence, which includes interdependence, empathy, cooperation, connection, caring, sharing, localization, and seeing the world with "connection consciousness:" a way of knowing and responding based on a deep, reflexive awareness that we are connected to one another and to all of nature.

Bottom-up living produced a system of metaphors through which humans perceived reality and related to their world. Humans evolved their bottom-up intelligence long before schools existed and developed their bottom-up morals and beliefs long before modern-day religions existed. The bottom-up connection revolution is reawakening these deep, core aspects of what it is to be human—an intelligence repressed and dormant since civilization and industrialization began. It's like a reunion with a lost piece of our soul.

About ten thousand years ago, changes occurred when humans began farming and domesticating animals, becoming dominators of animals and land and creating the need for policing by soldiers to protect crops and surplus food stores. That development soon produced a top-down world ruled by hierarchical, centralized control and patriarchy, which led to societies based on scarcity, slavery, serfdom, and feudalism.

Humanity was flipped from living their predominantly bottom-up lives to living their lives through primarily top-down, root, conceptual metaphoric filters. Wikipedia characterizes a "root metaphor" as the underlying worldview that shapes an individual's understanding of a situation. A conceptual metaphor takes one idea or concept to help understand another, or a whole world.

Hunter-gatherers' lives had depended upon equality, cooperation, interdependence, compassion, and openness with others in a small, local culture. The shift to a top-down social organization repressed their bottom-up heritage and spawned hierarchy, centralization, patriarchal domination, and secrecy. People lost their bottom-up native intelligence and their morals increasingly dumbed down. Narcissism replaced their impoverished emotional and social intelligence.

Humanity's experiment in civilization unfolded gradually and unevenly around the world. For most of humanity, it's relatively recent. Just 200–500 years ago, a significant percentage of the human race was still living in bottom-up cultures. Today, several hundred million— mainly indigenous—people continue to live in bottom-up cultures.

A confluence of forces has catalyzed the return to bottom-up intelligence, starting with the Women's Suffrage and Civil Rights movements. The internet, open-source software, smartphones, and digital life kicked it into high gear worldwide, transforming billions of people.

Two hundred million years of mammalian evolution and seven million years of human evolutionary programming have produced hundreds of neurobiological factors associated with bottom-up aspects of being human. When we see or act in bottom-up ways, we push our bottom-up epigenetic buttons, stimulating epigenetic factors to unfold and blossom into new ways of seeing, being, and doing. Today, that reawakening is well under way and radically changing the way we live, relate to people, do business, and make change happen.

BOTTOM-UP PARENTING AND EPIGENETIC POTENTIATION: THE WAY HUMANS EVOLVED

Psychologist Darcia Narvaez, author of *Neurobiology and the Development of Human Morality*, argues persuasively that humans, before civilization, developed in bottom-up, hunter-gatherer bands that engaged in ancestral parenting. Children were raised by the entire group. You didn't put a baby in a separate part of the cave. She stayed with the parents, just as how today, the philosophy of "attachment parenting" encourages baby-led-weaning and keeping the baby in the parental bed. Top-down parenting puts babies in separate rooms and lets them cry themselves to sleep—practices which indigenous peoples would have seen as life-threatening and stupid. Ancestral parenting potentiated hundreds of epigenetic neurobiological factors, meaning that it allowed the developing child to experience the full, optimal blossoming of hundreds of different brain and neurophysiological elements, producing a good, moral, deeply "connection conscious" human. These include neural pathways, hormonal factors, epigenetic factors that influence empathy, through mirror neurons, vagal nerve function, and hundreds more neuroendocrine functions.

The brain, at birth, is 25 percent of full adult size. Narvaez warns that if the child is not optimally cared for, epigentetic potentials never develop, and she reaches maturity with impaired moral functioning—meaning damaged relating to others, self, and nature.

Epigenetics Explained

Put a redwood tree seed, loaded with genetic potential in a cup of sand. What happens? Nothing. Add water. A stunted plant grows. But plant it in a mature forest, with adequate light and water, and the seed can reach its full genetic redwood potential. Epigenetics explains how genetic programming is repressed or environmentally stimulated to fully blossom. Like the Redwood seed, we each have thousands of epigenetic "seeds" waiting for the right environment to fully blossom. The bottom-up connection revolution is catalyzing your long dormant potentialities. If even a few of your repressed bottom-up epigenetic potentials are unleashed, this book will have done its job.

Top-down, powerful elites and those with authoritarian interests are also tapping this revolution to further consolidate their power. They are also exploiting the ideas and strategies described in this book because it's essential today to deal knowledgeably with emerging bottom-up changes and trends. Fortunately, simply using bottom-up strategies and thinking changes the way your brain works and the way you filter the world. You become a more bottom-up thinker as your bottom-up epigenetic neurobiological programming is awakened.

To probe the meaning and potential of bottom-up concepts from many angles, I've interviewed hundreds of leading thinkers on the subject. They include the founders of Twitter, Huffpost, Craigslist, and Zipcars; thought leaders like Bernie Sanders, Clay Shirky, Douglas Rushkoff, Joseph Nye, and Howard Gardner and leading whistleblowers, activists, diplomats, marketers, anthropologists, and psychologists.

NYU professor and digital thought leader Clay Shirky, author of *Here Comes Everybody*, told me that the technologies catalyzing the bottom-up revolution matter, "not just because they change the way people can coordinate with one another…they also matter because they let people imagine that their lives are different from the lives of their parents, from the lives of previous generations. And it lets them imagine that they can do things that previous generations couldn't do… People have a different sense of themselves and what is possible."

Expanding Your Bottom-Up and Top-Down Vocabulary and Thinking

In our conversations, our language is filled with the vocabulary and comparisons of bottom-up versus top-down characteristics and traits.

The following list attempts to systematically tie them together.

Bottom-Up Characteristics	*Top-Down Characteristics*
grassroots	elite
collectively	individually
equal, horizontal	hierarchical
sharing or distributed power	dominating
democratic, democratizing	autocratic
democratization	authoritarianism
decentralized/localized/distributed	centralized, global
free, letting go	controlled
connected	detached, boundaried, disconnected, isolated
cooperative, collaborative	competitive, consultative
sharing, public	selfish, controlling, holding
interdependent	independent, libertarian
compassion, empathy, caring	narcissistic, antisocial, sociopathic, bullying
commons/community owned	private, privatized
many to many	one to many
consensus	decree
management by worker-owners	management by boss
soft power (culture, arts, kindness)	hard power (weapons, money)
feedback-driven	policy-driven
open, transparent	opaque, secret, closed
participating, including	excluding
generative, empowering	extractive, parasitic, arrestive
open source, creative commons	proprietary, patented, copyrighted
questioning, challenging authority	dogmatic, authoritarian
passionate, all-in performance	emotionally disconnected, minimal commitment

Bottom-Up Characteristics	Top-Down Characteristics
systemic thinking	cartesian, separate, mechanistic, parts thinking
qualitative	quantitative
emergent	single vision
small	too big
simple protocols	complex rules
slow	fast
human decision	algorithmic
curved, circular, fractal, nonlinear	straight, linear
diversity	monoculture, restricted variety
biological, natural, ecological, organic	artificial, unnatural
collective/worker co-op	corporate
with	for (as in build with, not for someone)
trust, respect	fear
sustainable	unlimited growth
patterns of relationships	things and parts
mapped	measured
reaching potential	doing assigned role, stopping at assigned goal
empowering others, power "with"	power over (others)

The two words that came up most often in my interviews with hundreds of bottom-up thought leaders were *democratizing* and *collective*.

Another way to think about top-down and bottom-up behaviors, patterns, and characteristics is to look at the problems that are caused by too much top-down or not enough bottom-up in the mix. The following list of problems resulting from this lack of balance can apply to businesses, organizations, communities, and even many relationships.

- Top-down problem: Hierarchical organization—loses bottom-up input, discourages honest feedback
  Bottom-up solution: become more egalitarian, cooperative, and interdependent

- Top-down problem: Linear, mechanistic, and measured approach—counts and breaks down parts, but loses vision and creativity, and is rigid and inflexible
  Bottom-up solution: Employ systemic, nonlinear thinking and consider connection to systems, patterns, mapping relationships, interactions

- Top-down problem: Celebration of or emphasis on the individual discourages cooperation and collective problem solving
  Bottom-up solution: Facilitate teamwork and collective, cooperative culture

- Top-down problem: Dominating, fear-based authority and leadership—prevents, discourages, and resists sharing or distributing power, ideas, creativity
  Bottom-up solution: soften or eliminate hierarchy, communicate openly, share power, respect others, base authority on trust

- Top-down problem: Disconnection, distinct boundaries in situations—prevents teamwork, promotes management via bullying, isolating, and discouraging people
  Bottom-up solution: Facilitate connections by encouraging teamwork, attracting (soft power), cooperating, engaging, seeing and seeking opportunity with others

- Top-down problem: Autocratic, authoritarian leadership—holds on to power, doesn't delegate, trust, or respect others; didactic, know-it-all attitude, and discourages feedback
  Bottom-up solution: democratize, treat others as equals, and encourage questioning and challenging authority

- Top-down problem: Centralized system—loses touch with what's going on, becomes too algorithmic and disconnected from people, community, values, and answers
  Bottom-up solution: Decentralize and localize systems and networks

- Top-down problem: Controlled situations—rigidity inhibits ideas and discourages innovation
  Bottom-up solution: trust in others, loosen or eliminate hierarchy and authoritarian culture, encourage and reward independence

- Top-down problem: Selfish and controlling culture
  Bottom-up solution: support and encourage empathy, kindness, compassion, sharing, openness, and trust in others

- Top-down problem: Doing assigned role and stopping at assigned goal—leads to emotional disconnection, minimal commitment, and just doing what is required
  Bottom-up solution: Perform with passionate, all-in effort; work to reach potential, become whole

- Top-down problem: One-to-many communication—reflects narrow and shallow interactions which do not allow valuable feedback
  Bottom-up solution: Switch to many-to-many networked and systemic communication that encourages feedback

- Top-down problem: Decision by decree
  Bottom-up solution: decide by consensus, collaboration; encourage input

- Top-down problem: Power over others
  Bottom-up solution: Share power with others with love, care, and respect

- Top-down problem: Opaque, secret, closed culture—encourages corruption, abuse of power
  Bottom-up solution: Create a transparent culture that supports honesty and sharing

- Top-down problem: Expensive "hard power" that uses weapons, money, domination, threats, force and violence
  Bottom-up solution: "Soft power"attracts and encourages others; it uses culture and infrastructural help, and employs arts, creativity, and kindness

- Top-down problem: Top-down administration policy driven
  Bottom-up solution: Feedback driven

- Top-down problem: Extractive, parasitic practices and policies—lead to opposition, bad PR, bad will
  Bottom-up solution: Create policies that are generative and empowering—which build goodwill and add value

- Top-down problem: Proprietary, patented, copyrighted properties—limits peripheral and ancillary development of applications, particularly by synergistic third parties
  Bottom-up solution: Use open source framework and creative commons—opens creativity to the world. It worked for Bill Gates at Microsoft

- Top-down problem: Monoculture, restricted variety
  Bottom-up solution: Allow for diversity and flexibility, which produce higher yields

- Top-down problem: Unlimited growth, big structures and systems
  Bottom-up solution: Focus on small, local, sustainable, agile structures and systems

- Top-down problem: Artificial, unnatural, algorithmic processes and systems—they become unhealthy, unsustainable, toxic, rigid
  Bottom-up solution: Use biological, natural, ecological, organic, processes and systems

- Top-down problem: Selfish, narcissistic, antisocial, sociopathic, immoral, and corrupt individuals sought out and promoted
  Bottom-up solution: Emphasize bottom-up values and connection consciousness; seek out and promote caring, kind individuals with strong ethics, empathy, and compassion

Some of the words and phrases I've encountered the most in exploring the re-awakening of bottom-up thinking include "grassroots, collective, and democratize." The first two describe action. The last is an action. Bottom-up thinking affects the way things are done.

Since the bottom-up revolution has been happening below most people's radar, even experts in different arenas of this movement have not fully grasped it. Yet our new way of thinking and behaving is so pervasive that understanding just a small part of it has been the key to their success.

A three-thousand-year-old parable about blind spots tells of a group of blind wise ones who encounter an unidentified creature. Each tries to identify the creature by the sense of touch. One feels a "hose." Another feels "a rug" and another "a cow." Others feel "a tree trunk," "a rope," and "a long pole." They're all experiencing different aspects of a single entity, yet no one conceives the whole, which is an elephant. Before now, the concepts of both bottom-up and top-down have been understood in the same fragmented ways as the elephant in the parable. There are books on crowdfunding, social media, grassroots activism, bottom-up and top-down leadership, these concepts applied to programming, authoritarianism, hierarchy, and patriarchy. But so far, few if any people have woven these disparate topics together to reveal the full picture. I hope to consolidate the "whole elephant" to help you to more fully tap the power of bottom-up values.

We're transitioning from an information economy to a connection culture and economy. The same technologies catalyzing the bottom-up revolution are also enabling a large variety of other connections because they are much more affordable and easier to make happen. Clay Shirky brilliantly describes this development in his landmark book *Here Comes Everybody*.

It's essential to learn more about the aspects of connection, both what is already established and the recent ideas and new technologies. We also need to learn how to optimize connecting and minimize disconnections (which are occurring in epidemic proportions) to become a master bottom-up surfer.

Nevertheless, Top-Down Behavior Is Sometimes Necessary

This does not mean we should switch to engaging in only bottom-up approaches to life or business. The human brain and our human nature have both top-down and bottom-up ways of functioning. The problem is that most individuals and organizations are addicted to top-down thinking and doing. Bottom-up thinking is often neglected, rejected, or ignored. Marketing guru Seth Godin, referring to new ways of understanding our reality, says, "Learning how to see is essential and can be really expensive if you don't get it." The solution is to integrate and balance bottom-up with top-down. There are thousands of books written on top-down ideas, and none that cover the full realm of ideas considered bottom-up. This imbalance should be addressed.

WHY WE SHOULD CARE ABOUT HOW OUR BOTTOM-UP REVOLUTION AND CONNECTION CONSCIOUSNESS ARE REVERBERATING THROUGH OUR WORLD

If you don't "get" the bottom-up way of seeing and doing, you are already at a profound disadvantage in the worlds of business, diplomacy, and social and political change, and you are missing important opportunities to live a deeper, more fulfilling life with the people and communities you love and care about.

People born after 1980 who were marinated in the internet, smartphones, instant messaging, online gaming, and social media since they were teens or children, have literally developed different kinds of brains. These digital natives will probably benefit from understanding the dimensions and implications of top-down hierarchy, centralization, patriarchy, authoritarianism, and narcissism in our culture that preceded them.

Those born before 1980 were typically raised with more top-down, mechanistic brains, that produced more narrow ways of seeing, thinking, relating, and doing. By understanding the problems of top-down approaches and the possibilities of bottom-up thinking, you'll open new windows and doors to achieving your goals and dreams.

No matter what age they are, most people are like the blind wise ones and the elephant.

The bottom-up approach caught my attention when I realized that bottom-up responses to challenges and opportunities worked out to be much smarter, kinder, and more synergistic when I started using them as a central principle in operating my website, OpEdNews.com, which sees as many as 800,000 unique visitors a month. I realized that throughout history, when big changes have happened in the world, bottom-up actions and processes set them in motion, and even nature itself operates on bottom-up principles. Happiness, personal growth, change, and love are bottom-up concepts.

Understanding Our Connection Consciousness
"My spirituality is we are all in this together."
—BERNIE SANDERS, AT A 2016 CNN TOWN HALL.

Connection consciousness is an awareness, knowledge, and is a reflexive way of responding, based upon the many deep connections we have to one another, our communities, and the ecosystems of Earth. This consciousness perceives the self to include our relationship to a universe with which we are infinitely connected and integrated, including all matter, biological, energy and ecological systems. Pope Francis, in an address to the US congress, said, "We must move forward together, as one, in a renewed spirit of fraternity and solidarity, cooperating generously for the common good."

Connection consciousness produces a cultural, spiritual, and personal collection of characteristics that lead you to treat others and the environment well because they are a part of you. This results in kinder, more open and loving, caring, empathic people. You could say it represents another expression of the golden rule, "Do unto others as you would do unto yourself"—except that there are no "others." Everyone and everything is part of you, as you are part of the whole. When you gain conscious awareness of your connection to all others, you treat yourself well. You don't pollute your body—you don't feed it food with toxins. And you don't exploit or steal from parts of yourself.

Bottom-up connection consciousness can be incorporated into one's value system, where it is consistent with other values such as justice, fairness, balance, wholeness, equality, kindness, sharing, cooperation, and compassion. It is compatible with the ideals the Dalai Lama encourages—the practices of compassion and warmheartedness.

Becoming "connection conscious" can change how you relate to everyone and everything around you. If enough people develop a true connection consciousness, it could play a part in changing and perhaps saving the world. Martin Luther King, in his *Letter from a Birmingham Jail* said that we are all connected in a "network of mutuality" and that which affects any one of us directly affects everyone indirectly.

Aspects of connection consciousness include openness, honesty, transparency, receptivity, trust, kindness, caring, seeing connections, cooperation, nurturing, loving, and generosity. People who practice connection consciousness are generative, protective, considerate, empathetic, tolerant, eco-conscious, warm and openhearted, embracing, appreciative, and participating.

Connection consciousness has been a part of humanity for millions of years, and is normal for indigenous peoples. However, much of it has been repressed or forgotten in recent times due to patriarchal and hierarchical civilization and industrialization, which have produced technologies like clocks, writing, printing, and television. Twenty-first century, post-Industrial-Age humans have lost their connection consciousness. The Dalai Lama offers the solution. He told a group assembled at the Diplomatic Consular Corps of Karnataka and at National Institute of Advanced Studies, "What is important today is that we consciously cultivate a sense of the oneness of humanity, because we all depend on each other." Connection consciousness takes it a step further, so we cultivate a sense of oneness with everything.

Development of connection consciousness involves unblocking repressed epigenetic factors that we either never realized or shut off as we matured. For instance, birds and many animals migrate, knowing and being connected to the migration pathways. Homing behavior, too, is based on a connected way of knowing. I am certain that we have repressed—under our civilized cognitive veneer—some long untapped connection capacities. Who knows how deep a connection can run?

Embracing Human Experience Is Preferable to Being Dominated, Controlled, and Separated from Others

We grow by connecting. Connection consciousness opens one to embrace community, relationships, the ecosystem, change, new and uncertain situations, strangers, a risk of adversity, and others' differences. Embracing is a bottom-up connection behavior that enables us to connect with and appreciate all that is beyond our skin.

In contrast, top-down authoritarian consciousness is exploitive and predatory. It atomizes and categorizes; it controls and dominates. It creates boundaries and hierarchies and intensifies and strengthens separation based on race, religion, nationality, ideology, politics, economic status, and gender. A top-down approach seeks and manifests domination with power *over* others. It aims to define and control.

PROGRAMMING FOR POWER, CONNECTION, AND DISCONNECTION

People go through life with different levels of access to their own personal strengths and potentialities.

Back in the eighties, my company designed the Biopro software cartridge, which plugged into the back of a computer. We offered several versions: some, with more features and capabilities, cost hundreds of dollars more. To avoid making a different piece of hardware for each software version, we used an internal toggle switch component. The software version the buyer purchased was determined by how we set the switches. Customers never knew this or were affected by our manufacturing techniques. Like my adaptable hardware, everyone has the potential to do more. The secret is to know how to unlock that potential, just as knowing how to change the switch setting unleashed more power from my software.

Our culture has a huge effect on how we manifest our epigenetic potentials. As you learn about the roots, dimensions, and manifestations of bottom-up and top-down you'll hopefully change the way you connect with the bottom-up potential coiled in your DNA. It's also important to understand how we are disconnected and separated from our bottom-up nature—and most of us are very disconnected from our basic nature, except for the indigenous First Nation peoples who have held onto their cultures and languages. Disconnection is a normal state for many, intentionally induced by industrialized cultures.

How do you practice re-connecting? Here's an example. When Rhonda gives prayers of thanks and appreciation at meals, she thinks about whose hands touched the food to reach the plate—the farmer, the picker, the trucker, the grocery story produce clerk—and is thankful for all of them. Living a connection-conscious life, you will think about those kinds of chains and systems of connections. When you buy a product you will think about what effect it will have on the earth, the ecosystem, disadvantaged people, and the company that produced it. Companies would do well to think about how their brand is seen from a connection-conscious point of view.

CHAPTER 1

The Roots, Science, and Dimensions of Bottom-Up and Top-Down Thinking and Behaviors

This chapter explores ideas that will get you thinking deeper about bottom-up and top-down, so you'll develop the habit of seeing the "full elephant" instead of just the disconnected parts. We'll start exploring bottom-up as a value system. Then we'll dig into the roots and characteristics of powerful top-down dimensions that permeate so much of our culture. Next, we'll look at other big disruptive changes that affected human history—farming, civilization, the Gutenberg printing press, radio, TV, computers, and open source.

The chapter proceeds to cover top-down laws and control freaks. One sign of the ascent of bottom-up is the news that historians and history departments have shifted the field of history from top-down to predominantly bottom-up approaches. The next few chapter sections explore pairs of top-down and bottom-up dimensions—centralization versus localization, bigness versus smallness (such as government and corporations), and winning from a bottom-up perspective.

The last part of the chapter delves into the neuropsychological, evolutionary, primatological, and anthropological aspects of top-down and bottom-up. Then, finally, we dive deep into what I believe to be very valuable and hopeful areas—systems and chaos theories—that are the new, bottom-up scientific paradigms that have replaced hundreds of years of old, top-down mechanistic science. I'll discuss how they better explain our world, culture, and how change happens.

BOTTOM-UP AS A VALUE SYSTEM

I firmly believe that the bottom-up way of seeing almost naturally operates as a moral value system. Darcia Narvaez describes a communal or social imagination, by which people reflexively envision how other people will feel in response to possible actions. Most Westerners have lost this. Native Americans traditionally consider how a decision will affect the next seven generations. We need to learn from them.

Empathy connects people with other people, with animals, and even with nature. Other bottom-up *values* include:

- dispositions towards all things local

- compassionate or nurturing approaches to others, rather than exploitative or predatory approaches

- a sense of "we-ness," as compared to accentuated individualism

- democratization is preferable to authoritarianism

- cooperation and interdependence are preferable to dog-eat-dog competition

Bottom-up behavior and ways of seeing and doing are more humane, more natural, more noble, perhaps even more holy and spiritual. One great bottom-up example is the open source movement. Linux, one of the most popular operating systems, was built to be shared by thousands of people cooperating together under the supervision of Linus Torvald. Billions of people use the Linux that their Android smart phone operating systems are built upon. Robert David Steele advocates in his book, *Open Source Everything,* for the idea of open source—meaning nobody owns it, everyone shares it, and it's transparent—to be applied to, well, everything. And he claims it would lower the costs of…everything. Massively.

The opposite worldview to bottom-up values is Ayn Rand's Objectivism. In this system, the individual is all-important, and society is made subservient to the needs and rights of the individual. At its core, this worldview is top-down, selfish, and narcissistic. Even nature opposes such individualism. Josh Mitteldorf argues in his book *Cracking the Aging Code* that most living creatures have an altruistically programmed senescence by death-causing genes in order to protect the ecosystem and community from the individual.

RETHINKING YOUR RELATIONSHIP TO HIERARCHY, DOMINATION, AND CONTROL

When I was pioneering the field of positive psychology back in the early 1980s, psychotherapy and psychology were primarily focused on pathology and fixing what was wrong. I raised the question: "How much can you help people by teaching them positive skills that move them toward positivity and optimal functioning, as opposed to diagnosing and treating pathology and symptoms?" I take the same approach to bottom-up: "How much can adding bottom-up to your life and work make you happier and more successful, while remembering that there are many positive top-down systems or situations—and leadership is necessary?"

My hope is to inspire you to practice connection consciousness and to develop a more balanced perspective and practice regarding top-down ways, so that you live and work with hierarchy from a more enlightened viewpoint.

Hierarchy is a core characteristic of most top-down organizations and of some aspects of nature. The etymological root of the word comes from the old French, *"ierarchie,"* which means rule by a High Priest, and from the Greek roots meaning "holy" and "rule."

Google offers some definitions of Hierarchy:

- A system or organization in which people or groups are ranked one above the other according to status or authority

- The upper echelons of a hierarchical system; those in authority

- An arrangement or classification of things according to relative importance or inclusiveness

And here are two from Wiktionary:

- A body of authoritative officials organized in nested ranks

- Any group of objects ranked so that everyone but the topmost is subordinate to a specified one above it

Some synonyms for hierarchy include: pecking order, ranking, grading, rating, gradation, echelons, grouping, position, pyramid, scale, chain of command, and bureaucracy.

Hierarchies do exist in nature, like food chains. Wikipedia says, "Almost every system within the world is arranged hierarchically. By their common definitions, every nation has a government and every government is hierarchical. Socioeconomic systems are stratified into a social hierarchy (the social stratification of societies), and all systematic classification schemes (taxonomies) are hierarchical. Most organized religions, regardless of their internal governance structures, operate as a hierarchy under God."

Advocates of hierarchy say it makes for more efficient decision-making, especially under time pressures, and argue that it fulfills "fundamental psychological needs better than egalitarian social arrangements." Among those psychological needs, they cite one for power and achievement and another for certainty, predictability, and structure. They also argue that hierarchy "validates individual beliefs in meritocracy..."

But consider that need for certainty, predictability, and structure. I see that need not as legitimate, but as a problem. It fits the needs of authoritarian personalities—not the rare ones who are themselves dominators, but the majority who seek and need to BE dominated. So, yes, such people feel safer and better within a hierarchical system, but are they living up to their full human potential?

Let's look at an article by Stanford Associate professor Nir Halevy and his co-authors, who suggest that an advantage of hierarchy is that people know their place—and that this reduces uncertainty and enhances predictability in interactions with others. Again, this gives me a distinct sense of authoritarianism.

Gloria Steinem, in an HBO Documentary, *Gloria in Her Own Words*, proposes that outside of emergencies, like fire or brain surgery, hierarchy may not only not be necessary but it could be damaging. She argues that hierarchy tends to use the strengths of one person, while the alternative allows for the cumulative resources and strengths of a group.

Is hierarchy absolutely necessary on a battlefield or an operating room? Maybe, but asymmetrical warfare is the dominant form of combat today. Battlefield fighting is mostly obsolete. And who knows how much bottom-up, connection-conscious ecological and nutritional approaches to maintaining health, peace, and kindness could help eliminate the need for people to be in operating rooms, or for that matter, in battles?

Domination is a key element of the top-down worlds of hierarchy, authoritarian control, and maintaining the status quo. New studies have shown that when people are stressed, under pressure, or under the influence of alcohol, they are more willing to let go of freedom and accept authority—that is, domination.

I believe narcissism and narcissistic characteristics play a part in the domination aspect of patriarchy and perhaps also in the "power-over" effect that infects much hierarchy, versus egalitarian "power-with." One universally recognized aspect of narcissim is the need to control and dominate others. I explore this further in discussing authoritarianism.

Every sociopath and psychopath is a narcissist. Narcissists revel in controlling others. As hierarchies developed, civilization allowed narcissistic control and domination behavior to manifest itself more easily.

CONSEQUENCES OF AUTHORITARIANISM

Cognitive scientist George Lakoff proposes in his book *Moral Politics* that liberals and progressives tend to have a nurturing parent style while conservatives have a strict parenting, authoritarian father style. Lakoff says,

> In the strict father family, father knows best. He knows right from wrong and has the ultimate authority to make sure his children and his spouse do what he says, which is taken to be what is right. Through physical discipline they are supposed to become disciplined, internally strong, and able to prosper in the external world.

The problem is that such authoritarian parenting damages children. Gwen Dewar, of parentingscience.com, reports that children of authoritarian parenting are less resourceful, more likely to:

- have lower self-esteem

- become bullies

- abuse alcohol

- become depressed or be at higher risk for depression

- have diminished ability to make friends

- have diminished self-regulatory and moral reasoning

- have diminished critical thinking

Top-down *religion and power:* Historically, monarchs claimed that their power was God(s)-ordained. The Church backed the Inquisition along with some of the worst monarchies, dictatorships, and authoritarian regimes. Many religious orders, at one time, played integral roles in protecting and upholding the power of these autocracies. What functions do religions that support top-down monarchies and autocracies actually perform? They keep the common people in line—obedient and docile, so they support the ruler's claim to divine right. Bottom-up religion is discussed in chapter nine.

There were an estimated 45 million slaves in 2016, according to the Global Slavery Index. The slave exists in a system that allows coerced domination.

Insubordination

In the military; hierarchical order of command is enforced with jail or even execution.

In corporations; failure to respect the hierarchy can cost employees their jobs.

Top-down minds can produce top-down addictions. There are a lot of people who expect and need someone in charge, someone to tell him or her what to do, someone to dominate, to play the father—holy or paternal. Not many, but some slaves and free blacks fought FOR the Confederacy, such as the 1500 members of the Louisiana Native Guard. An 1864 book about General Benjamin Butler explained that they did it because "By serving the Confederates," they hoped "to advance a little nearer to equality with whites." This is the thinking of oppressed people.

People who enjoyed the benefits of slavery mocked slavery abolitionists and claimed it was an essential institution—that the culture would be destroyed if slavery was ended. They were wrong. Every aspect of every hierarchy should be examined to identify and eliminate unnecessary use of domination, control, and the abuse of power over others.

Holacracy throws out the industrial, predict-and-control authoritarian model of management and replaces it with a nonhierarchical, distributed approach to running an organization. A holacracy empowers everyone in the organization. All workers are treated as autonomous, equally given the opportunity to think and contribute creatively to the process of getting goals accomplished. Close to 1000 organizations have made the shift to holacracy, including the billion-dollar Amazon.com subsidiary, Zappos.com.

When a company shifts to holacratic management, some employees feel uncomfortable when they're unleashed from an authoritarian system and given responsibility. Some actually quit, because they prefer the superior/subordinate role structure. However, most thrive. Chapter eight covers holacracy in greater detail.

PATRIARCHY: A TOP-DOWN SYSTEM WRAPPED IN DIFFERENT STORIES

Patriarchal cultures are male-dominated. We see this in Taliban Afghans, in Saudi Wahabists, Ultra-Orthodox Jewish Haredis, and in some fundamentalist Christians. Patriarchal cultures posit that men are superior to women and should dominate and even own them. In these cultures, despite their subordination, women often embrace the patriarchy and the crumbs of power they're given, as though such an arrangement is better for them.

Scholars theorize that patriarchal cultures began in Neolithic times after people began to understand the concept of fatherhood—which was about the same time that farming and animal husbandry were developing. Women, who did most of the farming and caring for domesticated animals, were probably the ones to figure out that babies are produced in the same way that planting a seed leads to a plant growing. Some hypothesize that men and women were equals before patriarchy, and others propose that women, at one point, wielded more power than men because of their ability to bear children. It was because of this power to create, it's theorized, that women became the holders of power in the roles of high priestesses, queens, and the like.

I asked psychiatrist Jean Shinoda Bolen, who specializes in the study of Jungian archetypes and mythology, particularly feminine archetypes and myths, about the time before patriarchy when women were either treated as equals or reigned. She told me: "There was…a time when God was a woman… For 5,000 to 25,000 years prior to patriarchy in the West, we apparently had, in Western civilization, a mother culture—and it made sense, because if you did not know that a baby was made because a sperm and an egg came together and an embryo was formed, what you saw—what everybody saw—was that…women were the creators.

Women gave birth through their body…and it was a miracle… If you didn't know about the part the male sperm played, you'd assume God was feminine—that the great goddess was the creator. And so people did."

Then, one theory goes, when people figured out it took a guy to make a baby, the men decided THEY had the power. They were the sources of life, the progenitors. And power shifted from matrilineage to patrilineage.

In her book *Chalice and the Blade* Riane Eisler describes how Goddess-based, horticultural, matrilineal "partnership" cultures existed for thousands of years with equality between the sexes and absence of war. She proposes, based on extensive anthropological research, that the shift to patriarchal domination occurred because the application of bronze metallurgy led to use of weapons—blades—that were literally worshipped. Eisler says that the shift to patriliny and domination came with nomadic, herder invaders of peaceful agrarian people. Eisler argues that "at the core of the invaders systems were the placing of higher value on the power that takes, rather than gives *life*…the power symbolized by the masculine blade." She argues that in the invaders' dominator society, enslavement of women and "gentle, more effeminate" men became the norm.

Leonard Shlain, in his book *Alphabet and the Goddess*, theorizes that the shift from female power to male power was caused by the invention of writing, which shifted the way the brain worked from right brain holistic visual thinking to left brain linear, analytic thinking.

A multiplicity of elements of change—farming, land ownership, thing ownership, OWNERSHIP period, insight into paternity as a source of children, and development of the technologies of metallurgy, of writing and the written word—were all coming together to change how people thought, perceived, related, and worked. This series of interwoven threads of influence on humans pushed them inexorably toward a top-down, centralized, hierarchical, PATRIARCHAL culture. It's theorized that the idea of paternity led to the idea of property.

Top-down culture has led to the decline of the "commons"—the resources we all share—open land, schools, water, air, natural resources, roads, parking spaces, and trees. As Naomi Klein describes in her book, *Shock Doctrine*, recent efforts by University of Chicago, Milton Friedman model economists, and by neocons and neoliberals, have shrunk the commons, privatizing them far more than they have been for almost all of human history.

Jean Shinoda Bolen told me that the original Athenian democracy was a patriarchal culture but also a "rape culture that (democracy) only applied to men," saying, "In Athens, women were the property of men, and fathers could sell a non-virgin daughter into slavery if his daughter was raped or if he incested her. . . As soon as she was not virginal, she could be sold—she could become a member of the slave class. And the women could not testify in the courts."

The term rape, when used metaphorically, does not have to mean sexual assault upon a male or female. It can be perpetrated as predation, exploitation, theft, or strip mining. They all violate the sanctity of nature, of the whole, which the bottom-up approach respects, nurtures, and embraces.

In the United States, and in some other countries, patriarchy still plays a powerful role. Women are paid less and are told what they can and can't do. In the United States, some evangelical Christians, including some members of Congress, believe that women should stay home and be passive, subordinate, and obedient to their husbands, as Kathryn Joyce describes in her book *Quiverfull: Inside the Christian Patriarchy Movement*. Women in the US have been fighting for equal rights for nearly a century.

Bonnie Burstow, author of *Radical Feminist Therapy*, says, "patriarchy is part of hierarchy and rule. Everyone is treated badly." I asked her how it's bad for men. She replied, "Because it stops them from being full human beings. If you are turned into an oppressor, you are not a full human being. It profoundly hurts men. Men are socialized to take control. They are socialized to dominate. They are not socialized to be giving and caring, which are the most wonderful aspects of what we can make out of being human. So, and in that sense, men are profoundly cheated."

The bottom-up revolution can feel very threatening to people in patriarchal cultures. It won't be surprising to see patriarchal cultures resist or reject social and business manifestations of bottom-up. On the other hand, since some bottom-up technologies and ways of interacting are not directly contradictory to patriarchal rules and customs, they may actually help erode some of those old discriminatory ways.

The movie *Pleasantville* offers an interesting take on patriarchy's resistance to the feminine. It starts in a town shown in black-and-white, where women's sex roles are locked in tight. Tobey Maguire arrives and gets people to start thinking about other options—about colors, love, feelings. The black-and-white people start to manifest the full spectrum of colors—they become "colored." But the monochromatic men in the town prefer the women cooking and cleaning for them. They gather together, trying to stop the town's awakening, particularly its teens and a few "colored" women. They even put up signs "No Coloreds," refer-ring to people who appear in Technicolor rather than in black-and-white. The male teens do embrace the color change, which catches on. The last to accept it are the white males, who have been enjoying the advantages of the old system. That's probably how real-world patriarchy will fade out. But it won't disappear without a fight. Michael Kimmel, a leading expert on masculinity, and author of *Angry White Men*, told me, "Aristocracies historically don't like meritocracy. They don't like to play fair. They don't like for the best to win. They like it tilted…so that they get everything."

HOW WE GOT TO HIERARCHY AND PATRIARCHY

When man made the land-owning agrarian shift, he transitioned from living in integrated, connected harmony with nature, to living in hier-archy, parasitically controlling and dominating both nature and humans. This shift created slavery, rulers, class, caste, and disconnection. Did the metaphorical bite of the agricultural apple cause Adam and Eve to be expelled from the garden of Eden?

Daniel Quinn, author of the best-selling novel *Ishmael*, described Western culture's mythic rationale for justifying these top-down manifestations:

> Joseph Campbell is famous for saying that we have no mythology. I challenged that in *Ishmael*, saying that we do have a mythology— though not a mythology of Gods and Heroes. Rather, it's the story about the world and our place in it. And this mythology is that the world was made for man, and man was made to conquer and rule it. The world is a human possession, something that belongs to us to be used as we please. There is only one right way for people to live, and that's our way; and everyone in the world must be made to live the way we live.
>
> As we swept over the world, we arrived in a new world, and we found all these 'savages' living the 'wrong way.' We told them that is not the way God meant for people to live. They were 'mis-using' the land, so we took it away from them. Like Cain, we started tilling the soil, and killing off our brothers who did not measure up to our standards: pushing them into reservations, things like that. Part of our mythology is that we are the apex of evolution, the very top. It's the myth that has driven us forward for thousands of years.

Derrick Jensen offers a similar perspective in his book *The Myth of Human Supremacy*. Arguing that life is full of examples of genius in the world of plants and animals. I love his example of the invention of antibiotics. It wasn't Pasteur, who discovered pennicilin. It wasn't horsemen who discovered that moldy blankets could help horses with infection. It was the living mold that invented the antibiotics. Mold!! Human exceptionalism is clearly over-rated.

When I asked Quinn to explain the message *Ishmael* gives, he gave the following explanation:

> My message is that we should look at this mythology realistically, and think about our position in the world. Are we really the rulers of the

world? Were we put here, assumedly by God, to rule the world? Does that make sense? We're behaving that way. Is ours the one right way? Must everyone in the world be made to live the way we live? We've done a very good job of making everyone in the world live the way we live. But, look where it's put us. I couldn't have said this in *Ishmael*, but it was coming. Here we are in the midst of what biologists are calling the sixth extinction, as catastrophic as the fifth extinction that destroyed 75 percent of all species, including, of course, the great dinosaurs. Because of our impact on the environment, it's estimated that as many as fifty-thousand species a year are becoming extinct. This is where our vision, our mythology, has taken us. This is where our rule of the world has brought us.

I also asked Quinn, who also wrote the book *Beyond Civilization*, his thoughts on civilization, and he answered:

I wanted to know why civilization is hierarchical—why all civilizations (and there have been several) have been hierarchies. So I go back and look at the beginnings, how civilizations begin; and they all begin the same way: with people deciding to try a new way of life, deciding to live off their own food [which they raise themselves], instead of living off just the food that grows naturally all around them. They give up the hunting and gathering life, and become agricultural as farmers, and very quickly gather together into farming villages.

The reason that agriculturalists can stay in one place is that agriculture gives them surpluses, so that when the seasons change, they don't have to move on. But once the surpluses are there, they can't just leave them around in the open sitting around in piles. They have to store them. They have to keep them away from other animals and other people.

When I interjected, "Although, in the hunter-gatherer world there are no locks and keys, and all the food that's out there is free for the taking by anybody," Quinn replied:

Absolutely. That's why they are not hierarchies: it's that there is no one holding the key to the lock. Anyone can go and get whatever they want. But in the village, someone had to organize the storage and the guarding of the food. Once the food was there, the village was a target for peoples around them. So they needed to have armed guards. By this time, the division of labor was an established thing. People made pots, and cloth, and weapons; and the holders of the keys were their royalty. The armed forces that protected the storage (and themselves!) were the king's nobles. The artisans became the middle class. At the bottom, were the peons, who did all the drudge work, all the lifting and carrying, tilled the fields, planted and harvested the crops, and so on. And so, from the beginning, there very quickly appeared a necessary hierarchy.

For a long time, indigenous people were identified with the Hobbesian dog-eat-dog, law-of-the-jungle view of the world, or with Darwin's "survival of the fittest." They were seen as "uncivilized," as brutal savages whose lives involved nothing more than a constant struggle to survive. We now know that indigenous people, though they don't farm, nevertheless live in harmony with nature. People like the indigenous hunter-gatherer San people of Africa work only two to three hours a day to subsist. Subsist! We talk about subsistence living as a form of deprivation, while actually in the world of indigenous people still alive, primarily in rain forests, subsistence living works. They have 21 to 22 free hours a day. There is no unemployment and no mental illness. People are happy. Nowadays, more experts say the indigenous peoples of the world are the ones who are truly affluent.

We have much to learn from the few surviving indigenous peoples of the earth about their ways of living, relating, and working, and about their values and beliefs. It would be nice to add to our knowledge of how the hundreds of thousands of extinct indigenous bands and tribes viewed the world. We can use their perspectives to help us more gracefully undergo our transition from a top-down industrial era back to a bottom-up connection era.

I think where we're heading is in many ways similar to where indigenous cultures live, which can be a very good thing. When I interviewed Daniel Quinn, I also asked him about what he'd learned from his extensive research on indigenous cultures. He answered:

> Each tribe had its own identity, had its own laws, which were very bottom-up. They were not laws that punished people: they were laws that helped to make things right, rather than punishing what was wrong. They were not the same from tribe to tribe. The Sioux didn't think that everybody should have their laws, or should live the way they lived, and the Pueblos didn't think that everybody should live the way they lived. [In a tribe,] you're never sick all by yourself, you're never dying all by yourself, you're never poor all by yourself. The bringing up of children is not all your problem—it's the problem of the whole tribe. The function of the tribe is to make life work for everyone. If food is scarce, everyone is hungry. There aren't a few at the top who get to keep on eating. And if there's a lot of food, everybody gets more food.
>
> It's a much friendlier way of life than ours, where each of us is isolated, everyone for himself. That just doesn't work as a principle for people. People think we're rich, but what I saw in studies of indigenous peoples was how rich they were; not in toys, but in their lives, in the security they had. They had no jobs to lose; they couldn't become poorer unless they were all poorer.

Today, we're spiraling to a new era of cognitive and digital hunting and gathering. Hunters use Google, Amazon, Twitter, Ebay, Hubspot, and Craigslist, instead of spears and arrows. Gatherers use SEO, social media and big data to optimize the gathering of visitors and page views that are traded via webs and networks of ad companies for money that's deposited electronically. Thom Hartmann has written numerous books describing how people with ADD are like hunters in a farmer's world. He told me how he was invited to speak at a school system in Nunavut, the province in Canada inhabited primarily by First Nation, hunter gatherers. The ADD rate there exceeded ninety percent.

When agriculture catalyzed civilization, it offered mixed blessings. Perhaps it was necessary for humanity to take the path of domination, slavery, and hierarchy. But perhaps, too, it could have been done in a kinder, gentler way with more equality and justice. Perhaps we can change the path now.

THE HISTORY OF BIG CHANGE

Digital disruptors are accelerating and intensifying the rate of change happening in the world today. Since humankind began recording history there have been a number of notable game-changing, disruptive innovations

The emergence of words, language, and speaking changed the way hominids could communicate, enabling them to work together more effectively. Storytelling around the campfire probably shaped the evolution of the brain. Shlain, Ong, and Postman have described how the emergence of written language virtually reprogrammed mankind to be more left-brained, and perhaps, more male-dominated.

Gutenberg's printing press was another major game-changer. Before printing presses were available in the Western world, you had to be wealthy to own a book, which could take a monk a year to transcribe. Suddenly, with the invention of the printing press, many people could have books. The Gutenberg Bible was the first major book that was mass-produced.

When the first English-language Great Bible was printed and made available to the general public during the reign of King Henry VIII in 1539, the response was huge. Ordinary people wanted a Bible written in their everyday language, which they could read at home. Unfortunately, after Henry's death, the royal State, working with the Roman Catholic Church, decreed the death penalty for possession of an English-language Bible.

The Church had been the exclusive provider of God's word, and Gutenberg's press was a great bottom-up disruptor. Abruptly, top-down religion, which had dominated humankind for centuries, faced the threat of losing power.

Sound familiar? It's an earlier instance of top-down powers trying to suppress the new media.

The music recording industry made big changes when they waged their war against file sharing sites like Napster, Gnutella, Morpheus, and Kazaa. The big powers lost. They failed to see where things were heading. Then Apple's genius struck again, and iTunes became a huge success. It provided a way for people to hunt, gather, and find the music they wanted—song by song—rather than in the packaged way the old power brokers of the music industry had forced them to accept.

More recently, radio, movies, television, and computers have also been major disruptors. I'm hoping that the internet, open source software, and smartphones, which are catalyzing our bottom-up revolution, will make enough people "connection conscious" so that they'll voluntarily and consciously self-regulate the direction of the next stages of civilization.

TOP-DOWN LAWS, CONTROL-FREAKS, AND DOMINATION

A six-year-old brings a Swiss Army knife to school, breaking a rule. The school says it has no choice but to suspend the boy, based on school district "zero tolerance" policies. He may face charges. A TV commentator observes that zero tolerance shouldn't include zero common sense.

This is the work of top-down, centralized, dominator control-freaks. Someone decided not to trust school administrators and teachers, and pushed through a rule that took away trust and discretion from people who actually deal with children. School boards and courts should have rules that allow latitude and flexibility for administrators and judges. Laws that take away such prerogatives invalidate local wisdom and insidiously destroy community.

This is what happens when people with top-down minds decide they want to increase the control they have over their world. They have a problem with trust, so they pass rigid, inflexible laws. For centuries,

people accepted these kinds of laws, edicts, and rules. They were indoc-
trinated in the church and school unless they were the children of the
top-down power holders, in which case, as award-winning teacher John
Taylor Gatto told me, and as Glenn Greenwald and Chris Hayes have
written, they were taught to ignore rules made for the poor and the
common people.

Over fifteen years ago, I created a website, sphincterpolice.com, to
address the control-freaks in the world, who represent a virulent kind of
authoritarianism. Narcissists are control-freaks. Part of their pathology
is the need to control everything and everyone around them. Darcia
Narvaez says those characteristics are fear-based and a result of incomplete, dysfunctional parenting.

In our radio interview, Arlene Goldbard, author of *The Culture of
Possibility: Art, Artists & The Future*, described "consensus reality," a top-
down view of the world which many people embrace. We are constantly
bombarded with ideas—or memes—that sell the "story" to us for the
dominating powers. One is: "Things are the way they are because God
made [the world] that way (our monarchies and religions), because it is
the natural order of things, or because it is the best way." Goldbard suggests that the arts, whether visual, music, or story, can disrupt "consensus
reality" and get people seeing and thinking for themselves—leading,
perhaps most importantly, to a reconnection with community.

In his book *Domination and the Arts of Resistance: Hidden Transcripts*,
James Scott discusses how parades are powerful tools organized by
dominators to celebrate and dramatize their rule. He says, "A parade…
is a living tableau of centralized discipline and control… The scene vis-
ibly and forcibly conveys unity and discipline under a single purposeful
authority."

Scott also describes top-down rules, or laws. There are probably
millions of such rules throughout the world, designed to maintain
power and keep people under control or domination. It will require the
conscious efforts of many organizations and individuals to eliminate
these laws. Perhaps the first step is to prevent more top-down rules from

being put into effect. The federal "Dark Act," which forbids states from requiring GMO labeling of food is one example of such a top-down law. A whole popular movement must be mobilized aimed at toppling top-down, centralized laws that take power away from local communities and throw out local wisdom.

THE BOTTOM-UP HISTORY REVOLUTION AND HOWARD ZINN'S BOTTOM-UP PEOPLE'S HISTORY

In the academic field of history, the bottom-up revolution started some 50 years ago, perhaps inspired by the equal rights movement. Back in the sixties and seventies, history departments and authors of history books started to shift away from solely telling top-down histories of powerful people, nations, diplomacy, and military, toward exploring the histories of women, people of color, soldiers, food, workers, immigrants, cultures, and locales.

A *New York Times* article asking the question, "Are Traditional History Courses Vanishing?" reported that, while the number of history faculty members had more than doubled, the jobs were primarily for the new bottom-up specializations. That led teachers of traditional top-down history to complain they were being squeezed out. The article's author, Patricia Cohen, observed that starting in the 1960s and 70s, historian academics began paying attention to groups of people who had been ignored in history books—workers, immigrants, minorities, women. She referred to social and cultural history as bottom-up history and suggested that historians who studied diplomatic history tended to focus on the most powerful people—the old, classic, elitist history approach.

In 1975 over 75 percent of college history departments had at least one professor specializing in diplomatic history. By 2005 the percentage had dropped to less than half. It's reached a point, Cohen's article reported, that one top-down PhD history student described feeling like the last woolly mammoth at the end of the Ice Age, and that some historians treated his chosen specialty with "genuine derision."

This shift in how history is studied and taught is more than an academic change. When people routinely think about history from a bottom-up perspective, they begin to see and believe they can play a role in making history, rather than seeing making history as strictly for elites. It's one more factor fueling the bottom-up revolution.

"I don't think it's men who make history. Men, individuals, are the little motor, but the big motor is the masses. Individuals are only the little motor that sets the big motor in motion."

—FIDEL CASTRO TO DEENA STRYKER AS REPORTED IN HER BOOK
CUBA: A DIARY OF THE REVOLUTION

Howard Zinn's *The People's History of the United States*, one of the best-selling books on bottom-up history, started a whole movement of "people's" history books. Others include Zirin's *The People's History of Sports*, Pimpare's *The People's History of Poverty*, and Dunbar-Ortiz's *Indigenous People's History of the United States*. Interviewing Zinn, I said, "I think of you as the person who has written a bottom-up version of American history, looking at history from the perspective of the average people. Have you thought about it in those terms much?"

Zinn replied:

Well, sure, because most of our history is taught from the viewpoint of the people in power. Presidents dominate, Congresses dominate, Supreme Courts dominate, generals dominate, and nobody asks 'What about those people below?'

If you look at American history from the standpoint of the little people, of the workers, of the farmers, and certainly, of course, if you look at American history from the standpoint of Black people, then history looks very, very different. When you look at American history from the standpoint of the people on top…you are drawn into their way of thinking. It's like today, when the television stations and the newspapers all fasten on the existing president, or they fasten on the people who will be president, and they don't ask 'Well, what about the ordinary American?'

When you look at history from the standpoint of the people at the bottom, everything looks different, and then you recognize that the policies that we have followed in this country from the beginning have been policies that benefited the upper classes. It's not hard to see when you look at all the legislation passed by Congress all through history. It was legislation not to benefit the poor, it was legislation to benefit the railroads and the steel industries and the manufacturers and the oil companies.

Finally, bottom-up historians are actually writing and teaching about history in a way that changes things even more and faster, as they raise the level of self-awareness among the people who were ignored by top-down historians and histories. This is an essential step in helping them realize that they have the power to change their lives and cultures.

CENTRALIZATION VS. DECENTRALIZATION, GLOBALIZATION VS. LOCALIZATION, SMART VS. DUMB ALGORITHMS

One opposing "pair" of top-down and bottom-up concepts is centralization versus decentralization. I've heard horror stories about shifts made from local to centralized institutions.

We learned a hard lesson during the 2008–2009 Wall Street meltdown about the dangers of shifting from local bankers to centralized mortgage loan processing. Centralization, particularly with algorithms, dehumanizes and dumbs down decision-making and governance.

Venture capitalist and tech publisher, conference organizer, and online education pioneer Tim O'Reilly told me, "Our algorithmic systems, in the places like Google or Facebook, are a little bit like the Djinnis of Arabian mythology. You get to give him three wishes, and in the stories, the person who's giving the wish doesn't think it through, sufficiently well and it goes haywire."

He cites Disney's *Fantasia*, where Mickey mouse uses a spell to automate a broom carrying water, which goes out of control and causes a flood. Companies like Google and Facebook use crowd-sourced collective intelligence, in the form of big data to fine tune their algorithms, nanosecond to nanosecond.

I asked O'Reilly about collective intelligence, which has become one of the most powerful bottom-up factors in the creation of algorithms and artificial intelligence. He replied, "So many of the apps and services that we have today really are based on collective intelligence. That was sort of the central insight of the work that I wrapped the term Web 2.0 around (he played a key role in creating the term). All of the companies that survived the dot com bust, in some way or other, figured out how to harness the collective intelligence of millions of users. It was part of their edge, I think." Collective intelligence driven algorithms are the opposite of top-down, ivory-tower created policies, regulations, and algorithms that are rigid and nonadapting, which, I believe, were part of the cause of the 2008–2009 economic crash.

We globalized trade, meaning we centralized trade, with deals like NAFTA and CAFTA, and as Ross Perot warned, we heard the giant sucking sound of millions of jobs leaving the USA. Centralization and globalization have caused massive damage, hurting and brutally disrupting the lives of hundreds of millions of people by destroying local industries and jobs, circumventing locally passed laws, dispossessing indigenous peoples, and giving unaccountable transnational corporations powers that are dangerous to humanity and the ecosystem.

Centralization is sold as an efficient, rational approach to doing business by cutting out middle managers or intermediary elements in order to control things more directly. But in reality, localization and decentralization have been the way most natural systems and processes have evolved. Converting them to top-down centralized forms creates many problems, costs and, sometimes, disasters. I discuss this more extensively in Chapter Seven.

IT'S TIME TO FACE REALITY: TOO BIG IS TOO DANGEROUS

Just as hierarchy, centralization, domination, authoritarianism, and patriarchy are top-down factors, so are BIG things. Big money, big business, big religion, big government, big military—they're the major wielders, enablers and magnifiers of top-down energy and power.

E.F. Schumacher wrote, in his classic book, *Small Is Beautiful: Economics as if People Mattered*, about how bigness is massively problematic. The book was ranked one of the 100 most influential post World War II. It inspired the founding of the Schumacher Center for a New Economics, which promotes the "new economy," which includes the concepts buy local, local currency, self-sufficiency, and a just and sustainable global economy.

We Need Science, Economics, and Lifestyles Based on SMALL

Nature abhors just about anything that is too big. Gigantism is an abnormality that, in humans and most life forms, leads to pathology or death. It leads to the same result in human-created companies, government, political, and economic systems. Extreme wealth and the desire for money can be pathologically related to addiction, obsessive-compulsive hoarding, and depression or psychopathy. It is often the case that the need and desire for bigness can also be dysfunctional.

Fortunately, "*BIG*" (the notion, meme, and concept) is getting smaller. Nicco Mele, author of *The End of Big*, succinctly summarized his book for me in these words: "The last thirty-five years have seen a tremendous diffusion of power from institutions to individuals."

Advocates for "big" will argue that we absolutely need BIG and tell you why:

BIG is our destiny, inevitable, and better

BIG is required for scalability/mass production and efficiency

BIG is a sign of success

BIG is the greatest source of power

BIG is stronger

BIG is cooler

Actually, we can't be certain any of these claims are true, and we definitely don't know whether BIG is the only way to make them a reality. In many cases, we've never tried to accomplish what BIG things can do using a small or smaller approach.

Why do we need to get small? Because BIG is problematic for many reasons:

- It intensifies, potentiates, and enables narcissistic and psychopathic tendencies and behaviors.

- It is selfish and feels self-entitled.

- It parasitizes the commons, taking far more than its share of what it pays or compensates for.

- It is usually highly destructive to the environment and a major cause of the massive species die-off the earth is currently experiencing.

- It economizes by engaging in monoculture and analogous diversity diminishing unsustainable approaches.

- It buys/bribes power and influence, disrupting and corrupting democracy and justice.

- It destroys local community and culture. Think globalization and global trade pacts.

- Its centralization produces a disconnect from nature and humanity.

- It enables bullying.

- It becomes immortal, able to afford all forms of protection, creating dynasties.

- It evades accountability and regulation.

- It is more masculine/patriarchal.

- God is big. Has big become God?

- It produces manufacturing runs of irreparable, throw-away products.

- It generates unsustainable, metastasizing growth.

Economist Leopold Kohr was an advocate for smallness, and wrote in his book, *The Breakdown of Nations*, "Wherever something is wrong, something is too big." His message was that people who live in smaller states are happier, more peaceful, productive and happy. Kohr advocated for minimizing the aggregation of power.

SMALL IS SMART (SPECIFIC, MEASURABLE, ATTAINABLE, RELEVANT, AND TIMELY)

Bigness has evolved as a central dimension of civilization. But I challenge the notion that it is either a necessary or even optimal dimension. Perhaps the next step after BIG is "SMART small," which fractally raises freedom, democracy, connection, and humanity to the next level. Perhaps another way to morph big would be to make it distributed, like Bitcoin, blockchain, and the internet itself.

Examples of "bigness-need" that impose unnecessary risks: consumerism: always needing more and bigger

- gas-hog cars: think Hummer and massive SUVs

- breast augmentation

- use of steroids by weightlifters to get bigger muscles

- mega-mansions, mega-churches, mega-malls, mega-stores

- expensive high fashions and luxury cars, purchased simply because they're big money

To counter these trends we must shift to using small companies to build things currently built by massive companies. We must shift to governments that are decentralized and local, so they can be made smaller, more transparent, and accountable.

WHAT DO WE DO ABOUT TOO MUCH BIG?

Trying to tackle BIG head-on won't work. BIG is most powerful when it defines the territory and the terms. The solution is to start living small and going local. Become a consumer of local products purchased from local small businesses. Practice a SMALL lifestyle. You don't have to do it all at once. You can ease into it, just as people who are working on becoming vegetarian or vegan gradually discontinue eating meat.

Also, treat people as individuals, not as parts of a big system. Talk to them. Connect with them. Shift them from an extension of something bigger to someone with a face, heart, and soul. Here are more ideas for shifting support for less big and more small in your lifestyle:

- Support local co-ops and CSAs (community supported agriculture).

- Avoid big box stores and centralized, corporate-owned franchises. If there are no locally-owned stores, and your only choice is between a locally-owned franchise and a nationally-owned franchise, pick the locally-owned franchise.

- Make it a fun practice to discover small, locally-owned businesses. Get to know the owners. Let them know that you value the fact that their small business is part of the fabric of the community.

- If you go to big stores, like supermarkets, limit your purchases to healthy, necessary items. Identify aisles you don't need to go through at all, usually the middle aisles, and be proud of yourself for fighting the BIG system every time you bypass them.

- Purchasing on-line? Find smaller companies to buy from. Avoid the big mega-companies worth billions. Buying from Amazon? Make purchases from small sellers, not directly from Amazon.

- Expect to pay a little more for items you get from small businesses. Consider the small cost difference to be an investment in a better future and a stronger community that you can feel good about supporting.

- Some areas have organizations that provide certificates for genuine small, local businesses to display. Look for them. If there are no such organizations in your area, create one. Anthony Flaccavento, author of *Building a Healthy Economy from the Bottom Up*, recommends BALLE (Business Alliance for Local Living Economies).

- Whether it's cars, furniture, or sporting goods, think used and reconditioned. Some products just stand up better in spite of intentional obsolescence. Also, find local people to repair appliances, shoes, and clothing instead of throwing them out and replacing them.

Change the Channel

The mainstream media play a huge role in maintaining BIG—in business, consumerism, and belief in BIG and the system that supports it. Consider doing some of the following to change things:

- Create your own content and channels.

- Identify the worst shows, and let advertisers know you won't buy their products if they continue advertising on them.

- Stay away from the biggest internet websites/channels.

- Stop watching TV altogether, or at least unplug from cable, as millions are doing.

- Seek out local entertainment—theater groups, performers, clubs, music venues, art galleries.

- Join book clubs, writers' groups, and discussion groups.

Needed: A Science of Small and SMART Big

We need to fund research aimed at developing SMALL business approaches and solutions to problems that are usually only addressed by big business. Look at all the touted advantages of big business and then identify small ways to do them as well or better, for the same or lower cost. Part of the research will identify quality and cost benefits that are not usually included in the BIG business solution equation. Noam Chomsky has told me how corporations don't pay for "externalities" like air and water pollution. There are also positive externalities for small businesses, like supporting local families, paying local taxes, and maintaining local clean streets. A scientific approach to small business would identify small ways that are more profitable—for the business and for the local community—and would also encourage BIG companies to embrace SMALL approaches and lead to legislation that supports this.

When I told Douglas Rushkoff, Professor of Media Theory and Digital Economics at CUNY about my take on BIG, he replied that being big is, not, of itself, always bad. It's when being large aims for unrestrained, unlimited, extractive growth, that it's a problem. We were discussing his new book, *Throwing Rocks at The Google Bus*, in which he argues that taking companies public usually ruins them because they are forced to just aim for big and fast, instead of building a long-term company that supports consumers and the local community as well as investors. According to Rushkoff, there is not an absolute need to eliminate what's big, but we absolutely must change the way we think about BIG. Kelvin Campbell, proposes the idea of "massive small," the idea of tapping the collective power of a multitude of small ideas and actions to produce significant results.

Campbell argues, in his book, *Making Massive Small Change* that "Many things need to be conceived of at scale; there is nothing wrong with having big ideas or big plans. Big ideas do not mean big solutions in the same way that big plans do not mean radical or wholesale change." And he concludes, "So…we still need big shared visions, but they must be capable of releasing the collective power of many small ideas and action that will add up to make a big difference."

START ERODING THE BENEFITS OF BIG, AND BEGIN REDUCING ITS ADVANTAGES AND ATTRACTIONS

- Reduce or eliminate tax breaks for bigger companies.

- The US government imposed a 92 percent tax rate on the highest portions of the highest income brackets under Eisenhower in the early 1950s. There was a thriving economy. Bring that tax level back for wealthier individuals and bigger companies.

- Drastically raise dynasty taxes on inheritances over $5 million per person. Eliminate billion-dollar inheritances for born-on-third-base children.

- Pass legislation that makes it less attractive, even unattractive, for BIG companies to acquire smaller businesses or merge. For example, require that the number of local employees be retained for five years, and give bigger tax breaks to smaller companies. Motivate companies to find ways to stay small or become smaller.

Long-Term Big Goals for Ending BIG

- Eliminate billionaires and make it illegal to become a billionaire. Anyone with that much wealth has too much power. Start with big taxes on estates and end dynasties.

- Make it more expensive for BIG corporations to operate. Motivate them to break up into smaller operations that are legislated to be more profitable, ensuring a win-win outcome for all, including investors.

- Make it BETTER for investors if big companies break up.

- Create legislation that makes it more attractive to engage in open-source practices and which discourages proprietary patents and copyrights.

- Eliminate corporate welfare, which costs tens of billions of dollars.

- Replace the biggest government operations, including the military and intelligence agencies, and rebuild them with small principles in mind, with accountability and transparency being high on the list.

- End corporate personhood.

- Establish and enforce a corporate death penalty for criminal corporations.

- Develop energy and transportation systems that don't depend on BIG. Replace Big Energy, especially nuclear plants, massive power grids, and transportation systems with small, local systems, using wind, water, and solar energy.

- Regulate the banking and finance system.

- Establish public banks for states, cities, counties, and municipalities.

- Create oversight models, principles, and agencies for tracking, regulating, and preventing BIG. Maybe call it "Little Brother."

- Adopt the approaches and models described in Kelvin Campbell's book *Making Massive Small Change.*

Though taking on BIG is a big project, there are millions of small ways to address it or get involved.

BOTTOM-UP WINNING: WIN-WIN IN BUSINESS, GAMES, WORK, AND LIFE

How does bottom-up winning look compared to top-down winning? How do we all share the win? Can you win without there being a loser? The answer: Seek win-win approaches to do win-win business and to play win-win games.

Let's start off by considering definitions of winning and losing:

"Win" as a verb: to get, to get possession, to obtain, to gain, to achieve, to acquire, to secure, to overcome, to achieve or gain victory, to succeed/be successful, to make, to finish first, to induce increased attraction or more friendliness, to accept a proposal or offer, to defeat others or all, to allure, to court, to charm

"Winning" as a noun: a victory, the position of a competitor who comes in or finishes first

The etymology of the word "win" derives from several origins: from Old English "winnan"—to fight, struggle, work, bear; and from Old High German the word "winnan." Also to struggle from Old Norse is "vinna," a possible variant of "winnow"

Top-down winning considers the victor to be the one who dominates, who defeats, or who takes victory by inflicting defeat, loss, and damage. This kind of winning is based on Hobbesian "law of the jungle," "winner-take-all" values by which the opponent is seen as the enemy to be destroyed.

In contrast, bottom-up winning seeks an optimal outcome for all involved, so everyone wins. Characteristics of bottom-up winning include kindness, sacrifice, cooperation, trust, transparency, and sharing of resources. When you consider that one of the original meanings of "to win" is "to struggle"—the outcome where everyone wins is a more reasonable, and therefore preferable, alternative.

Taking the Bite Out of Win or Lose Games

The best way to get better at a sport is to play someone better than yourself. Fortunately, the best players will often play against all levels of players, patiently sharing tips. Angel Roman, one of my gym's best racquetball players, plays all levels. He doesn't throw all he has at weaker players, but lets them win some points. I lose to Angel, but I've learned a lot from him about how to play better. When I play others, I consciously thank Angel, Chuck, Ben, Noah, Hansa, Manish, Dan, Larry, Fred and others who have taught me specific skills and techniques. And I pay it forward and play gently with people I can easily defeat, so I'm helping them learn. When YOU face win/lose situations, try to turn them into we-all-win outcomes.

Remember, by simply taking a bottom-up approach—by working, cooperating, and engaging in shared participation—you're taking the first winning step for "WE."

Dr. Linda Seger wrote, in her book, *The Better Way To Win: Connecting, Not Competing, For Success,* ". . . scientists and mathematicians have created games that can test who's more likely to win—the competitors or the collaborators." Seger described how one game theorist, Robert Axelrod, who's spent his life researching cooperation, found that "nice guys can and frequently do finish first." Axelrod reported that in studies of numerous conflict situations, the top dog was not the most ferocious person, but rather, the most cooperative person. The reason was the predatory exploiters ran out of prey, and in the long run, that nasty approach would destroy the environment needed for success. Seger concludes, "The survival of the fittest is not dog-eat-dog where clearly few survive, but where dog learns to live cooperatively with other dogs. Being cooperative does not mean being a pushover. Axelrod discovered the best way of playing any game, even the game of life, begins by cooperating."

Do winners always have to produce losers? Do wins have to produce losses? No. It has never had to be that way and doesn't need to be that way anymore. People can be victors without the need for victims.

THE NEUROPSYCHOLOGY OF TOP-DOWN AND BOTTOM-UP

As founder and organizer of a brain conference that ran for 15 years, I've discussed my theory that emerging bottom-up web and smartphone technologies have literally changed the neuropsychology of humans, changed the way their brain works, with hundreds of brain experts. Every single one agreed.

Then I found Darcia Narvaez's book, *Neurobiology and the Development of Human Morality: Evolution, Culture, and Wisdom*, which is described in my introduction. Narvaez, like Daniel Quinn, proposes that for millions of years, mothers had the help of the whole band of hunter-gatherers to care for a baby, so the newborn or infant was never left alone, crying himself to sleep. The whole band would get involved in loving, caring for, and raising the baby and in raising the child as an integral, equal part of the community. Narvaez calls it the "ancestral nest."

When ancestral parenting doesn't happen, the child's full, optimal epigenetic potential is not reached. Contemporary Western industrial culture makes it difficult to provide the nurturing that human babies and children received for 99 percent of human history. Civilization compartmentalized our lives and broke the chain of continuity, love, and nurturing that our indigenous, pre-civilization ancestors and hominid predecessors maintained for millions of years. But the epigenetic DNA programming, which I believe wires bottom-up metaphorical filtering into our perceptual processing, is still deeply encoded in each of us. That's why we respond so stronly when bottom-up technologies like social media and the internet stimulate us. Our neuroendocrine programming is engaged and activated by them.

THE TOP-DOWN AND BOTTOM-UP BRAIN

MIT neuroscientist Earl Miller, who researches top-down and bottom-up brain processes, explained to me that in neuroscience top-down "executive" brain function, primarily in the prefrontal cortex, uses knowledge we've acquired and synthesizes it, in order to decide what to pay attention to and how to act on the raw bottom-up information our senses deliver.

According to neuropsychologist Robert Thatcher, only two percent of the brain is dedicated to what is characterized as bottom-up input—sight, hearing, touch, smell, and balance. "We only have two percent coming in and we make the rest up. That's why two people looking at the same incident have very different views," he said.

"No wonder there is so much misunderstanding in the world," Dr. Thatcher observed. "We are creating reality all the time, and expectations of what the future will be." Some people shut out almost all the bottom-up raw input.

Physician and Native American healer/Lakota shaman Lewis Mehl-Madrona, author of *Remapping Your Mind: The Neuroscience of Self-Transformation through Story*, explains the concept of changing our stories, saying: "We're forced by the nature of our brains to do a lot of top-down processing. We need a story to tell us how to separate foreground from background, what objects to pay attention to and to ignore. Once you have a workable top-down perception story, you may never discover there are different ways to organize the pixels. Most of our stories on how to perceive the world are in place by age seven. It takes an effort to go bottom-up." In his workshops, Mehl-Madrona helps people identify stories they are unconsciously living so they can take a different view of the world, to rewrite the stories they live their lives through "by re-storying."

The Bottom-Up Brain Revolution and Toddlers

While the brain functioning of people born after 1980 has become more bottom-up, neuropsychological change is continuing to accelerate. Two-year-olds are operating iPads and accessing iPhones with Siri or Alexa. They view videos, play games, and even navigate the App Store and download apps, tapping what Nico Mele calls radical connectivity. These digital kids are experiencing a sense of self-agency that people born before 1980 never imagined as children. Who knows how that will change them as they grow up? The brain revolution is just getting started. The question is, how will it change what it means to be human?

Top-Down and Bottom-Up Psychological Dysfunction

I asked Dr. Miller for some examples of unbalanced top-down and bottom-up thinking leading to psychological disease or dysfunction. He replied, "ADHD (attention deficit hyperactivity disorder) is a primary one—an affliction of people who have trouble staying focused because they are easily distracted. Some people with prefrontal cortex problems lose sight of the goals, the context, and the big picture. Their minds are buffeted by the bottom-up sensory inputs and they have very little top-down control. They lose the forest, the big picture, and get lost in the trees." They don't have enough modulation of their bottom-up brain function, so their sensory experience is like drinking from a fire hose. Brain biofeedback, also called neurofeedback, teaches people to voluntarily control their brains so they can focus better and inhibit distraction.

Obsessive compulsive disorder is an example of a condition that results from top-down overactivity. Other top-down brain disorders include delusions, hallucinations, and schizophrenia, in which, as Bob Thatcher describes, the brain makes things up. Personal rigidity and inflexibility, being very driven or opinionated, can also be based on top-down overactivity.

THE BEGINNINGS OF BOTTOM-UP MORALS OF FAIRNESS, CARING, AND EMPATHY

It has been estimated that there are at least 50 different genetic factors that can contribute to creating a psychopath, and 150 epigenetic factors that can be activated to maximize creation of a moral being. The evolutional genetic programming of caring, empathy, and the sense of fairness dates back at least two hundred million years in early mammals.

Primatologist Frans de Waal, director of the Living Links Center at the Yerkes National Primate Research Center, and one of *Time* magazine's "100 Most Influential People," has shown that animals have bottom-up morals and demonstrate fairness and cooperation.

Dr. de Waal's research focuses on primate social behavior, including conflict resolution, cooperation, inequity aversion, and food-sharing. I interviewed him to learn about animal morals and evolutional and anthropological aspects of fairness, caring, and altruism.

My first question to Dr. de Waal was: "After almost forty years working with primates, what's the number one thing you've learned?"

He answered, "When I started, primates were usually depicted, like all animals, as competitive, aggressive, and selfish—this whole view of nature as a competitive place, a dog-eat-dog world. The main thing that I've learned is, yes, there is plenty of competition—there's no denying that—but there's also plenty of cooperation."

Dr. de Waal's research on cooperation confirmed similar reports from other experts I've interviewed, dismissing "rule of the jungle" and "survival of the fittest" theories as simply untrue. I asked him to explain bottom-up morality, which he describes in his book, *Bonobo and the Atheist.* He said, "The top-down view of morality is, of course, the dominant view that morality comes from God and that God told us how to behave. After God's word became less popular during The Enlightenment, the philosophers told us, 'Well, maybe it doesn't come from God. It comes from reasoning and logic. We reason ourselves to moral principles and then we apply them to society, and that's the top-down view.'

"The bottom-up view is exactly the opposite," de Waal continued. "You have moral tendencies that you're born with, and, actually, we have evidence that young children, even one-year-old children—you can show them a puppet-show with good guys and bad guys and they already have preferences for one or the other. So moral judgments actually don't necessarily require a God, or a philosopher, for that matter.

"Many of the tendencies that you see in young children you can also see in other primates, such as the tendency to help others, to be empathic to others, to be sensitive to fairness, to have a tendency to cooperate with others and to maintain good relationships. All of these tendencies are part of our usual moral systems, and so all of these things can be acquired by our species without God and without philosophers. And that's the bottom-up view, basically that morality comes from within. That doesn't mean that religion or the philosophers have no role, but it means that the tendencies are already there."

According to de Waal, moral fairness and caring are mediated or supported by empathy, and mammals and even birds show signs of empathy. As he explained, "Mammals evolved two hundred-million years ago, and, whether you are a female mouse or a female elephant, you need to react to your young. The thinking is that maternal care is actually the origin of empathic responses, because you need to be sensitive to the emotions of others if you want to raise them." There are also dozens of studies of rodent empathy, de Waal reports, which have shown that even rats and mice respond to the emotions of others and sometimes help others who are in a predicament.

Dr. de Waal described an experiment in which two monkeys, sitting side by side, are given a task and rewarded for it either with cucumber slices or much more desirable grapes. If they both get cucumber or both get grapes, things are okay. But if one monkey gets grapes and the other gets the less desirable cucumber, the monkey who gets the grapes becomes upset that the other monkey received an inferior treat. According to de Waal, the same fairness response can be found in many species.

Relating his findings to the Occupy Wall Street's protest against inequalities and the one percent, de Waal said, "[Humans] are very sensitive to inequity, just like those monkeys." He added, "Inequity has all sorts of consequences and our experiments indicate that it's a very profound and very ancient reaction to react negatively to getting something less than somebody else. It has enormous consequence, probably also health consequences in human society."

Primates and elephants not only cooperate to achieve common goals, but will even help others when they're not going to be rewarded themselves—evidence of altruism and interdependence.

Dr. de Waal described an experiment: "You put two chimpanzees side-by-side. They can exchange food for tokens. They get a bucket full of tokens of two different colors. One color, if they hand the token to us, they get food, but the neighbor in the next cage gets nothing. For the other color, if they hand it to us, they get food, but the neighbor also gets the same piece of food. So the one who does the exchanging will always get some food for what he does with us. The only difference is that one color feeds only himself and the other color feeds the two of them. We found that over time the chimps started to prefer the color pieces that would feed the two of them. Chimpanzees do actually care about the well-being of others."

Dr. de Waal then broadened his discussion, "The bottom-up view is, of course, very much a biological view, and neuroscience is also very much a bottom-up science at the moment. We think, for example, that our behavior is based on reasoning. But often our behavior is based on intuitions and emotions that we barely control. We automatically choose this or choose that, and then afterwards we come up with wonderful reasons for why we did this or why we married that…but actually our decisions are not necessarily produced by that kind of reasoning. So that's the view that is becoming very popular—actually also in psychology—that we are sort of bottom-up creatures."

Dr. de Waal is suggesting that while our hard-wired DNA programming plays a big role in our intelligence, we tend to repress or ignore our feelings, intuitions, and wild imaginings. His words suggest to me we could do even better if we trust ourselves, let down our boundaries, and open ourselves to all the systems we are already connected to.

Mirror neurons play a key role in our ability to feel empathy and caring and explain how the bottom-up connection between two people, and even between humans and animals, is wired. I asked Dr. de Waal about them. He said mirror-neurons "blur the line between your own body and somebody else's body. The mirror-neuron discovery is very interesting because they were discovered not in humans, but in macaques in a laboratory in Italy. The first discovery actually had to do with human-animal connections. They did experiments where a human reaches with his hand for an object, and [when] the monkey sees that, his mirror-neurons respond in exactly the same way as when the monkey himself reaches for the same object."

That's why the neurons involved are labeled mirror neurons. The monkey mirror neurons don't make a distinction between the monkey's own movement and somebody else's movement. Besides mirroring physical movements, mirror neurons also create mirror feelings when we see someone else expressing and experiencing emotions. The tie between mirror neurons and empathy is pretty obvious.

BOTTOM-UP SCIENTIFIC PARADIGMS: WHY BOTTOM-UP, SMALL ACTS CAN PRODUCE MASSIVE RESULTS

Systems theory and chaos theory, essential bottom-up concepts, have been giving me hope for over 30 years—ever since I learned chaos can lead to higher levels of order. Even more, they explain why bottom-up change can be so powerful, even if only a tiny number of people set it in motion.

Before systems theory existed, a top-down, mechanistic approach to science—the Newtonian/Cartesian model—predominated for hundreds of years, providing a take-things-apart-and-count-them approach to understanding and explaining the world. That worked for simple physics and chemistry, but not for more complex biological systems, eco-systems, and sub-atomic particle systems.

A new, more bottom-up systems-theory model evolved in the mid-twentieth century which, in addition to basing its study on parts and quantitative analysis, also looks at processes, relationships, and patterns and assumes EVERYTHING is connected in different systems and networks.

I interviewed Fritjof Capra, co-author of *The Systems View of Life,* which takes systems thinking and applies it to economics, health care, social change, and most of the big social and ecological justice issues. Systems thinking offers a valuable, deeper way to think about bottom-up, connection and connection consciousness, providing concepts worth knowing: chaos theory and nonlinearity, fractals, complexity theory, attractors, and emergence.

A central characteristic of the systems view of life is nonlinearity, which chaos and complexity theories are based on. It assumes that all living systems are nonlinear networks. I asked Capra to explain. He replied:

"Linearity is a straight line. Anything that's not a straight line, a curve, circle, or cycle, is nonlinear. A network is nonlinear because a network goes in all directions, not just in one straight line. When you influence a living system, the effect goes around in circles…called feedback loops. So, whatever we put out in the environment eventually will come back to us. We build cars and factories that use fossil fuels, and they emit greenhouse gases that change the atmosphere, which then have many… severe consequences of climate change, which is a feedback of our human actions. And that is because the whole planet Gaia is a living, nonlinear system."

Nonlinear science is primarily the study of relationships and patterns. Patterns represent the dynamics of how a system behaves. System patterns are called attractors, which can be stable or unstable. When they're stable, the system continues to behave the same way. As Capra explained it, when the attractors are unstable, a totally new behavior can emerge, "because the system branches off into a new behavior and a new branch of the attractor." Capra says this is "one of the most important results of complexity theory, the discovery of *emergence*—that there can be a spontaneous emergence of new forms of order."

Let's return to my comfort, chaos theory. Ilya Prigogine won the Nobel Prize in chemistry for his theory that living things are NORMALLY far from equilibrium or balance, and that in chemical reactions a period of even explosive levels of chaos can lead to higher levels of order. Out of the chaos, new patterns emerge. Capra observed, "This spontaneous emergence of order has been recognized as the basic dynamic of development, of learning, and of evolution."

When you're experiencing chaos in your life, remember Prigogine's theory, embrace the chaos, and take comfort, knowing that it will lead to higher levels of order. But keep in mind, top-down people and powers also take advantage of chaos. Naomi Klein, author of *The Shock Doctrine*, reminds us, "It's in those moments when fear and chaos are sucking up all the oxygen when we most have to ask whose interests are being served by the chaos. What is being slipped through while we're distracted."

I asked Capra, "How does this tie in to economics and our world today?"

He explained that, according to complexity theory, a small "disturbance in the system" can cycle and be amplified "to such an extent that the entire system becomes unstable and then breaks through to a new form of order... It can happen also in the social realm—for example, in a human organization... Somebody says something and it's a new idea. But the person doesn't even consider it very important—just an idea. But it disturbs the system in such a way that the other people in the discussion throw it around back and forth in their network, and it cycles around the organization. It gets amplified because everybody contributes something—a new interpretation, a new comment. It may get amplified to such an extent that people realize they can't go on working like they did: They have to do something new—a new form of organization, a new order, new behavior. That's the phenomenon of emergence. And in economics or in society at large, it can happen that the small group, say a small NGO, a nongovernment organization, comes up with a different way of viewing things and it spreads and it changes the system."

Fractals represent another important chaos theory concept. They're repeating natural or mathematical patterns that occur at different scales within a system. Try a Youtube search for "fractals in nature."

To summarize, nonlinear Dynamic/Chaos theory describes how, in living systems, change happens when a small event or repeated pattern becomes an attractor, leading to emergence of breakthrough changes. These produce bigger and bigger effects throughout the system. Such an emergence can lead to massive changes, even though it started with very small acts at smaller, fractal levels.

To put it simply, systems thinking and chaos and complexity theories teach us that small actions can produce huge changes, like the "butterfly effect." Capra observed, "In the linear world, small causes have small effects, and if you want a large effect you have to achieve it by adding up a lot of small causes. But in the nonlinear world, a small cause can have a huge effect. That's why seemingly small acts by a single person or small group can change the world."

This new systems way of thinking about change gives me hope that the bottom-up revolution can happen in spite of the daunting, seemingly invincible top-down power system and sociocultural structure built by and composed of transnational corporations, billionaires, and trillion-dollar economies.

Top-down thinking, built upon limited mechanistic thinking, takes a narrow, quantitative approach that fails in many ways to deal with reality.

The mechanistic scientific model contributes to the top-down metaphoric perceptual filter. It has created a deeply embedded mindset in society that has led to nonsustainable ways of thinking about how we live, do business, and even relate to one another.

Take, for example, the ideas of control, ownership, and domination. The mechanistic view of the universe, which dictates that everything is a machine to be controlled, provided a scientific sanction for the manipulation and exploitation of nature that became typical of modern civilization, as Daniel Quinn described. But Capra says, "If we deal with living systems, with living beings, then control is not the best approach... The appropriate approach to life is communicating, by engaging in dialogue."

Bottom-Up Systemic vs. Top-Down Mechanistic Management

Capra describes the problem with top-down mechanistic, hierarchical management in this way: "As a machine must be controlled by its operators to function according to their instructions, so the main thrust of management theory has been to achieve efficient operations through top-down control... This largely unconscious embrace of the mechanistic approach to management has now become one of the main obstacles to organizational change... Transcending the mechanistic view of organizations will be as critical for the survival of human civilization as transcending the mechanistic conceptions of health, the economy, or biotechnology."

Capra gives examples: "If you think, for instance, of business organizations, then there is still this Newtonian model of trying to design an organization either with the help of outside experts or from the top inside, and if the design doesn't work, then they talk about re-engineering the organization. These are all very mechanistic terms—the legacy of the mechanistic worldview."

The mechanistic approach stunts innovation and prevents the freeing up of emergent ideas. Kelvin Campbell observes in his book, *Making Massive Small Change*, "We have lost the ability to build successful human habitats. Our current plans treat the city as an ordered mechanical system where every variable must be entirely understood and managed, painstakingly controlled and legalistically prescribed for."

Individualism vs. Interconnection

Capra describes how the mechanistic way of "seeing individuals as independent and not connected to anything else is really the dilemma because we are all embedded in social systems and in ecosystems, and everything I do has an effect on the rest of society and has an effect on the ecosystems of the earth." Whether we talk about energy or environment, climate change, politics, economics, and so on, Capra says, "None of these issues or problems can be understood in isolation. They're all interconnected...systemic problems which need systemic solutions. Another way of saying this is that a systemic problem has harmful consequences in many areas and a systemic solution solves problems in many areas."

Capra spelled it out, "The fundamental dilemma underlying all these problems seems to be the illusion that unlimited growth is possible on a finite planet. It's an irrational belief that is held by virtually all our politicians and corporate economists. I see it as a clash between linear thinking, projecting out into the future in a linear way...pursued relentlessly by promoting excessive consumption—a throwaway economy that is energy and resource-intensive, creating waste and pollution and depleting the earth's resources and the nonlinear patterns in our biosphere, the ecological networks and cycles that constitute the web of life. *It seems that the key challenge of our time is how to shift from an economic system based on the notion of unlimited growth to one that is both sustainable and socially just."* (The emphasis is mine.)

Capra says growth itself is not bad. It's a central characteristic of life. But, he explains, "growth in nature is not linear and unlimited. When you look at an ecosystem, you see certain parts that grow [and] others that reach maturity, decline, and then disintegrate. [These] release and recycle their components, which become resources for new growth. We need to . . . distinguish between good growth and bad growth. The good growth should continue. The bad growth should decline."

"Growth is the closest thing we have to a global deity."
—NAOMI KLEIN, MOVIE, *THIS CHANGES EVERYTHING*

If we are to transition to a future that includes bio-diversity, sustainability and the continued existence of the human race, we must replace our top-down mechanistic filters with connection consciousness.

THE ROOTS OF CHANGE: STRATEGICALLY ADDRESSING AND EMBRACING DISRUPTION AND EMERGENCE
Peggy Holman, author of *Engaging Emergence: Turning Upheaval into Opportunity*, has developed a practical approach to emergence, the order

that arises out of chaos—facilitating it and making the most of it when it happens.

"Emergence," Holman offered, "tends to be about the interaction of people or things coming together in a novel and, in a sense, a more complex, yet more simply elegant way." She offers 'emergency' as an example of a word that shares the same root, saying, "If there's some kind of emergency, think about horrific storms. Some people start organizing and getting food. Some tend to the injured. Some put up a website so you can find your loved one. People, in a sense, self-organize to get stuff done, and out of the disorder of an emergency, a new order arises."

All Change is a Process of Emergence.

Holman says, "All change begins with some kind of disruption. If there were no disruption, there'd be no need for change. What does that disruption do? It means that the assumptions about business as usual, about how things work, no longer serve. Things break apart and we move into this experimental stage, and ultimately something new emerges and comes back together in a comprehensible form."

"How do we as human beings organize to get stuff done?" Holman asks, then answers, saying, "I come back to this prevailing notion of the idea that 'no one is in charge.' One of the major transitions that we're in, is that we're moving from our principal organizing metaphor as hierarchy, and thinking in terms of pack animals, to an organizing metaphor around networks. And there, you can think more in terms of flocks of birds, ants, bees, or animals that work in the collective. As people pursue what matters to them and discover others that care about similar things, we begin to be connected, not just to ourselves and others, but to our sense of a larger social body. And in that spirit of connection, our differences become a source of creative tension for breakthrough ideas that nobody could have come up with on their own."

I asked Holman to detail her step-by-step approach to embracing and making the most of emergence. She begins with the idea that change starts with disruption, which causes "things as we know them to break apart…" This doorway from disruption takes us to a place of experimentation. When we are in that situation, Holman says, we must ask ourselves two questions: "What do we want to conserve that still has value, and what do we want to embrace that wasn't possible before?"

Holman offers some strategies for engaging in this experimental stage:

Think about how to prepare to "engage with this area of mystery. Not knowing, as we go into this open, divergent, chaotic kind of space, how do I ensure that I am equipped as possible?" The trick is to embrace the mystery of it, knowing that you don't necessarily know the answers, nor, at the early stage, want to know the answers. She advises, "Find an attitude of possibility, looking towards what's possible, and following the energy, which generally shows up, and where things get lively—where the emotional roller coaster is most alive. That can look like anger, fear, or even joy."

I related to Holman that I've had a few encounters with opportunities for success. I call it "riding the roller coaster." It makes you feel incredibly alive. For me it meant flying in Lear jets and doing million-dollar deals with CEOs of billion-dollar companies. You never know, when you light the metaphorical cigar and take a puff, whether it will blow up in your face. Or you can trip and fall, or move forward and have big things happen. It's very disruptive and changes everything.

I said to her, "You have to embrace it and love wherever it takes you. Right?"

Holman agreed, adding, "that's where we're most alive—I think of it, a lot, as jazz. The more I practice my scales, the more discipline I have in my life, the more equipped I am when the moment comes to let go and jump in, and trust that I am equipped to deal with what shows up.

"The next layer, in terms of the practice of engaging, is preparing myself to 'host.'" What does it mean to 'host' others? Holman advises "Focus on a willingness to invite those who have a stake but don't necessarily see things the way I do. To be welcoming to who and what shows up creates the set of conditions in which we can be present to each other in a more authentic, profound way—such that our differences become the source of creative response rather than a reason to fight with each other."

Holman went on to explain, "The heart of these practices is engaging. Ask possibility-oriented questions as a doorway in because they clarify intention, and they have a spirit of invitation in them. And then, there's the leap of faith, a stepping into the not-knowing, to act. And out of that, then, to reflect—and particularly to reflect with others on, 'What are we learning?' 'What do we now know that we didn't know before?' Out of which [there's] a new coherence. We begin to get glimmers of where we're going. One of the lessons is that any great shift is actually many, many, many increments happening over time. Generally, the first time we try something, we don't necessarily get it right, and if its intent is really important to us, we'll learn from that, pick ourselves up, dust ourselves off, and try it again."

"Making change," Holman elaborated, "is a lot like growing bamboo. You water it every day for four years and nothing happens, and then it grows 90 feet in 60 days. There's an awful lot of groundwork by the time things 'suddenly blossom.' Just knowing that certainly has kept me going. That's something that people trying to change things, whether they are corporate, social, or political, really need to think about—the whole idea that beneath the surface things are happening, that growth is occurring—preparing for a sudden burst of growth that doesn't happen, sometimes, until much later."

Holman summarizes five guidelines for working effectively with disruption:

1. **WELCOME DISTURBANCE.** "Disturbance is the doorway to change and creativity. Rather than fighting or resisting it, become more capable being present to what shows up, getting curious about what it has to offer, and what can we do with it. It becomes an entryway into possibility, and curiosity becomes a tool. Just that idea of welcoming disturbance can be life changing.

   "University of Arizona Professor Gary Schwartz, an old friend, has a cardinal rule: 'Be prepared for the unexpected.' For over twenty-five years I've been saying, 'Be prepared for moments when you encounter situations that you didn't plan for.' Have a plan—a set of instructions for yourself—on how to respond to such opportunities. I've given myself permission, when I encounter something unexpected, to break my routine, to readjust my schedule, and to just stop and interact."

2. BE A PIONEER. "Experimentation accelerates the feedback. It's where we find out, 'Well, that didn't work,' or 'That did! We want to do more of that.'"

3. ENCOURAGE RANDOM ENCOUNTERS. "[Get] back to the notion of 'No One in Charge.' Go talk to people you don't usually interact with. Show up in their world and do some listening, observing, and learning as part of that experimentation. Invite them to play with you. It's very often at the intersection of unexpected partnerships that breakthroughs occur."

4. SEEK MEANING. "What is the intention that sparked in the first place? Disruptions wouldn't be disrupting if we didn't care. So, there is some deeper meaning that may be implicitly or unconsciously guiding us. The more we can seek meaning, [the more] we will find kindred spirits, and find the experimentations that help us emphasize that."

5. SIMPLIFY. "What's a simpler way to talk about it?"

Peggy summed things up: "If you're in the moment and facing disruption and you're not sure what to do, ask a question that points to possibility. It's like my 'hip pocket' idea, the most compassionate and creative act that I know to do." She shared a story as an example:

I have an African American colleague who was in New Orleans. He would go play his guitar in this park across from where he was working. One day, out of the corner of his eye, he saw these three young men—lots of tattoos, shaved heads—sneaking up on him. So he put his guitar down, stood up and very softly said, 'Stop where you are.' And they stopped, and then started telling him in not very pretty language that he didn't belong in this park. It wasn't for people like him, and they were going to make an object lesson of him. He, at that point, whipped out a possibility-oriented question. 'Okay, before you do that,' he said, 'can I ask you a question?' and said: 'What is it in your life experience that led you to wanting to do this? Forty-five minutes later the four of them were deeply in conversation about their worlds and experiences and life. Needless to say, it was a pretty profound shift for all four of them.

BOTTOM-UP CHANGE IS NOT OPTIONAL

We live in a predominantly top-down world that is spiraling both BACK and FORWARD to a new, more nonlinear, systems-embracing way, similar to how indigenous people existed, which Zeitgeist video series creator Peter Joseph calls "neo-Neolithic." You can't avoid this emerging bottom-up connection revolution. So you might as well learn how to navigate it and embrace it, perhaps in the way Peggy Holman advises.

CHAPTER 2

The Connection Revolution

CONNECTION POWER AND DYNAMICS

The bottom-up connection revolution has shifted us from an information era to a connection era. This chapter takes a deeper look at old and new ways of connecting, at aspects of disconnection and at ways to optimize connecting.

THE TRANSITION FROM AN INFORMATION ECONOMY TO A CONNECTION ECONOMY

In a family or an indigenous band, at a kitchen table, or around a campfire, the whole group can talk to one another. That's many-to-many communication. The bottom-up ability to speak many-to-many was the norm in prehistoric hunter-gatherer bands. Later, however, in big tribes, villages, states, and nations, where there were thousands of people who did not know one another, many-to-many communication was replaced with top-down, one-to-many communication.

In civilization's early days, one-to-many royal decree messaging was inscribed on stone or parchment and displayed in the town square. You had to go TO the message to receive it. Later, Gutenberg's printing press allowed a shift from hand-inscribed books for the wealthy and powerful to pamphlets, books, and newspapers that could be widely distributed. This development connected people in new ways, providing access to new ideas and information and also to the power that information imparted—which shifted the balance of power. In the modern advance to democracy, pamphleteers like Thomas Paine used the printing press as a tool to build bottom-up grassroots energy. Emerging postal services, followed by the telegraph also began connecting people.

Radio, then movies and television, also dramatically increased and radically changed the nature and character of one-to-many communication. But those media were still in the model of one person addressing many, not a two-way conversation or dialogue.

All these means for REMOTE connection reduced face-to-face connection. Until the 1950s and '60s, when air conditioning became common, neighbors sat outside on the front porch talking to one another. Air-conditioning drew them indoors, watching TV in isolation.

Today, digital technologies are creating a similar disconnection, reducing face-to-face, smell-each-other's-breath, real-voice, direct-eye-contact, shared-mutual-environment connections. Compared to in-the-flesh contact, digital connections are weaker, not as dynamic or whole-brain-engaging.

Email enables any person to send a message to many people at once, and all of them can respond to the original sender, or to all. This is the reinvention of many-to-many connecting, without the need to sit at a kitchen table or around a campfire. In the early '90s, Compuserve and AOL offered forums and discussion groups where people from all over the world could join in online conversations. Text messaging enabled real-time conversations with many people at once. People around the world could digitally contact multiple people simultaneously. Kids grew up in a world where many-to-many connecting was the norm. Now, young people text thousands of times a month, and use group texting apps like Snapchat, WhatsApp, and Facebook Messenger.

Social media—Facebook, Twitter, Pinterest, Instagram, WhatsApp, plus blogging and other apps—make it even easier to let your "friends" know what's on your mind, even if you haven't directed the thought to them directly. Blogging and video blogging put the power of one-to-many in anyone's hands. You don't have to decide who to have a conversation with. Post a new entry to your blog and wait to see who responds in the comment section, where many-to-many conversations come alive.

The one-to-many media have also changed. TV and radio News anchors and hosts have embraced social-networking technologies like Twitter and Facebook. When they are broadcasting, they are also inviting, tracking, and sharing Twitter responses and Facebook postings. Some, like top-ranked progressive radio host Thom Hartmann, use bulletin boards as a way to stay connected to and maintain a two-way conversation between host and listeners.

Psychology professor Gary Schwartz, from the University of Arizona, has shown just how intimately we are connected. Using EEG electro-encephalographic brain monitoring combined with ECG electrocar-diographic heart monitoring, he's demonstrated that if you and I are in the same room, the electromagnetic energy produced by my heart can be detected in your brain. We are connected to and touch each other in so many mysterious ways!

New Connections Are Changing Young Brains

In the 1930s, a movie scene might last two to five minutes. Today, television and movie scenes can be a fraction of a second. Long scenes last ten to twenty seconds. Maggie Jackson, author of *Distracted: The Erosion of Attention and the Coming Dark Age*, suggests that the trend towards diminished attention span and other factors are leading to a shallowing of the way people connect—not only to their environment but to one another. Nicholas Carr, author of *The Shallows: What the*

Internet Is Doing to Our Brains, told me how the shift to shallower is affecting our social norms.

Carr warns, "We lose a lot of the fundamental processes that give richness to our thinking and intellectual lives," Carr said. "Our most sophisticated, deepest emotions, like empathy, arise from brain processes that are quite slow to emerge. There's one line of theory [that] if we're distracted all the time, we're not able to activate the processes that give rise to our deepest emotions."

There's been a huge uptick in ADD and ADHD. Many have suggested it is because people have been conditioned to shift their attention much more often, by changes such as shorter scene durations, the replacement of news reports with short sound bites, and an exponential increase in the choices of what to view on TV, smart phones, and the Web.

When you are sitting on a porch, face to face with your neighbor, you don't simultaneously compose several emails, talk with four or ten other people, and watch TV. It's rude. But today's technology makes it easy to do all those things AND stay "polite." That may be good in terms of efficiency and convenience, but we pay a heavy price. By giving up face-to-face warm-body time, we lose the stimulation of the parts in our brain, like motor neurons that are connected to our empathy, our hearts and feelings, and our spirit of connection to Mother Earth. Pope Francis said, in his TED Talk, that we live our lives through relations with others and that our very existence is integrally tied to our interactions with others. What effects will a major diminution of these kinds of connections have, long term, on human brain functioning or relationships? The impact will be big and is well under way.

The Connection Economy
As our culture transitions from top-down back to more bottom-up ways, we are also shifting to a more connected economy that is radically changing the way business is done.

When I learned Facebook had passed Google on some traffic metrics I had an "aha moment." I realizing we'd shifted from an information era to a connection era. It appeared to be a clear case of a primarily connection-oriented site overtaking the world's most powerful information-oriented site.

Even Google's original search is built upon the connections and links between websites. Some of the algorithms that decide top search ranks on Google look at how many other sites connect/link to a site that fits the search term requirements. Google also provides connection tools like Gmail, Google Groups, Google Hangout (face-to-face through video), and Google Drive, a cloud-based word-processing program that allows multiple people to collaborate on texts, spreadsheets, and so forth.

Marketing guru Seth Godin has been talking about the shift to a connection economy for years. He told an inbound marketing conference (bit.ly/GodinConnection), "We are leaving the industrial economy and entering the connection economy. Only by working together, by integrating into communities that connect, can we create value now." Godin emphasizes, "You are in the business of connection... Connection is the asset of the future," and value is created where connection occurs.

Godin says connection is built on the following:

1. coordination—getting people to show up, work together, and create value as a group

2. trust

3. permission—the idea of delivering anticipated, personal, and relevant messages to people who want to get them

4. the exchange of ideas

And Godin proposes that connection is based on two fundamental principles—generosity and art. He says, "We don't want to connect with a selfish person" and "you gain connection by earning it—by being generous and being an artist."

The full blooming of the connection era will take maximum advantage of all the social networking technologies combined with smart phones, wearable technology, geolocation technology, and the Internet of things (IoT,) which Wikipedia describes as, "the network of physical devices, vehicles, buildings and other items embedded with electronics, software, sensors, actuators and network connectivity that enable these objects to collect and exchange data."

You'll be able to set up preferences for being notified in different situations. For example, you might want to be to be notified when you're walking or driving past a store or restaurant that offers products you've expressed an interest—say, in cases where they are discounted X percent, or your friends have recently made a purchase there. Some apps already do some of this.

Imagine apps, in the not-too-distant future, that offer you two discounts. When you use your account number to make a purchase, you'll be offered one discount for sharing your purchases with your friends, and an additional credit if any of your friends make purchases based on your sharing.

The Ability to Track Connections Makes It Possible to Treat Them as Assets

It can be valuable to have more and/or better connections. meaning with people who are more connected, with more followers and influence. In the past, having connections could get you better seats at a theater or restaurant, get you or your kid a job, or get you out of paying parking tickets. The new kinds of connections can get you income, discounts, free samples, and access to people and things. Amazon Vine offers free products to their top reviewers, some valued at $700 or more. We now know that in the 2016 election, connections were used extensively to identify who to target for political gain.

The connection economy is also flourishing at membership websites and affiliate programs that profit from connecting people. (This is discussed in Chapter Four)

HOW IS THE TRANSITION FROM AN INFORMATION ECONOMY TO A CONNECTION ECONOMY CHANGING THINGS?

No one suddenly threw a switch that converted us to a bottom-up connection economy. We've been moving steadily in that direction for some time, with lots of technologies and approaches that are already developed. But the culmination is still far off. The connection economy will continue to evolve and develop, integrating with and enhancing the information economy.

If you're in the information business, don't worry. The information economy will probably expand, just as we use MORE paper now than we did before computers. We'll be SHARING information as we expand our connectability with the new science of connection, which opens new dimensions and parameters to be considered.

Weaponized Connection Power

Imagine a weapon so powerful it's invulnerable to missiles and so massively distributed that, like the internet, it is nearly unstoppable. Imagine, too, that the weapon does not poison, explode or fire, but has effectively defeated the US military time after time. It's a weapon so different it could be ignored and unnoticed as a weapon altogether, even though it powerfully affects vast portions of the civilian population.

That weapon is CONNECTION. When armies and nations use the power of connection to form ties with targeted people or peoples, they win allies who will often sacrifice their lives fighting for them. General David Petraeus used such a weapon in Iraq by building schools and infrastructure and by helping communities—so successfully that when he retired, he was made director of the CIA. The connections made by intelligence agencies, called "humint," for "human intelligence," are among the most valuable and powerful assets available for spies.

When people reach out, build or create bridges, and CONNECT, they produce phenomenal results in warfare, in marketing, in publicity, in politics, in healing, and in happiness.

One of the world's leading thinkers on diplomacy, Joseph Nye, author of *The Future of Power*, has written about the potential of the power of connection, to get people to care about you or your country. There's more on bottom-up power in Chapter Five.

Photo Connecting

I go to a high school reunion. Another attendee posts 150 photos. Someone else labels one with my name. I dutifully go to Facebook to check it out. *Voila!* Connection enabled. This photo-naming software doesn't just ask the person who posted the images to name faces. It allows anyone with access to the images to add to the image database. So months after a photo has been uploaded, you may get a notice that your face is on someone's photo on Facebook, Instagram, or Flickr, or any of the many other photo-sharing venues where social networking is enabled and promoted.

Those extra labels produce extra page views and add glue to the digital connection matrix. Put them all together, and you have a massive digital database of connections that can be used by intelligence agencies like NSA. In fact, NSA uses metadata—analysis of the connections between individuals via photos, phone, email, etc. to identify potential suspects and targets. NSA whistleblower Bill Binney says NSA tracks the metadata for seven billion people.

BEING A CONNECTOR OR BRIDGE

In 2000, before the internet and social media had exploded, Malcolm Gladwell introduced "connectors" in his best-selling book, *The Tipping Point*. He described them as people who know a lot of people and have a "knack for making acquaintances" and for connecting people together.

Ethan Zuckerman, author of *Rewire: Digital Cosmopolitans in the Age of Connection*, delves into how connection has evolved and changed in the digital world. He makes the point that people who are able to bridge cultures "have certain superpowers. They are able to sample from what's best in a variety of global cultures and recombine those influences in creative and novel ways. They can translate what's wonderful about a culturally specific art form and make it accessible to a new audience. These people build *connection bridges,* and corporations are looking for them."

Zuckerman, Director of the MIT Center for Civic Media, says that "a bridge figure is more likely to be able to translate insights from other markets and less likely to be trapped listening only to complaints." He suggests people tend to surround themselves with similar people— whether it's politically or geographically, they are living digitally-circumscribed lives.

If you're going to become a bridge, a connector with 'superpowers,' it's important to consciously extend yourself, to tap the pulses of the different aspects of the world. Make sure you don't get stuck in the "filter bubble" Eli Pariser describes in his book of the same name. Filter bubbles are created by search companies and Facebook. They use algorithms to determine what you see and don't see. I've set Google's advanced settings to turn off personalization functions because I want to see the full range of results, not the ones Google's algorithms predict will interest me more. I suggest using additional search engines, including exotic ones from other countries, to evade the filter bubble results the biggest search sites are likely to automatically inflict upon you.

Rewiring for Deeper, Smarter, Serendipitous Connection

"Connection is the source of inspiration; it's the source of new ideas," Zuckerman told me in our interview. But he is concerned that, even though we have incredible possibilities for connection, we end up demonstrating "homophily," paradoxically flocking together with people like ourselves. We have access to more information than we ever had before, but we're not using it.

He explains, "The internet could be an amazing space for serendipity. We have that potential to have those unexpected and helpful discoveries, but I feel like we're really falling short of that potential much of the time because we tend to get stuck in a rut of the same information over and over on the topics that we are interested in and the topics that our friends are interested in."

How do we go beyond our silos and flocks? Zuckerman suggests we should create technologies that "help us engineer serendipities that help us discover people who have other ways of looking at the world."

What kind of person finds such connections? Zuckerman talks about cognitive diversity, bridgers, and xenophiles, envisioning a very bottom-up kind of floating up of all the different, cognitively diverse, local ideas so that they are more accessible globally and people can have a bigger collection of different options and solutions. When local ideas and, perhaps equally important, conversations are translated in terms of both language and culture, they can be made accessible globally. Zuckerman created his website, globalvoices.org, with thousands of writers from all over the world to facilitate a global conversation and "to help everybody have access to a much broader range of thoughts and perspectives." The writers function as "bridges," he explains, "having one foot in their home countries and one foot in an international conversation. We look for stories that help with cultural bridging."

Xenophobes avoid the strange and different. Zuckerman seeks to encourage xenophillia and says, "Xenophiles find a lot of their inspiration, a lot of their new ideas from intercultural encounter and exchange. A lot of what they're finding that sort of shapes their thinking, that pushes them in other directions, comes from encountering other cultures." He offers Dhani Jones, a former Cincinnati Bengals football player, as an example.

"He would spend his off-season traveling around the world learning new sports in different countries and would often play them at a very high level. Dhani was learning something about the world, learning something about sport as a common bond, about his role as a communicator. His receptivity to identify and connect with people in other cultures really allowed him to use xenophillia as his path towards exploring other cultures."

HARNESSING THE POWER OF NETWORKS
"If you want to go quickly, go alone. If you want to go far, go together."
—AFRICAN PROVERB

Now, let's take this bridging idea a step further—to groups or organizations. Studies have shown that a diverse group of people can actually perform better than a select group of brilliant, but very much alike, high achievers.

Manuel Castells, in his book, *The Rise of the Network Society*, tells us that more and more there is a historic trend in which some of the most important functions and processes within social structures are organized around networks. This new, emerging development is changing all kinds of things including our experiences, the nature of power, and our culture.

The book *Connecting to Change the World: Harnessing the Power of Networks for Social Impact* begins by declaring that we've shifted from an organization era to a network era, stating, "A network is a radical version of decentralization that in its most robust form can eliminate altogether the need for an organization." I interviewed two of the three authors, Peter Plastrik and Madeline Taylor.

The book cites Joe Trippi, the first campaign manager to use online organizing for a presidential primary and a huge early influence on my thinking on bottom-up. Comparing a top-down, tightly controlled campaign to the peer-to-peer kind Howard Dean and Barack Obama ran, Trippi described the need for a more bottom-up approach, "Every political campaign I have ever seen was built on the top-down military structure… This kind of structure will suffocate the storm, not fuel it… The important thing is to provide the tools and some of the direction… and get the hell out of the way when a big wave is building on its own."

Plastrik and Taylor described how generative social impact networks are "designed to be a platform for generating multiple, ongoing kinds of change, not just accomplishing a single outcome… A generative network is a social relationship platform—a 'human operating system'—for spawning activities. It's a unique and renewable capacity, and this makes it especially useful when taking on complex, unpredictable, large-scale problems like climate change, homelessness, or education system performance, which won't yield to a silver-bullet solution."

In our interview, Peter Plastrik, co-founder of the Innovation Network for Communities, offered this as background: "Back in the nineties a number of people started to write about networks as a way of solving problems, as a way of organizing. What they were preaching was a decentralized, bottom-up way of organizing, rather than a top-down centralized way. Organizations still matter. But increasingly there are things that organizations can't solve on their own. And so we see the world as having organizations as well as networks. And now there are networks of organizations."

Plastrik says the millennial generation, the largest in American history, is "really interested in communal, collaborative ways of working [and] less interested in the lone-entrepreneur or baby-boomer conflict-oriented culture." I agreed. It would blow my mind when my millennial son's grade for a group assignment would be based on his study group, regardless of how much work or quality my son provided. The other students could slack off, and I'd say to him, "That's not fair," and he'd reply, "Dad, that's the way it is."

The authors studied complexity theory to understand networks. "What did you learn?" I asked. Plastrik replied: "A complex dynamic system is most alive, has the greatest potential, when it exists in a balance point between a large amount of chaos and a large amount of order. Too much order and the system is not creative, is not innovative. Too much chaos and the system can't get its act together, can't actually produce things. And so complexity theory taught us to look for the balance point between the chaos and the order." The art of managing a network through its evolution includes operating in the tension between too much structure and not enough structure.

Network Mapping, Analysis, and Density

Madeleine Taylor, an anthropologist by training, and co-founder of Network Impact, which provides social-change agents with strategies, tools, research, and consulting expertise to design and use networks. explained that "social network analysis is a set of tools and processes for understanding the relationships and the structures of a network. In social network analysis, the social network relationships are represented as connections or links between nodes."

Plastrik explained, "That connectivity structure tells us a couple of things. One, there is no dominating hub in that network that is connected to everybody and running things. It really is a highly decentralized, bottom-up system. And two, people in that network can touch each other, can reach each other very efficiently, and can then tap each other's networks, too. So, if you're a member from Philadelphia and you're connected to the member in Seattle, you're not just connected to that member; you're connected to that member's own networks. And they may well say, 'Oh, you have a question about this? I'm not the right person, but here's the right person in Seattle to answer that question and I'll connect you.'" The mapping process reveals the enormous amount of *reach* network members have.

Reach enables you to use the network to find people one or two nodes away who may have the information or resource you're looking for. Plastrik offers an example of when a person has a burning question about something he's trying to do, but is not sure about how to do it, he could put a call out to the network. He could ask: *Who's worked on this before? Who has some advice for me?* And he will get responses from all around this network because of his reach.

Dr. Taylor says, "The rule of thumb is that three links out, you're blind. You really can't know what friends of friends of friends are doing directly through those relationships. You need a denser network with many more connections among nodes for that to be effective. The reach is shorter. Density is really just a measure of the number of links between members in a network, a description of how connected everybody is to everybody else. In many networks you're wanting to increase that density so that those pathways to information and insight are shorter."

They reference Malcolm Gladwell's book, *Tipping Point*, which suggests networking is built into our genes—that we are social animals and learn these skills in our families and social and professional networks.

Top-down culture tends to discourage some of the positive aspects of network connecting, innovating, and adapting. Taylor says, "Organizations have bosses and networks have coordinators." Plastrik says, "When these networks get together it's very different from being inside an organization. The net-centric way is—bottom-up—relationship-based, not structure-based. And very much trust-based. When do you decide whether or not you're going to help that person meet somebody else? I don't just do it automatically. I do it based on the trust I have in the person asking me for a referral. Do I know this person? Do I understand their motives? Do I believe that they won't waste this other person's time if I make the connection for them? There's a whole set of these issues around trust that are based in relationships that are a part of the work that these networks do." When I asked Craigslist founder Craig Newmark, "What's the next big thing on the web?" He replied that it was *trust*.

A network is a gift economy. Plastrik explains, "If you're a member of a network, it's not just about what can you get from the network, it's also about what you can give to the network. If you are just in the taking business, you're not going to last in a network. And a network built around people who are simply there to *get* is not going to become a generative network. There's a reciprocity that's involved in a network. There's a generosity that's involved in a network. There's a gift-giving without an expectation that if I do this, you will do that. It's a place where people give, give, and give because of the pleasure of it and because of the potential of it."

Taylor adds, "The term in anthropology is *generalized reciprocity*. It's not just an exchange between individuals, where I may have something to offer you and you offer something back in return. It's that I offer something to you with the understanding that the network will benefit me—not necessarily through you, but through some other member or through some activity that the network engages in. So it's the sense that there's not only a give and take between individuals, [but] that you give to an individual and they stand for the network and then that network gives back to you." I'd say that families, good friends, and tight-knit communities also function this way.

This suggests that some people won't fit well into networks, particularly narcissistic people who lack empathy and others who demand that everything revolve around them. Plastrik confirms this: "It's not that you have to have no ego, but you have to be able to submerge your ego and let the network's needs be what drives your behavior, not your own needs all the time." Plastrik questions whether highly egocentric people can use this kind of organizing effectively, and whether they can be good network citizens, saying, "We've seen examples where it's just not the right fit for some people."

Connectivity is an essential element of networks, Taylor says. "If people aren't connected to one another, don't build relationships, then none of the rest can happen. They can't align around a common set of goals and develop a strategy. They can't come together and implement joint actions. Connectivity is the base of any network enterprise. It's hugely important to think about at every stage of a network's development."

Weaving is essential for making connectivity happen—in building connections and relationships at conferences and meetings. Plastrik explains, "If you think about a typical conference, it's not designed around weaving. It's designed around people getting information. They clearly can meet each other if they want to. But there's nothing necessarily intentional about walking out the door two days later with a lot more connections, a lot deeper relationships, and trust." Weaving, encouraging good connectors to help facilitate relationships between network members, makes that happen. Plastrik advises, "Weaving is one of those early stage things that you have to do well in a network. And if it's not getting done, the network will have a lot of trouble getting on its feet."

THE ANATOMY OF CONNECTION AND CREATING BETTER BOTTOM-UP CONNECTIONS

It's amazing how similar connecting is to having a positive experience. I started working with what is now called Positive Psychology around 1981, when I called it Positivity Training. By 1984 I was presenting at national psychological and health professional conferences, using it with clients and participants in my workshops. Around 1988 I developed the Positive Experience Anatomy model, concluding that positive experiences and the good feelings associated with them are the basic building blocks for our capacity to be happy and to love, trust, have fun, take risks, and face adversity. I've presented this model at national Positive Psychology conferences in the US and Canada.

My model leads to another logical conclusion: It makes sense to develop an understanding of, and skills for, having more, better, stronger, deeper, more meaningful, and longer positive experiences. To that end, my model breaks positive experiences down into categories of "before," "during," and "after." In this section, I apply it to a particular category of positive experience: namely, maximizing connecting and connections. I detail the steps needed to find as many opportunities as possible and then to make better, deeper, and more powerful connection experiences happen.

* * *

THE SIX STAGES OF THE CONNECTION EXPERIENCE

Here's the list of the six stages presented followed by a detailed discussion of each one.

1. Optimize your connection reflexes. Be prepared for connections mentally and physically.

2. Improve your skills for anticipating planning, scheduling, and researching connections.

3. Recognize, identify, initiate, and embrace connection opportunities.

4. Intensify, expand, prolong and deepen your connection

5. Store Positive Connection Experience memories

6. Integrate and use the connection experience later.

1. OPTIMIZE YOUR CONNECTION REFLEXES

Develop your capacity to respond fully and deeply to connection opportunities, mentally, physically and emotionally, so you don't miss potential connections. Be relaxed, feel comfortable, and express strong positive emotions.

Maintain healthy habits, a positive attitude, and self-talk.
You will then have robust positive emotional reflexes and lots of bounce and energy to make the most of connection opportunities whenever they appear, so you'll have the energy to be as vivacious as you want. The energy you have available will determine the opportunities you can embrace.

Develop and seek positive and stabilizing social factors in your life.
Seek positive people, things, and activities. Avoid negative factors, thinking, and people.

Practice warmheartedness.
As the Dalai Lama advises, be compassionate and kind.

Practice using more smile muscles.
Strengthen your smile reflex.

Practice increasing your eye contact.
Develop a fast "smile-at-strangers" reflex.

Develop the habit of generosity.
Share your knowledge, your connections, and your material possessions.

Give yourself and others a break.
Cultivate positive expectancy—what psychiatrist Christian Hegaseth calls positive paranoia—expecting good things from the world.

Get organized and focused.
The better you organize your things and your time, the fewer hassles you'll encounter, and the more you'll be able to focus on getting and staying connected.

Anticipate, Plan, Schedule, and Research Connections.
Do this not just for meetings or "doing lunch," but throughout each day of the week. Study your own behavior patterns, your inner and outer resources, and your environment in order to build a connection

knowledge base that helps you zoom in on connection opportunities—planned or unexpected. Schedule connections and plan your reaction to unexpected connection opportunities.

Stretch to Flow: Fresh Challenges Sharpen Your Skills.

Positive psychology pioneer Mihaly Csikszentmihalyi's research reveals that we are happy and that we grow and stretch our capabilities when we test or challenge ourselves to go slightly beyond our current capabilities. Attention narrows and concentration on the task increases. People often lose track of themselves and seem to merge with their task or their environment, experiencing a feeling of elation or transcendence, called a flow state. To enjoy life more, we need to continually create challenges for ourselves, as artists do when they confront a blank canvas. So, remember, when you face a situation that seems a bit daunting—but possible—consider it not a wall, but a doorway to connection.

Develop the Habits of Living in the Moment and Creating Challenges for Yourself.

Staying in the moment is a primary element of flow. Focus on the road rather than the destination. Csikszentmihalyi says, "Flow is a sense that humans have developed in order to recognize patterns of action that are worth preserving and transmitting over time." Staying in the moment deepens connection.

How do you stay in the moment? Keep all your senses wide open and receptive. Seek out art, novelty, beauty, good abilities, gifts, and the positive ideas and acts of others. Maintain a healthy sense of humor and relate to each day with playful respect, ready to embrace the challenges it brings to you. Challenges take different forms. An exciting challenge for one person may be un-noticed by a thousand others. As you master one moment's challenge, seek another that is even greater.

Creating challenges in your life is not a new idea. Thomas Carlyle said, "Men do less than they ought, unless they do all that they can." Psychologist Abraham Maslow explained that the reason we feel so good when we meet or create challenges is, "the appetite for growth is whetted rather than allayed by gratification. Growth is, in itself, a rewarding and exciting process."

You don't have to conquer the world as you take your beginning steps to stretch and embrace challenges. Give yourself credit for small steps. They could set off emergent changes.

Your powers may astonish you. Know what they are and how to use them.

"It is in men as in soils, where sometimes there is a vein of gold which the owner knows not of."

—JONATHAN SWIFT, *THOUGHTS ON VARIOUS SUBJECTS,* DELPHI CLASSICS COMPLETE *WORKS OF JONATHAN SWIFT*

The philosopher Schopenhauer said, "There is really no enjoyment other than in being aware of our powers and using them." How can you know your powers if you don't test them and use them regularly? William James said, "Compared to what we ought to be, we are only half awake. We are making use of only a small part of our physical and mental resources… The human individual thus lives far within his limits…possesses power of various sorts which he habitually fails to use." You can't just coast and expect connections to come to you. Connection requires work. Some may come to you, but you can also make them happen. Always respect and treat workers as individual people, not just as service providers. Be kind, caring, and genuine. It's incredibly simple, but you'll be amazed at how it changes things.

You can't authentically connect without courage—without the audacity to expect, to want and go for the deeper connections and interactions that brighten and bring more meaning and even power to your life. Have the courage to say to yourself, "I'm breaking out of the routine. I'm challenging myself, taking a risk and experimenting with a new connection." People's biggest fear is that they'll make fools of themselves. Self-criticism and its avoidance cause this problem. People are often afraid to expose themselves to risk, even though the payoff is virtually certain. I've seen it many times in my lectures and seminars. I announce that an exercise will feel good, and then I ask for volunteers. Only a few hands go up. Then, having demonstrated that the exercise feels good, I ask participants. "Did it feel good?" It always does. But always, there are still many people who won't take the opportunities and will just wait for them.

For several years I co-led agoraphobia therapy groups. The key to progress was to use simple relaxation, self-regulation skills, and cognitive behavioral self-talk, to take small steps that stretched and challenged the clients' fears of losing control and being stuck.

The point is, take risks! It doesn't matter what you try, so long as you are exercising and building your courage muscles. You'll begin to easily handle formerly impossible-seeming challenges, and you'll enjoy discovering new "mountains" that become easier and easier to climb. And, as these become an integral part of your most inner self, your attitude will unfold from cautious and fearful to eager and anticipating. Remember, George Patton said, "Courage is fear holding on a minute longer."

2. IMPROVE YOUR SKILLS FOR ANTICIPATING, PLANNING, AND RESEARCHING CONNECTIONS

Expand your knowledge base to connect smarter.

The more you know about the world and the people around you, the more likely you'll be to recognize connection opportunities of greater depth and complexity. Research and plan the situations that will produce connection experiences: meetings, meetups, networks, vacations, excursions, parties, and conferences. Consult experts and acquaintances, and use all available resources.

Cultivate your creativity.

It takes imagination and creativity to recognize opportunities that can be turned into valuable connection assets. Practice fantasy and mental imagery; speculate on implausible possibilities; suspend your disbelief. Research sources for building creativity.

Review and analyze your positive connection patterns.
Identify which positive connection categories and areas you tend to focus on and which areas you currently neglect that are worth additional attention. Maximize your positive connection opportunities by identifying positive connections that:

- you can build into your regular daily, weekly, monthly, or annual schedules.

- you enjoy but don't make happen often enough.

- you rarely or never have (but could).

- you are usually too busy to connect with (you rush past them).

EXERCISES
The next phase for improving your connection skills is to practice boosting your positive connection reflexes.

Routinely practice strong smiling.
Pump smile iron with different smile muscles, to prepare your smile muscles and reflexes to maximally embrace each connection opportunity. Get into the habit of smiling more throughout the day. A smile acts like a magnet, attracting warmth, friendliness, and happy connections.

Do emotional stretches.
Before and after exercise, you stretch to loosen your muscles and stay flexible, so you can do more and hurt less. Use emotional stretching exercises to prepare yourself for times when you expect to have a connection opportunity. Prepare for a party with connection potential by mentally and physically rehearsing. Pump some extra smile iron. Mentally rehearse warm greetings. You'll be more prepared, psyched, and ready to make the most of the event.

Develop a schedule which allows you to learn and play.
Schedule positive connections into your daily routine, so you always have good connective moments to look forward to. When you travel,

choose the more scenic route that exposes you to locals and nature, even if it takes longer. Take art, music, quiet, learning, and people breaks in addition to coffee breaks. Schedule time to enjoy intimacy or family moments. Don't over-schedule your life.

Plan how you'll react to unscheduled opportunities for connection experiences.

Give yourself permission in advance to take time off when unanticipated connection opportunities appear, so you're able to spontaneously enjoy surprises. Develop an inner dialogue which gives you permission to act with spontaneity. Practice making statements to yourself like "This is one of those moments when I allow myself to take off some time to make a good connection." Say the statements out loud. "This is one of those moments!" "This kind of moment is good for me!"

3. RECOGNIZE, IDENTIFY, INITIATE, AND EMBRACE YOUR CONNECTION OPPORTUNITIES

"To improve the golden moment of opportunity, and catch the good that is within our reach, is the great art of life."

—SAMUEL JOHNSON, *THE PATRIOT*

Look for opportunities for love or growth.

Know how to recognize your opportunities so you can grab them. The best connection experiences involve love, growth, kindness, sharing, cooperation, accomplishment, synergy, giving, or receiving. When your heart trembles or starts to glow or fills with warmth, that's a connection opportunity recognition cue to move toward whatever is inspiring your feelings.

My Smelling-the-Roses Kissing Experiment: A Semi-Scientific Study

I met Marvin the flower seller in Dallas after I presented a workshop. Marvin stopped a couple walking on the sidewalk. I overheard him say to the young lady, "I'll give you this rose if you kiss him." She smiled, grabbed her partner, and proceeded to kiss him passionately for about

45 seconds. When she finished, Marvin said to her, "You kissed him so good, now I can ask him for some money." Her companion gladly paid Marvin the four dollars for two roses. They walked away laughing. When I questioned Marvin, he told me that he makes a good living getting people to kiss, rarely having to give away the roses. He explained that most fellows gladly paid for the kiss he'd prompted.

I decided to create my own experiment to test the old "smell the roses" metaphor. Would people take time to enjoy a kiss for a chance to "smell the roses?" I paid Marvin for a dozen roses, allowing him to offer his rose-for-a-kiss deals without having to ask for money afterward. I could then measure how many people would decline or ignore the roses. Approximately one out of three people refused to take a rose for a kiss. They were so intent on their destination that they could not adapt to any opportunity. Some of the most ardent and playful kissers were well over fifty years of age and proud that they could still be playful and passionate. Remember: When life offers you a rose—grab it!

Here are some more strategies for recognizing and initiating connection opportunities:

Take action. Preparation is important, but don't let it keep you from getting started. Change your activity or pace. Speed up. Slow down. Move if you are still. Become still if you are moving.

Persevere to achieve. The Bible says, *A just man falls seven times and rises up again.* The Koran says, *God is with those who persevere.* Pick yourself up from setbacks, smile, laugh, hold your head up straight, put extra bounce in your walk—even if you don't feel it—and pat yourself on the back, telling yourself that it is all part of the learning process.

Set mini-goals—easily achievable small steps.
Experiment. Try new activities, things, and experiences.

Take control—of anything! This will prime your confidence to try more challenging things. It's a safe way to practice taking risks. Start by taking control in small ways, such as cleaning a small area of your home—a drawer, a closet—or fixing or mending something.

Turn adversity into opportunity. Learn to endure difficult times with calm, optimism, and hope. Chaos theory demonstrates that life can and usually does get better and more organized after things get stirred up. The next time you're in a difficult situation, when problems or chaos enter your life, think about and embrace the possibilities. Consider the challenges to be cues to start seeking and creating higher levels of order from which you can introduce new and better emergent options into your life.

Forgive. Anger, resentment, and grudges can create barriers to important connections. Forgive, and replace anger with compassion and love. Healing yourself will open new doors to connection.

Let go completely. Meditate or use biofeedback, guided imagery, and yoga to achieve deeper levels of calm and quiet.

Smile with your whole body. Crinkle your eyes. Walk with a happy bounce. Your happy demeanor will be contagious, inspiring good feelings in the people you encounter, creating a feedback loop. You smile. They smile back at you.

4. INTENSIFY, EXPAND, PROLONG, AND DEEPEN YOUR CONNECTIONS
Intentionally brighten connection experiences. When you see how easy it is, you'll begin to recognize many more occasions when you can deepen the connections in your life by using the following techniques.

Increase the complexity and depth of your connection experiences.
When you find yourself enjoying a connecting moment, make it better, more powerful, and more memorable by bringing in additional

connection experience factors. Smile to yourself (with any part of your body). Increase your energy output by connecting with someone in a deeper, more heart-to-heart way. You can do that by sharing, touching, giving, showing, teaching, empathizing, or sympathizing.

Turn shallow connections into more deeply shared ones. If you are having a shallow connection then speak up. Share how you are feeling. Share smiling eye contact. Laugh, make feeling-good sounds—mm, ooooh, aaaah. Think about or express appreciation. Deepening a connection makes it better, stronger, more complex, and more memorable.

Keep a connection diary. Refer to it to identify elements of past connections that can add new dimensions to your current connection experience. Increase the complexity by finding a way to use the situation to challenge your skills.

For instance, Jim added a connection anecdote to his diary: he wrote that when he was watching a lunar eclipse, he reached to hold his girlfriend's hand, making the moment better.

Pump your Pleasure. Boost your emotional expression. Smile with more of your body. Wave your arms. Shake, shiver, and vocalize your feelings. Hum, laugh, shout for joy. Singing wakes up your happiness homunculus—the part of your brain that sets your nervous system happily dancing when it recognizes positive experience stimuli. Make singing a habit, even if you're tone deaf. Add musical inflection and change pitch intonations to your voice and speech, as US Southerners and the French do. Dance!

Enjoy tears of happiness. Enjoy the good tears which help you to more fully express joy, empathy, and sympathy. Let yourself be emotionally touched and moved more easily. Instead of trying to hold back tears, encourage them. Our bodies release endorphins and oxytocin, when we produce tears, creating a kind of emotional glue that connects us.

Deepen connection intensity by consciously including more senses in the experience. Smell the surroundings. At the theater, feel the warmth of the shoulder next to yours and remember the cold air when you step outside during intermission. Note the texture of the fabric of your clothes and savor the meal you eat afterwards.

Expand or contract your focus. Unfold and expand your perceptions from a narrowed to an open focus. It will connect you more completely with your environment. Or go the other way. Narrow your focus to concentrate on small details.

Intensify the connection experience with positive self-talk. Psych yourself with superlatives. Tell yourself, "I'm having a great time. Wow, we're really connecting." Use self-talk to welcome the connection or to banish the fear of letting go and opening up to connection.

Tie-in other memories. Put your current connection experience into the context of past good memories to make it even stronger and more meaningful. For example, intensify the enjoyment of planning a meeting by remembering the gratification you experienced from the success of your last meeting. By adding roots to the present, you will begin to strengthen your vision of the world as a happy place, loaded with positive connection opportunities.

Anticipate and love future connecting. Not the completed connection, but the process of creatively connecting, breaking the ice, building bonds, and finding connection points.

Count your blessings. Connections are gifts. Humans and many animals evolved to experience and enjoy connections. When you make a connection, remember that this is something in our DNA that's wired into your being, that's tapping a part of your ancestral self.

If you are a person of faith, consider the idea that God or a higher power is in the connection. You are tuning in to God's wavelength. Feel connected with and thank God or the higher power you believe in. Feel God's presence or role in your connection experience. Feel or experience grace or gratitude.

5. STORE POSITIVE CONNECTION EXPERIENCE MEMORIES

Positive memories are biologically designed to be fragile and easily forgotten because the endorphins which contribute to warm glows and thrilling feelings also block memory consolidation in the brain. For that reason you must work extra hard to preserve memories of your positive connection experiences. When you are having a positive connection experience, remember to intentionally create a memory. Take mental, emotional, and sensory snapshots of special moments.

I think of a wonderful connection memory: *Riding a fast, scary water slide with my two-year-old, and by whoopeeing down together, teaching him how to shout with joy to turn his fear into fun.*

Underscore positive connection experiences as success experiences. These can strengthen your self-esteem and your expectations for more successes. No matter the size, any positive connection experience is a success. Add every occasion of making a good connection to your success list. Instead of minimizing achievements with excuses like it was "just lucky" or "an accident," affirm and enjoy each connection and own credit for making it happen. Luck is what you work your butt off to put yourself in the path of.

Take a post-positive connection experience stretch. After a good experience, do a "post-positive connection stretch." Stretch the positive emotional elements of the connection beyond their original strength, without inhibitions, as you would have done if the circumstances had allowed. These positive emotional "after-shocks" can become merged with and strengthen your memory of the event.

After winning an Oscar for her role as supporting actress in *Ghost*, Whoopie Goldberg calmly thanked the audience. Then, according to *USA Today*, she went backstage and shouted, "I'm fucking thrilled!" That stretched the experience and created an emotional "echo" which reprogrammed the memory of the excitement and happy feelings she kept hidden from the outside world, but felt inside.

Record your experience. Use your smart phone or diary. Send off a letter, email, or tweet, share your experience on Facebook or Instagram, or text a note to a friend, write in a journal, or make an analog or digital collage. Use one of the many "count your blessings" apps available.

6. USE YOUR CONNECTION MEMORIES AS RESOURCES LATER

The positive connections you've had throughout your life are among your greatest assets and can help you face adversity and new challenges more effectively. To perform better in a new connection experience, select a related memory. Then perform an emotional transplant, super-imposing your feelings from the past positive connection experience into the present moment. This cloning of your best moments' feelings will enable you to act with strength and confidence, even in stressful and unfamiliar new situations.

* * *

CONNECTION DILUTION, ADDICTION, AND DANGERS OF DISCONNECTION

Increased connection can also bring increased disconnection, distractions, and dilutions, especially when the connection is in an addictive form, like screen or phone addiction, which can disconnect people from other people. But it can also heal disconnections created by our top-down mechanistic culture and economics.

The Internet of Things—Billions of Connections

By the year 2020, experts have estimated there will be 20-50 billion devices connected to the Internet of Things (IoT).

All those billions of things will also be connected to billions of people through AI interfaces such as Siri, Alexa, and Cortana, which use artificial intelligence to add glue to the digital connections. Those billions of things and the AI interfaces have the potential to dilute our connections to other people and to the important social connections that nurture our ability to be caring, compassionate, connected and human.

Already, many people spend hours every day on social media, text messaging, and blogging. There's an ever-growing range of ways to stay connected. It can turn into digital-connection addiction, particularly for people who have lived their entire lives connected to the digital world. Psychologist Mari Swingle, author of *i-Minds: How Cell Phones, Computers, Gaming, and Social Media Are Changing Our Brains, Our Behavior, and the Evolution of Our Species*, warns that digital screen addiction often leads to depression and substance addiction.

Globalization's Liabilities

Globalization, which has produced a massive onslaught against face-to-face connection, is bad for communities and families. The documentary film *The Economics of Happiness*, produced and codirected by Helena Norberg-Hodge, shows how globalization affected communities and small businesses. Norberg-Hodge spoke eloquently about globalization and connection as a guest on my radio show, saying: "If we were to choose to turn the whole ship in the direction of localizing instead of globalizing, we would start to rebuild the fabric of connection, of our connections to one another and to nature. And those connections—there is so much evidence around the world—are necessary for our well-being, for our happiness, and for a sense of meaning and purpose in life."

"BIG," as I discussed in Chapter One, also kills connection and community. People used to know their grocer and the people who owned and managed the local clothing and hardware stores. Those stores would be community gathering spots. Big box stores—Walmart, Target, Kmart, and Amazon—killed small stores and the tapestry of community they supported. These top-down, centralized operations also siphon local money and good jobs out of communities.

Today's world has lost many of its strong, deep connections. Some researchers refer to strong ties, like the ones between frontier people who helped each other build barns and homes, and weak ties, like connections between people on Facebook who barely know each other. Strong connections with friends, neighbors and families have been replaced by weaker connections in fandoms for TV characters and talk show hosts, and by digital connections with fellow gamers on massive multi-player games like World of Warcraft and on social media and blog sites.

The Varieties of Disconnection

Disconnection is an intentional, divide-and-conquer goal of top-down, often patriarchal, authoritarian regimes, economic systems, cultures, and religions. Hate, racism, bigotry, hierarchy, patriarchy—all act to separate and disconnect people from one another.

Darcia Narvaez's moral epigenetics model would suggest that indigenous people are likely to have more empathy and are more likely to share, to be interdependent, and to connect. Civilization brought not only hierarchy, authoritarianism, and centralization, but also disconnection. Absence of empathy is an important dimension of disconnection and a core part of the problem with narcissists and psychopaths who are unable to engage in authentic connections with others. Consumer culture and commercial technologies also lead to disconnection, alienation, and loneliness.

Clay Shirky discussed the effects of television with me. "One of the hard things to explain about television is why people watch it," he observed. "There's good stuff on TV. The hard thing to explain is why we watch so much of it. It's really the number one use of free time worldwide. It turns out that watching television makes us feel less lonely. But the terrible irony of this is that when we watch television, we are typically more disconnected. So the awful feedback loop of television in an era where it's hard to connect to one another is that watching television ameliorates the effects of loneliness, but it actually worsens the conditions of it."

Antonio Lopez, author of *Media Ecology*, told me, "One of the things that eco-psychologists or eco-activists talk about is that we, in our Western culture, are very disconnected from our landscapes. We are disconnected from our environments." He had an experience during a Hopi ritual in which he felt very connected, and he emphasized, "It is not just Native Americans who practice rituals who are connected to Earth."

Lopez describes the idea of a Chakaruna, a bridge person. He explains that "Chakaruna is a Quechua word. The Quechua are the descendants of the Inca. They live in Peru and Bolivia. Runa means bridge and Chaka means person…" He describes how shamans and healers in the region came up with the idea: "In the center circle, you have the elders, the healers, and the shamans, who are essentially communicating directly with their communities and also the earth, the animals, etc. In order for them to reach out to the outside world, the shamans, healers, and elders need these bridge people [whom] they call 'Chakaruna,' people who have a foot in both worlds. [They] are people who may have an indigenous background or a multicultural background. [Their role] is not based on race or ethnicity; [they're] just people who have perceptions that exist in different worlds. You have a foot in the world of the indigenous or the sacred, and you also have a foot in the modern technological world. These…people are very important, because [they] are the kind of people that are going to be able to go back and forth to bring these ideas from the indigenous and the sacred to our current reality. I believe that James Cameron is one of these Chakarunas. His movie, *Avatar*…was a bridge to a certain kind of eco-spirituality that a lot of people resonated with."

We need to get back to connecting with nature. Indigenous ways and rituals can help us reconnect, to re-remember. Start by just putting yourself in nature. Take walks in the woods, along beaches, rivers, and streams. Touch trees. Native Americans talk to them. There are rituals that help connect us to the earth, to our culture, and to each other. Find them. This connection to nature is really essential to happiness—to being a whole person who is an integrally connected part of the earth.

Mary Pipher is a psychologist, activist, and author, most notably of *Reviving Ophelia*, which opened up an important discussion about the challenges adolescent girls face. I noted to her that she wrote in her book, *The Green Boat: Reviving Ourselves in Our Capsized Culture*, that people are in denial about the problems humanity faces, writing that "anytime we humans disconnect from reality, we enter individually and collectively what could be called a psychotic state."

Pipher said in our interview, "We are at a kind of a psychotic state as a culture. Individually, most of us are able to lead sane lives with people we love, paying our bills and enjoying our communities and participating in meaningful work. But collectively, we're teetering toward the edge of a cliff without discussing where we're going. And that is really psychotic behavior. Bateson said, 'The unit of survival is the organism and its environment.' And for us to deal with this, realistically and openly and collectively in conversation, is a survival strategy. The basic moral issue is if we do not expand our moral imaginations so that we include the whole web of life in our circle of caring, we will destroy ourselves. But the survival issue is we simply cannot survive as organisms without an environment that's hospitable to us."

Robert Wolff, author of *Original Wisdom*, (also titled *What It Is to Be Human*,) spent time living in the jungle with the indigenous S'gnoi hunter-gatherer dream people of Malaysia, who were wiped out decades ago by logging. He cites this quote from White River Sioux Jenny Leading Cloud: "We Indians think of the earth and the whole universe as a never-ending circle, and in this circle man is just another animal. The buffalo and the coyote are our brothers, the birds, our cousins. Even the tiniest ant, even a louse, even the smallest flower you can find—they are all relatives." Then Wolff observed: "We, modern Man, walked out of the circle. How can we deny our relatedness to all that lives? We cannot act as if we owned the place and do with it what we want. That is not how a planetary ecosystem works. We are part of it, whether we like it or not. An ecosystem is not something you can resign from. It's like the head saying, 'I am better, more spiritual, than the body' and then proceeding to abuse, reshape, pollute the body. When the body dies, the head dies. We have done exactly that! And because we cannot see that what we are doing can only lead to our own extinction, we pretend that everything is fine—'*Progress, more and bigger. An economy that must 'grow' every year.*' Even a moment's thought should convince us that if one lives in a closed ecosystem, there is no *more*. The only way to live in a sustainable world is to live within our means. Anything more is stolen from our neighbors."

Gregg Levoy, author of the best-selling book *Callings*, and his newer book, *Vital Signs: The Nature and Nurture of Passion*, says we have been "disconnecting energies and tyrannical energies within us, that we repress." In his chapter "Call of the Wild," he discusses wildness versus civilization. I asked him to summarize it. "Part of living passionately," he told me, "is reconnecting with the part of us that is wild, that is original, that is natural. We talk about our natural-born selves, right? That's the essential part; that's the wild part. Try to be not so civilized. That's why I love this poster that's on the wall of the kitchen of a friend of mine. It shows a picture of a woman down on her hands and knees scrubbing out a bathtub and a caption that says 'a clean house is a sign of a wasted life.'"

Smiling for Pay, and Paying the Price in Disconnected Feelings

Even smiling has its risks. Psychologist Arlie Russell Hochschild, author of *The Managed Heart: Commercialization of Human Feeling*, warns that commercialized "smiling for pay" can be dangerous.

Do you disconnect your on-the-job-face from your real feelings? Flight stewards are trained to be warm and friendly and may find that, after a flight, they are all revved up and excited from too much "turning on" of feelings. Or they may depersonalize themselves to cope with the demands of keeping their happy faces on. Inside, behind the happy mask, there may be a cold lump that does not warm up easily when it is off the job. Hochschild suggests that many people in today's society are forced to put their feelings up for hire to earn a living.

Disconnection from emotions, from compassion, from empathy, from nature, and from people is a major component in my conception of top-down.

Mythologist and storyteller Michael Meade told me, "Connection is a movement of the soul… We live in a culture that is disconnected from its own soul… You see a kind of non-full connection that happens through social media and the internet, computers and all. Everyone desires to be connected, and yet that's not a full enough connection. The connections that are meaningful have soul in them. The places we love are the places we feel the most connected to, and that kind of a deep and loving feeling is soulful connection. That's what makes a person feel secure and valuable in the world, and, mostly, the modern world lacks deep connectivity."

Besides the aspects of disconnection tied to the loss of ancestral parenting that Narvaez describes, there are also cultural influences that cause it: traditions and cultural beliefs. For example, some cultures discourage the facial expression of emotion, an important means to enabling connection. Some individuals have problems expressing emotion, which is called *alexithymia*; others have an inability to feel emotions, which is called *euthymia*. Some cultures encourage masking emotional expression. A study of cadavers in one such society found that smile muscles had literally atrophied. Patriarchal culture tends to produce "macho men." It discourages men from expressing more "feminine" feelings like kindness, sympathy, and love but considers their expressions of anger and aggression okay.

What are the effects of disconnection, separation, and repression? Disconnection from people, sometimes called "alienation" or "anomie," causes some people to forget about the suffering and humanity of others and to lose their capacity for compassion. Disconnection can also manifest itself as separation, which underlies such social pathologies as separatism, apartheid, segregation, racism, bigotry, and caste systems.

In the broadest terms, disconnection can be understood as the loss of human connection to nature, to other people, and to our true inner selves. Bottom-up connection consciousness and connection skill-building are the answers.

CHAPTER 3

The Powers of Top-Down and Bottom-Up Language, Story, and Myth

Our brains, our psychologies, and our cultures are wired with language, story, archetypes, and myths to be bottom-up. Understanding how this works increases our power over our lives and our ability to communicate.

THE METAPHORIC FILTERING WE LIVE BY

George Lakoff and Mark Johnson write in their book *Metaphors We Live By*: "Metaphor is pervasive in everyday life, not just in language but in thought and action. Our ordinary conceptual system, in terms of which we both think and act, is fundamentally metaphorical in nature... and plays a central role in defining our everyday realities... The way we think, what we experience, and what we do every day is very much a matter of metaphor." They explain, "The essence of metaphor is understanding and experiencing one kind of thing in terms of another." They argue that "human thought processes are largely metaphorical" and that such metaphoric filtering can hide aspects of our experience.

Top-down and bottom-up are systemic metaphoric concepts that provide a collection of perceptual filters through which we view the world. Industrialized peoples primarily experience and process their world through a top-down, mechanistic system of metaphors, which include control, power-over, domination, hierarchy, centralization, separation, disconnection, quantification, linearity, patriarchy, order, rigidity, and exploitation.

In contrast, indigenous people—and now our post-internet, connection-era digital natives—live through bottom-up metaphors associated with nature, systems, networks, collective cooperation, interdependence, democratization, localization, commons, sharing, connection, and empathy.

Top-down root metaphors function as filters which lead to people having a very different way of engaging with the world than those who process their lives through bottom-up metaphors. An individual with primarily top-down filters might see individuals who perceive the world through bottom-up filters as communist, lazy, parasitic tree-huggers. And people who see the world through bottom-up filters, might consider people who live through top-down filters to be insane, weak, deranged, evil, and selfish. And, according to their filtering systems, they may be right. Koko, the famous gorilla who communicated through sign language, said, "Humans are stupid. I cry. Fix Earth. Protect Earth. Nature see you."

BOTTOM-UP AND TOP-DOWN FRAMING AND LANGUAGING

Roy Peter Clark's book *The Glamour of Grammar* got me started thinking about the idea of bottom-up and top-down language. The book characterizes slang and local dialect as bottom-up language, in contrast to the properly spoken, top-down "King's English."

Clark told me that H.G. Wells observed during World War II, that in order to be effective, propaganda should be from the people, using bottom-up dialect and local slang. If you look at political campaign ads, you'll see that many use that approach. The candidates talk with a local accent. Hillary Clinton spoke with a stronger accent when she campaigned in the Deep South.

Masters of the language-spin game build "framing" phrases and messages that have power, values, and ideology built into them. These are top-down phrases designed so opponents will unintentionally make use of the words, even amplifying the desired message, in discussing their own views.

Frank Luntz is, for the conservative right, the master of creating framing language that tricks the opposition into using words that sell an ideological message. He's created phrases like the "death tax" to negatively frame the estate tax, for example. My frame is to call it the "dynasty tax" because it helps prevent ultra-wealthy multi-generational dynasties.

The Left has George Lakoff, author of *Don't Think of an Elephant*, who bases his framing approaches on moral ties to politics.

I brought up a conversation about framing I had with former US Senator Barbara Boxer to George Lakoff during our interview. It was just a short time after attending an invitation-only progressive media summit meeting held by the Democratic Senate Outreach committee. I concluded from the conversations at the meeting that the Democratic leadership was pretty clueless about the concept of framing. Lakoff observed that there's a huge difference between the Democrats and the Republicans, explaining that Democrats tend to be academics, trained in liberal arts and enlightenment reason, so they pursue logic, trying to get people to see and act on "the truth."

But Lakoff says that peoples' brains really work through empathy, through social connection. Democrats in Congress don't understand that, and think the way to gain support is simply to tell people the truth, getting the policies out there and telling them the economics and then "what's in it for you." But that's not as effective as tapping their values, which are tied to their emotions and the story they live in terms of the people they are connected to.

Lakoff explained, "Libs and Dems don't understand what communication is about…. [It] works by using language and repeating it over and over again. That evokes the conservative worldview. And they've been doing this for year after year after year. They have think tanks that create that language. They have language experts like Luntz, that create the language. The language reflects their moral system. They have training institutes that train tens of thousands of conservatives every year in how to use the language…and they're getting their message out over and over and over every day, twenty-four/seven."

Democrats have long known everything about this system, Lakoff pointed out, "And they've done nothing, because according to enlightenment reason, that would be propaganda. That would be repeating yourself…not just saying it once and people will reach the right conclusion. They don't. That's not how brains work. The Republicans have a system that fits how brains work. The Democrats do not have such a system."

Lakoff explained how framing is used by right-wing advocates "The way that brains work—every word is defined in terms of a frame—a brain circuit. A frame is a system of circuits. Politics is a moral system. That is how people think about what is right. They use language that will evoke their moral system. They repeat it, day after day, year after year. And when it is repeated it strengthens synapses in the brain. It creates permanent circuits. One of the most interesting things about the brain is that circuitry is linked up in such a way that certain circuits are mutually inhibitory in the brain. That is, there are certain circuits [that], when active, inhibit—that is, turn off—other circuits and vice versa. So you have two moral systems that reside in the same brain—where one is turned off and one is turned on."

Languaging, i.e., manipulating people through choice of words and changing the meaning of our language by framing uses top-down strategies created to "infect" the language of the masses and tap into their neurobiology.

George Monbiot described to me how he envisions making change for a better world happen. "Produce a better and more compelling narrative of change ourselves, before the other side does." Monbiot says that it's essential to "show people a better future and a way of reconnecting and a sense of belonging and a sense of having control over their lives," and the way to do it is with story.

"You cannot take away someone's story without giving them a new one," Monbiot told me. "If you just try to confront a story with facts and figures all you get is reactive denial because we are creatures of narrative. We confront a world which is phenomenally complex. We can't understand it by trying to make sense of all the facts and figures. We understand it by looking for a story that makes sense to us. Telling a story, you've immediately engaged our minds. And that is the power of narrative."

Monbiot has observed that in politics and religion the most successful stories all have the same format, which is what he calls the "Restoration story: Disorder afflicts the land, caused by nefarious and powerful forces acting against the good of humanity. The hero of the story may be one person, may be a group of people, may be an institution, confronts those powerful and nefarious forces, and against the odds overthrows them and restores order to the land. That is a successful story that has worked again and again over the centuries. It's a fundamental truth about politics but also about religious revolutions."

Monbiot believes that it takes powerful new stories which infect people's minds to replace the stories people are living—stories that are not working for them. And those stories should include the values we want to instill in the people.

Susan Strong, author of *Move Our Message: How to Get America's Ear*, offers a bottom-up approach to framing, "I advocate using ordinary life, ordinary daily-speech metaphors, for conveying our message. The method I teach, 'American Framing Steps,' helps people form their own message and find the appropriate American political metaphors."

She's basically proposing that we take language that's already in use in America that can be metaphorically applied from one area—where people already know it, love it, and embrace it—to another area. Citing the example of corporate regulation, she offers this advice: "Many Democrats have unfortunately gone on and used the word 'regulation.' Professor Lakoff very rightly says, 'Don't use their language!' What I've put out there is, 'Play by the Rules.' It's not a new phrase. *It's not necessarily important to find a new phrase. It's important to find the right phrase.* And what that does is shift you completely out of the story that the Republicans are telling, which is 'regulation is bad for business,' etc., over into the sports metaphor, a piece of it that progressives and liberals can use, which really evokes the idea of fairness, everybody playing by the same rules, and ultimately calls up the American idea of the Rule of Law."

Strong is tapping into the roots, the narrative and connections that people have for that story. She offers three approaches to dealing with framing or "languaging" created by the opposition:

1) "Choose another commonly known metaphor that evokes a familiar story as part of our cultural heritage."

2) "Tweak something the opposition has put out. An example would be 'Stay the course,' [used] during the Iraq war when Bush was president. Remember how we couldn't seem to shake it? Then I and others working on the issue of the Iraq war put out 'Change Course!'"

3) "Create something brand new. 'FrankenFood' is an example where a professor who was writing about GMO food, and very upset, wrote a letter to the *New York Times*. And, as you know, it's just gone viral."

Strong says her preference is to be positive and frame what we want to have happen, which is targeting the five or ten percent of people who are swing voters, not the people who have already firmly decided how they're voting. She advises that people should study their audiences and "[frame] their own message as a problem-solving story, because that's part of…the core American dream. We solve problems!"

Our dominant top-down culture has produced many words that have top-down or patriarchal framing that start with non- or anti- because the root word is top-down, patriarchal, mechanistic, or linear, such as "nonlinear," and "NGO" for "nongovernmental organization." Other top-down words are chief, top, uncivilized, fellowship, mankind, fellow man, and many more. Top-down framing traps are pervasive in our language. Bottom-up words include open, we, gather, and together.

BOTTOM-UP AND TOP-DOWN STORIES, ARCHETYPES, AND MYTHS

At the first Storycon Summit Meeting on the Art, Science, and Application of Story, which I founded and organized, Cathy Pagano, a Jungian counselor and mythologist, presented on archetypes. She says examples of bottom-up archetypes include the Round Table of the Knights of King Arthur and the gathering around the campfire.

Jung suggested that archetypes are a deep part of our human and cultural identity. It is only natural that there are powerful archetypes that represent the bottom-up behaviors of sharing ideas, joining in unity, and cooperating to develop power. Pagano says, "Archetypes are primordial, the very basis of life here on Earth. Archetypes are the inherited instincts that make us human, shaping the way we behave, perceive, and understand life. While Jung saw them as existing outside the human psyche, they are also part of our psychic make-up. Archetypes in themselves are unknowable until we perceive them through the archetypal images that all humanity shares. So, in many ways, they are the original bottom-up energies of life."

Myths are similar to archetypes. A myth is a full story, compared to an archetype, which is usually a specific character or element of a story. Pagano says, "Myths are archetypal patterns that take on flesh. Just like fairy tales, they describe how humans need to meet life in different crisis circumstances."

Mythologist Pamela Jaye Smith, author of *Inner Drives, The Power of the Dark Side,* and *Symbols, Images, and Codes,* offered her take on myths: "My favorite definition of myth is: the stories we tell ourselves to explain the world around us and within us. We also use myths to justify and legitimize the world we have created."

Though some myths have been used to wield power, the role of mythology is very bottom-up. Myths are shaped and evolved over many generations to become a part of the deep narrative of the culture. Today, modern cultures may not relate to the old myths of creation, of the pantheistic gods of nature—the sun, the moon, the river, the sky. But every culture has narrative stories that define the culture, the community, and every person has stories that define how he or she fits and functions in the world.

Today we have access to a newly emerging art and science of story. As the cost of making movies has risen above $200 million, financial considerations have inspired an effort to understand scientifically how to use myths, metaphors, and the elements of story to make stories more engaging and powerful.

I was inspired to start my Storycon Summit meeting after reading Robert McKee's book and taking his seminar on story structure and screenwriting. I came to the realization that stories are incredibly important in our lives—that they define who we are and the story business is one of the biggest businesses in the world.

Sure, we understand that stories on TV and in movies, newspapers, books, magazines, and on the internet add up to a business in the hundreds of billions. But there are many other fields built upon stories. Lawyers tell stories to juries. Psychotherapists help us identify and change the stories we live our lives by. Religion is dependent on its founding stories, and sermons are built with them. The most effective politicians give stump speeches woven from stories. Some of the most effective marketing campaigns are built upon stories. And there are many other applications and fields of endeavor where stories play an integral, essential role.

Some stories develop memes, the ideas or messages that become viral. Rupert Sheldrake has a theory that when a critical mass of people say or do something, it creates a "morphogenic field," which makes it more likely that the behavior will be replicated. The more people say or do a particular thing, the more likely it will be replicated, a highly bottom-up phenomenon. Some scientists mock the notion. But one of the most daring scientists I know, University of Arizona professor Gary Schwartz, entered a contest to develop a study to prove morphogenic field theory, and won. He had students look at words in Hebrew. Some were real words, some were nonsense words. None of the students could read Hebrew. Gary predicted that the students would be able to identify the real words because they were regularly used by millions of people. It turned out he was correct. It's a powerful concept: what you put out, what you do or say, makes it more likely that others will do or say it too.

I've come to believe that hominids, perhaps even before homo sapiens, shared stories, probably about hunting and gathering, and that telling and processing stories shaped the evolution of how our brains process experience and relationships. It is often said that we live our lives by the stories we tell ourselves and by the stories our communities and religions tell to define both themselves and ourselves. We exist in a state of story consciousness, thinking in story, seeing and perceiving in story, and communicating through the use of language that uses brain functions and anatomy shaped by story. Our stories filter our experience. We create shared stories by consensus, a bottom-up process. Robert Wolff's book, *What It Is to Be Human,* describes how the indigenous Malaysian Sgnoi jungle tribe started each day with a unique form of crowdsourcing by sharing another kind of stories—their dreams—and then used that information to decide what to do that day.

If we can understand how stories work and how we function as characters within our own and others' stories, we can empower ourselves to play a greater role in scripting the stories we will live in.

REVERBERATIONS OF STORIES THROUGHOUT HUMAN HISTORY
Since their earliest existence, humans have lived with myths that have explained their beginnings and the world around them. Those stories imbue in the listener, reader, or viewer a deep sense of resonance with the thousands of other generations that have experienced the same stories.

Lewis Mehl-Madrona, MD, a Native American healer, believes that stories are the webs that most effectively connect us together.

MYTHIC POWER

Ever since stories have been told, people have sought the secrets and wisdom of the ancients. Myths and archetypes are vessels that carry this wisdom. When you tap the power of mythic wisdom, it is like downloading into your mind, your heart, and your spirit the universal intelligence of mankind—the planetary consciousness. You begin to make choices and decisions with the help of the distilled wisdom, vision, and awareness passed down and built upon by thousands of generations. You access an understanding of human patterns that enables you to anticipate, in a way, what will happen next. This is not fortune telling, not precognition, and not knowing the future. But it IS a powerful, *real* ability to be better prepared for the future.

The mythic powers are right in front of you, so accessible you may not even believe they have the power I claim. One regrettable result of the West's technologization of the world has been the forgetting or rejecting of these powers. Many people will ignore the energy and raw power of mythic wisdom throughout their entire lives. Others, however, have adopted this path to inner power and now take it for granted as a natural part of their life. Indigenous peoples tend to be much more aware of and in touch with these natural powers. I invite you to try it on for size and see if it works for you using the approach I describe below.

The mother of all myths, the repository of a profound wisdom that has been told billions of times, is called the Mono-Myth, or the "One" Myth. This is the archetypal myth that perhaps, better than all others, tells the story of what it is to become a full human, to live a life that taps all the power, courage, and potential you possess.

Joseph Campbell called this Mono-Myth "The Hero's Journey." And it truly is the journey of the hero or heroine. Yet, it is also something as simple as the process of individual growth, transformation, and change. Cathy Pagano suggests that the *heroine's* journey is different from the male hero's patriarchally shaped journey. She told me, "It's about taming the dragon and accessing its wisdom. The Hero's Journey is the patriarchal or man's Mono-Myth. And a father's daughter's myth. But there's another step for women beyond it. That's going on to leave that myth behind and just BE a vessel for the powers within us."

Why is it useful to know about the Hero's Journey and how it works?

The Hero's Journey is all about change, transformation, and growth—really, about being reborn as a new, improved person, often one who makes a difference. Let's explore how you can apply an understanding of it to your life and work or even your company or organization.

Joseph Campbell studied hero myths from many nations, tribes, cultures, and religions before publishing his classic book, *The Hero with a Thousand Faces*. In this book, ranked as one of the hundred most influential of the twentieth century, he described a common pattern all of the heroes shared.

Just about every blockbuster movie includes a theme of a Hero's Journey. This is because the Hero's Journey is the universal experience we all go through when we embrace the opportunity for personal change. I've presented at conferences my talks about how making decisions after being diagnosed with cancer, or deciding to get help for chronic headaches, or deciding to take or seek a new job, or deciding to leave or begin a relationship, can all be beginnings of a heroic journey. Once you learn the stages and the experiences associated with the Hero's Journey, they'll start to feel familiar. You'll recognize times you've been through this, and you'll definitely see the pattern in movies.

Why is the Hero's Journey a bottom-up experience?

The archetypal myth of the Hero's Journey tells the story of a person who has made a decision to "answer the call." It narrates the stages the hero goes through in seeking that new start. That includes interacting and forming alliances with people or learning from people who, in most cases, he encounters for the first time. It doesn't get more bottom-up than this!

Carl Jung characterized the Hero's Journey as the process of "individuation," where the male child goes through the stages necessary to become an adult by confronting his father's dominance over him as part of what we describe as the Oedipal Conflict. The son must form a new relationship with the father, so he can transition from being a dependent boy who sees Daddy as all-powerful and owes him his obedience, to a man who stands equal to, and, being in the prime of life, perhaps even stronger than, his father. It's not a big step to see this as a process of learning how to stand up to authority and patriarchy.

The hero myth is about justice, courage, fairness, and redemption. This is portrayed archetypally through the overcoming of top-down entrenched power by a hero or heroine whom agents of that power had tried to destroy, lest he or she undo the established order of things. Very often it is the story of someone born into royalty and power. Then it is taken away because the child is perceived as or prophesied to be a threat. The journey is the path by which the hero attains his full powerful self. Examples of such heroes or heroines include Moses, Wonder Woman, Luke Skywalker, Princess Leia, Frodo, Harry Potter, and Hermione Granger. And even the Buddha left his parents to find rebirth in an authentic self. Blame patriarchy for there not being more female heroines. Disney has made progress offering powerful heroines in the form of Moana and Pocahontas.

We're talking here about mythic stories and archetypal heroes who define the virtues of courage, bravery, goodness, and caring-for-community. Such stories are about questioning, challenging, and overcoming traditional authority and conquering and ending or replacing the existing power structure, the status quo, or the way life has been motoring on automatic pilot.

The Hero's Journey is the journey you follow, when either by choice or circumstance—you find yourself at a turning point which presents an opportunity to make a life-changing decision. If you don't choose to make a decision that thrusts you across the threshold of a new journey, then you stay the same. You miss, avoid, or reject the opportunity to start on a heroic journey, and, in a sense, allow the possibility of creating a new, better, stronger, more heroic YOU to die. Instead, you continue leading the life you've had. Some people live their entire lives in a kind of semi-dead state, never accepting the call to adventure that is the call to a new heroic journey. From a mythic perspective, they are rejecting the opportunity to grow, to live nobly, and to face tough challenges that can strengthen them and build not only their own character, heart, and spirit, but also their ability to help their community and the world around them.

This section's goal is to help you learn to recognize the times in your life when you've already accepted the call to change, as well as future calls to new heroic journeys that can take your life to the next levels.

To begin, let's make a few lists, starting with a list of a few of the heroic figures in your life, organization, or company, and why you see them as heroes. Try to include people other than close relatives in your list.

List the evil villains you consider the worst in your life, in history, in the world, and why.

List the guides, teachers, mentors, and advisors who have helped you, whom you have trusted, and whose guidance and advice have benefited you.

List the allies, friends, and colleagues in your life who are or have been resources and assets that add meaning and perhaps even safety to your life.

List the new knowledge, tools, abilities, techniques, etc., that you have acquired.

By starting with this inventory, you'll be able to tease out some of the heroic journeys you've already completed, or at least, begun in your life.

The Hero's Journey, or Mono-Myth consists of a series of stages that look like this:

1. The hero starts in an **ordinary world**, and then something happens to nudge, itch, annoy, invite, threaten, or wake him up, and, in some way, issues a "call" to do something different, or to stop doing what's customarily been done. Some describe this as "The Call to Adventure." Gregg Levoy has written an extraordinary book, *Callings*, which is dedicated to helping people learn to recognize and connect to such calls.

2. The hero—or heroine—must choose whether or not to **accept the call**. If she does, then she crosses a threshold into a new world to begin the heroic journey, symbolizing the beginning of a new life, of being reborn.

3. Crossing the threshold is characterized by Campbell as the willingness to face primordial fears. For example, many cultures have stories about people who go out into parts of the woods beyond the bounds of the village where they encounter a mystical, powerful being that can kill or eat them. However, if those people have come with the right mindset and answers, the same powerful being will gift them with wonderful boons, such as fertile crops and abundance.

Crossing the threshold means you go out beyond your ordinary boundaries to face the unknown. This is where you find the deeper, previously untapped parts of your full potential that have been there all along, residing in your subconscious self. This is bottom-up stuff. You are tapping the power of what is deeper than your normal conscious mind. Bottom-up power is exactly that—tapping into the resources, strength, and potentials of systems and cultures and people which have been there all along, but not yet connected with, not yet engaged, or not yet fully tapped or realized. We might consider this a mythic way to describe epigenetic unfolding.

There are archetypal threshold guardians (friends, family, jobs, coworkers, beliefs, stereotypes, and possessions) who intimidate you and attempt to dissuade you from accepting the call and making the crossing. Fortunately, there are also mentors; teachers, friends—particularly new-found or long-lost ones—ministers, employers, coworkers, therapists, coaches, storekeepers, books, the internet and websites that help you face the threshold guardians and cross the threshold. Crossings are not too easy, or they won't be meaningful. The challenges strengthen and teach you.

"When a difficulty falls upon you, remember that God, like a trainer of wrestlers, has matched you with a rough young man. For what purpose? you might ask. So

that you may become an Olympic Conqueror; but it is not accomplished without sweat... No man has had a more profitable difficulty than you have had, if you choose to make use of it as an athlete would deal with a young antagonist."

—EPICTETUS, DISCOURSES (108 AD)

Sometimes it just takes a moment's contact. But take the mentor factor seriously. Heroes create themselves through a bottom-up process, sculpting themselves from a social clay. They are not islands. Mentors help them. Antagonists help them, even tricksters. This archetypal collection of mentors, threshold guardians, tricksters, allies, and antagonists is an important bottom-up dimension.

4. Once the hero crosses the threshold, the first step usually involves, symbolically, entering a womb-like situation—going under water, underground, or into the dark. This can be confusing, disorienting, scary, temporarily overwhelming, or intoxicatingly exciting. Upon crossing the threshold the hero becomes like a newborn, a blank slate ready to learn and grow on the road while seeing the world with new eyes and a beginner's mind, letting go of top-down, authoritarian preconceptions of how things are.

5. The hero passes from this "womb" stage to beginning the journey by "going on the road," taking a series of new steps that will gradually build a stronger, wiser, and more powerful new person. The road represents the process of growing into the skin of this new person. The hero must develop the ability to crawl and then walk to find friends, allies, and enemies and to develop the new skills and find the tools that will empower him to achieve the tasks and goals that the call to the Hero's Journey initially prompted him to accomplish. My son Noah, who grew up learning about the Hero's Journey, pointed out to me that the road of challenges is as bottom-up as it gets. You are formed into a hero by your interactions with the people and places you encounter on the journey.

The road is not easy. You are supposed to fall down, then get up, then fall down again. It forces you to encounter new challenges, difficulties, antagonists, and conflict. The road's job is to challenge you until you are sufficiently strengthened to function in your new role as a powerful, heroic master of the new universe you've crossed into and co-created.

6, 7, and 8: To fully achieve the peak, optimal potential of the person you crossed the threshold to become, you must have a meeting with the Goddess, an atonement with the Father, and the experience of Apotheosis. What this basically entails, in non-archetypal terms, is a re-evaluation and redefining of your masculine and feminine energies and of your relationship to authority and the god or Higher Power you relate to. These relationships must evolve so you can both tap into your own new power and face and challenge top-down power.

9. At some point along the road on the Hero's Journey, you'll face a very nasty, almost overwhelming, antagonist who forces you to fight for your life. You can't run away from this challenge. You actually need it—to test your strength and to forcefully slough off any final ties you have to your old self. You may have to face a few antagonists before you finally learn how to thoroughly overcome them and let go of your former self.

Often there's a top-down or anti-bottom-up narcissistic or psychopathic aspect to antagonists. These bad characters usually fit in several categories that may combine or overlap:

Top-down: evil kings, generals, crime kingpins, bullies, or greedy corporate or wealthy types

Psychopaths: people who are narcissistic, self-centered, uncaring, disconnected, or have zero connection consciousness, except for their ability to charismatically manipulate people

Bad Groups: gangs; evil, corrupt systems that help criminals; crime syndicates; corporations; armies; bands and minions of evil people

Once you've successfully battled with antagonists enough times, with a final very close call from which you emerge triumphant, you will have accomplished a good portion of the goal of your heroic journey: namely, becoming a master of the universe. However, if the hero stops at this point, he's fallen into a top-down trap—transfixed by the glamour and power he's achieved.

10. The final stage of the Hero's Journey is "the return." You must return from whence you came, bringing with you the healing elixir, power, or thing that you originally crossed the threshold to obtain to rescue or heal the ordinary world. Only by returning to your original, ordinary world and reconnecting with it, having made two shifts—from dependent to powerful and from powerful to interdependent—can you truly complete the Hero's Journey, which must end with your feet in both the heroic and ordinary worlds. A true hero possesses great power but acts with bottom-up connection consciousness, helping and respecting others.

Consider civilization as a five- or ten-thousand-year heroic journey. Humanity itself, or at least vast swathes of it, may be at a point where we are waking up to discover that top-down civilization has enchanted and deluded us long enough. Now, perhaps, we are ready to return "home" to consider the Hero's Journey as a model for exploring humanity's potential to return to its ordinary bottom-up world where we no longer need to be more powerful, more wealthy, and to let go of and share the power, the magic, the mastery, and expanded consciousness achieved in the heroic world with the community of the ordinary world. This is the way of relating to one another that Jesus, Buddha, Muhammad, Moses, the Goddess, and thousands of indigenous tribes and cultures have taught.

How about bottom-up Group Heroes?

There is also a top-down aspect to the Hero's Journey, especially as it's represented in movies, where it's common for one hero to singlehandedly save the day. After the Fall 2011 Occupy Wall Street movement, I watched the movie *The Avengers*. I exited the theater wondering whether it was necessary for a top-down "superhero" to be the one who saves the world. Why not a super *community*, with the spirit of Occupy Wall street, where the people, the 99 percent, become the composite hero embracing the Hero's Journey. That would be more bottom-up.

Historically, change has been brought about from the bottom up. This suggests that telling stories based upon bottom-up strategies, practices, and character arcs in books, movies, television, and games could support and encourage more bottom-up seeing, thinking, and believing. It could shape expectations, visions of possibilities, and the way people apply their imaginations, creativity and passions.

Blockbuster movies could play a powerful role in further catalyzing an awakening and transition to bottom-up connection consciousness. Christopher Vogler, a veteran story consultant for major Hollywood films like *The Lion King* and *Fight Club*, adapted the Hero's Journey concept for his brilliant book *Writers Journey*. In it he explains how to apply the Hero's Journey theme to novels and movies. When I asked him if he'd be willing to discuss the idea of creating bottom-up Hero's Journeys on my radio show, he enthusiastically replied, "Woohoo." So we went deep, discussing how such a story could work, how it had been done, and which mythic elements and archetypes might be involved.

Vogler explained, "The very idea of what a hero is will shift from culture to culture. I've found in some places around the world, they don't think in terms of one person making a difference. It's a community working together or a family working together. The interest in the story is from this more collective point of view."

He gave some collective movie examples. "Think about the *Three Musketeers*. It's really four Musketeers. If you put all four of those guys together with their very different qualities you get a complete human being. All the possibilities are expressed." He went on, "You can see it very nicely in *The Lord of the Rings,* where the whole first movie is about building something: this team, the Fellowship of the Ring. There's one person who's carrying most of that responsibility, but it's really a collective sort of approach to storytelling."

Vogler suggests that a hero does the hard thing for the greater good. "How would that look for a group of people?" I asked. He replied, "In order to operate in a group in this very collectivist way, you have to submit your ego; you have to give something up; you have to sacrifice in the interest of what's good for the group. Any time people stand up for their rights, they're risking a lot. They're risking their freedom.

"Individual heroes separate themselves from their ordinary world," Vogler continued. "Sometimes they have to go alone deep into the darkness of the earth or into the belly of the beast, where they have their lesson, and they're transformed. Those same experiences can be added on the collective level. Your group can be isolated, can be separated from the rest of the culture, and experience the same feelings in this collective way that you do for the individual. In fact, sometimes the [story is about] the whole country or maybe the whole world changing its consciousness about something and facing the fear and overcoming that fear and then becoming stronger because of it."

I raised the idea that the Hero's Journey is about a character arc. Vogler replied, "It could be the development within one person or it could be the development of a new consciousness within a whole nation." He referred to an interview I did with Marina Sitrin, author of *Horizontalism*, where she described how the Argentinian people protested:

> This thing of the cacerolazos, it was called, which was the idea that people spontaneously, to protest something, would go out and just bang pots and pans. Hundreds of thousands of people . . . just, without any leader at all, just decide, 'You know what? This is too much and we have to make some noise about it.' People have attempted things like that. The famous example is in Paddy Chayefsky's movie, *Network*, where the broadcaster has just had enough and he's reacting as a normal human being reacts to the craziness he sees all around him and goes: 'Go to your windows and shout: I'm mad as hell and I'm not going to take it anymore!'

This is just a taste of Vogler's thinking. Hopefully, some screenwriter or novelist will read this and envision an idea on how to write a bottom-up Hero's Journey movie that becomes a super hit.

Steven Barnes, television writer (*Twilight Zone, Outer Limits* and *Stargate*) and author of *Lion's Blood*, told me, "The idea of a communal 'hero' is solid, and the rules already established: Robert McKee specifically states that a group can function as a single protagonist/antagonist if they all share the same goal: ('The Dirty Dozen' or any sports team story)"

I interviewed David Korten, author of *The Post-Corporate World: Life After Capitalism*, a book primarily about economics. But he brought story into the conversation, saying, "So many of our really meaningful stories by which we understand ourselves in our world fall either in the category of Empire stories or Earth Community stories. And they're either affirming the legitimacy and necessity of hierarchy or they are affirming the benefits and importance of community and partnership and our human capacity to be responsible, to be caring.

"Certainly in our current culture the Empire stories are so embedded in our culture that we get them from science; from churches; we certainly get them from the corporate media. It's partly because we have been living under empire for so long and we're so conditioned to empire stories that we rarely step back and say, 'Hey, wait a minute!'"

Some of the most classic, archetypal movies often start out in the Empire mode. Think *Star Wars, Avatar, Hunger Games,* and *Braveheart* where the empire story and characters represent the beginning of a typical Hollywood story arc, when the system, the bad guys, are in control or threatening the "world." Then the story arc takes the culture or world to a better place, post-dominating-empire culture. I replied to Korten, "I think that's really what you're describing as the post-corporate world, too."

In Korten's vision of the post-corporate world, a different story has replaced the top-down dominator, empire story. It's the bottom-up connection-conscious sharing story. Steven Barnes, says, "Want to replace the old story? First you have to interrupt the old one, anchor pain to it. Then people will WANT to change—and you offer them your new vision."

DOUGLAS RUSHKOFF'S VISION OF NEW STORIES: PRESENTISM, NARRATIVE COLLAPSE, AND NONLINEAR STORY

Doug Rushkoff has been a digital visionary, seeing patterns and trends for over 20 years. I interviewed him about his book, *Present Shock*. He argues, persuasively, that we are shifting to a new kind of nonlinear story. Rushkoff suggests that the linear beginning, middle, and end kind of story that Aristotle described (in "Ars Poetica"), which tends to be oriented toward a future and a destination, is being replaced by a form that is more oriented to the present.

Rushkoff says we're going through "narrative collapse," explaining that it stems from "the idea that, if you're living in a world without time, then there's no time for stories. There's no beginning, middle, and end; there's just these ongoing stories." He observes that people have stopped looking to the future and are looking at the present, saying,

"In the 20th Century (for example), we organized movements by having goals. Martin Luther King would have a dream, and then we would follow the charismatic leader: march down Broadway arm in arm. Declare our goal, and then strive towards it. We keep our eye on the prize, and the ends justify the means. Race to whatever it is. Stick a man on the moon, and stick the flag in, and declare that we've won. The war against Communism and the Russians: we're going to fight this Cold War...had the goal of eradicating the world of Communism, and we'd know when we won. The world doesn't really work that way anymore. Even our entertainment doesn't work that way. When I was a kid we were playing fantasy role-playing games. You're not playing a fantasy role-playing game in order to win; you're playing it in order to keep the game going.

"So I feel that, in a lot of areas...culturally, as we move from movies with beginnings, middles, and ends to things more like *The Simpsons,* that just go on, and the audience reward has more to do with making connections than it does to getting to the end...or [with] movements like Occupy, which were much less about stated goals or demands, and much more so about process."

Rushkoff then elaborated on the concept of The Aristotelian Arc.

"This idea of, we follow a character from a beginning, through a middle, to an end. We watch someone else make a series of choices that put them into danger, and bring us up the inclined plane of anxiety; and so this character makes the critical choice that saves the day, or changes the world, and then we get to sleep. Then we get that denouement, and conclusion, and sleep. It's this male orgasm-curved shape of narrative that has really driven our culture and our society since then. It's campaigns, it's moon shots, it's team sports."

All in all, Rushkoff offers us a glimpse into the way our culture is shifting from a top-down masculine energy to an energy that reflects the values of a more archetypally feminine bottom-up zeitgeist.

Metaphors, language, archetypes, myths, and stories play an incredibly important role in how we process our experiences and form our perceptions. Hopefully this chapter's tools will help you.

CHAPTER 4

Applying Bottom-Up Thinking and Strategies to the Internet and Social Media

This chapter focuses on how to practically apply bottom-up approaches to tap the power of the web. It offers specific strategies to find information, get support, raise money to promote your services, your work, your company, your product, your book, or your advocacy issue, and make online aspects of your business more bottom-up. Internet tools and social media have created a much more level playing field so that any person or organization today can have a voice, particularly if you incorporate the following bottom-up, connection conscious practices.

This chapter explores bottom-up approaches to tap the power of the following resources and technologies:

WEBSITES: Considerations to explore with your team are domain names, content, community email mailing lists and mailing programs, and multiple membership levels. Also explore free and paid visitor and member retention, repeat visits, search engine optimization/SEO, and identification of in-house content resource assets.

BLOGGING: Explore reasons to blog, the possibilities blogging offers, how to interact in the blogosphere, and your staffing, time, and investment costs

FACEBOOK: Use it to evaluate competition, check out key people and potential employees, create community, build your brand, and promote and spread your message.

TWITTER: Reach beyond followers to find clients, uncover relevant news, identify competition, and discover third-party websites and tools that can maximize your Twitter efforts.

LINKEDIN: Tap first-, second-, and third-level connections of your friends and colleagues.

CROWDSOURCING: Explore how to crowdsource images, products, analysis, planning, and funding ideas; and build a donor/supporter base.

WEB METRICS: There are many sites and tools to help you assess how you, your work, and your site are doing. They include Google Analytics and Google Trends.

BOTTOM-UP THINKING ABOUT THE DIGITAL ECOSYSTEM

Be findable and connectable on and through all media.

There are biological receptors which respond to specific hormones and biocompounds. In the digital world, it's important to develop receptors that allow people to find and connect with you.

- Make it easy for people to contact you by giving them multiple digital contact options through email, Twitter, Facebook, LinkedIn, Instagram, and texting.

- Have a comment section tied to your content. Disqus, Facebook, and Wordpress offer easy add-on options.

- Maximize your findability with search-engine optimization (SEO). There are SEO companies, and you can learn how to do some on your own.

- Tag content with keywords to help searchers find you and help search engines optimize your content.

- Manifest a Wikipedia page for you, your company, and your products.

- Start a YouTube channel. Google owns YouTube and favors it in search results. You don't have to do full video. A video that uses audio with a static image will do. One way to create video content with relative ease is to do online video interviews using Google Hangouts, Zoom.us, Skype, other video tools, or use your smart phone. Or narrate a PowerPoint slide show to video.

Be shareable.

Make it easy for people to share your content and connect it to your connections. Make sure your platform has sharing links for Facebook, Twitter, LinkedIn, Reddit, and email, and on the mobile version, for texting. Even if your content is great, it won't reach its optimal potential for being found by others if it's not easily shareable.

Actively connect.

Being findable and shareable is passive. The media ecosystem is not static. It is alive and dynamic. Regularly and fully engage with your media ecosystem, and your connections will flourish. Remember: After investing time and effort to create content, you'll increase results by taking the time to share it. Connecting builds your personal network/ system of promotion and interdependence.

BOTTOM-UP SOCIAL MEDIA WEB PRESENCE AND REACH CONSULTING

Bottom-up thinking can help you get an effective handle on social media. The next part of the chapter will show you how social media consulting works, so you can either use the ideas on your own or more knowledgably assess and hire experts and tell them what you need

A bottom-up *social media* consultant or coach analyzes the current interests, needs, resources, and strategies of an individual or organization and develops new strategies for integrating bottom-up social media and analog tools and approaches. The consutant evaluates:

- Current needs, objectives, goals, knowledge, and strategies

- Performance of online and social media being used

- Reach, profile, assets, liabilities, metrics

- Current staff resources

- Current business and career model

- Potential content resources

The consultant then reviews the profile you provide and does online research and analysis using tools like Alexa and Google Analytics to gather metrics on your organization's and your competitors' online and social media presence.

Taking the bottom-up approach can transform the way you understand and relate to your work and your clients. It can change your company and may well change your life.

While discussing the findings with you, the consultant will recommend strategies with specific steps for reaching your goals.

Bottom-up social media strategies and approaches can be applied to the following:

- **WEBSITES**: SEO, membership, retention, content creation, sharing, marketing, user interface, and experience

- **RELATIONSHIPS**: community, staff, advisors, board, volunteers, recruiting, retention, membership list-building, and motivation

- **PROMOTION**: marketing, sales, prospecting, researching competitors, branding, and content

- **PRODUCTS SERVICES AND ASSETS**: development, feedback, endorsement, and trust building

- **EVENTS**: pre-event, community, relationships, content development, and invitations

- **PUBLIC RELATIONS**: In the new bottom-up world, PR is a two-way process. There are tools you can use—at no cost, except for staffing—for tracking your brand, your people, and your industry. PR is also used to defend against adverse events.

A BOTTOM-UP CONSULTING CASE EXAMPLE

I did a social-media consultation and staff training project for the office of a psychologist—who'd written a book—and his partner, a social worker. They offer direct services, sell CDs and downloadable MP3s, and run workshops.

We started with a conversation aimed at identifying what they were currently doing and their goals and needs. They wanted to expand sales of their digital content and start doing online "webinars."

Then we discussed their website. It was a static "brochure" with no images above the fold, the part of the page visible without having to scroll down. The photo of my client's book, a main factor in his brand recognition, was well below the fold, as were the important links.

We then checked out some competitors' websites, which were as bad or worse. We discussed how some people prefer text, but that their website ignored visual people altogether. We identified images they could use and explored ways to make the site more interactive.

I probed into the skills and experience possessed by their five employees. Four did email. Two did some web design, along with Facebook, Twitter, and Google Alerts. Most of those skills, however, were unknown and untapped by their employers. We discussed how they could be utilized and the effects they might have on other job responsibilities.

I proposed creating an email list. People who want to subscribe are the easiest to get. But you can also motivate people to sign up as members by giving them something extra, for example; access to additional content, extra privileges at the site, such as commenting, seeing an article as a single printer-friendly page, sending messages to writers or commenters on the site, and access to advanced stats.

My clients wanted to build their mailing list for marketing purposes. I suggested a free e-newsletter as a motivator for sign-ups. They asked, "But what do you send to subscribers?" One of the owners said she'd tried to do a blog but that it was too time-consuming and too much work, even though she likes to write. I pointed out that they had over 50 professionals certified in their psychological approach who could write the articles and fill a blog with content.

"But they'll write things that are wrong," one of the principals voiced, in concern.

"So you add a comment and correct it, or make an edit before the submission goes live," I replied.

"It'll be a teachable moment," the other partner added.

Again, the idea of extra work raised its head. Where would the time and resources come from? That's the challenge of social media: finding time and staff resources. Social media can work magic, but requires a time commitment to make the magic happen.

Knowing the untapped resource this group was ignoring, I pursued the possibility of bringing in professionals they'd certified as content producers. These were smart, creative entrepreneurial therapists who could bring a lot to the table. And they were ripe for becoming part of an online community in a community blog site. I explained that writing for the site wouldn't take as much work as they supposed. They could recruit volunteer editors and provide writers' guidelines to assuage their quality control concerns.

We weren't just talking about implementing technology. We were talking about a quantum shift in this team's career—a transition from being just two top-down people carrying the water to becoming a more bottom-up, cooperative community, which would nurture the emergence of an environment that would birth the next generation of innovators and practitioners.

"This could be the next phase of your career, a way to take your work to the next level," I observed. Later, one of them suggested that it could be a paradigm shift for them. But this was not something they were going to immediately embrace. They were feeling trepidation about passing on responsibilities to staff. I assured them, "You are sitting on an incredibly powerful resource—these people—and it takes TRUST to tap that power and turn it into an asset." They started to get it.

Our discussion moved to Twitter. The previous week I'd worked with a medical credentialing organization and after some analysis of their market demographics and Twitter keywords and potential hashtags, I concluded that Twitter probably wouldn't be useful to them. But as I walked the psychologist's group through how they could use Twitter for lead prospecting, media development, publicity, and relationship development, their eyes kept opening wider and wider.

One staffer had some Twitter experience and skills and was willing to put some time into Twitter work. We discussed how to use Twitter in a bottom-up way to find potential journalists to write stories on their work and how to connect with influence leaders.

Next we explored Facebook. Younger people are using email less, but they love Facebook, Snapchat, WhatsApp, and Instagram. The same content sent out in the team's e-newsletters could be posted on their website or blog, and then linked to their Facebook page and then, as I discuss later, it could be shared, reaching people who don't do email.

We wrapped up the consultation by summarizing the action steps the group could take:

- Redesign the website front page with more graphics and content above the fold.

- Follow more people on Twitter.

- Add website URL and email address to key contact points in the office, ads, business cards, bills, and stationery.

- Start a blog and invite certificants likely to be contributors.

- Change email addresses for status update notifications for Twitter and Facebook to the staffers who will do the answering, since the owners didn't want to put in the time.

- Have the owners do audio and video recordings and webinars that can be transcribed for text and archived as podcasts. These would serve as another kind of media content asset to build the mailing list and membership.

I left feeling I'd helped them develop some new ideas and skills and helped them to envision another stage in their business and lives—an inclusive, bottom-up approach that would greatly increase the odds that they'd build a lasting legacy.

BUILD A PLATFORM: THE CENTRAL STEP TO ESTABLISHING YOUR BOTTOM-UP STRATEGY

Most web strategists, publicists, literary agents, and marketers agree that building a platform is essential, whether you're an author, speaker, artist, consultant, or run a company or a nonprofit.

Your platform is your tool for putting your best face forward. In one place, it pulls together all of your strengths, kudos, and references so that people can get to know the YOU you want them to know. A good platform gives potential clients, customers, editors, partners, or agents an idea of your accomplishments and capabilities.

Perhaps you've received awards or honors, written articles, or been a president or board member of an organization in your profession or community. Or maybe you've been a guest on a local radio show, or had an article written about you, or have had some unique or interesting experience. A professional license, education, credentials—they count, too. All are elements of a platform. Facebook, Twitter, LinkedIn, Stumbleupon, Instagram, Pinterest, and so forth are valuable, as well, but they're best used to support and link back to your *platform*. And then you can link back to them from your platform.

The following aspects of your work are usually covered:

- unique capabilities: skills, knowledge, expertise

- media exposure: YouTube links, interviews, articles you've written, your experience

- visibility: followers, readers, listeners, friends, etc.

- endorsements: blurbs, reviews, etc.

- reputation: press or possibly a celebrity profile

- marketing ability

- projects and accomplishments

- education

Here are some things you can do to create a platform, or enhance the one you have (details come later):

- Create or update vision and mission statements that embrace bottom-up connection consciousness.

- Identify key words your project is related to and include them in the text.

- Research competing and related projects, organizations, websites, and platforms for ideas and inspiration.

- Create a name for the project that's available as a domain name. Then register the domain name, paying for at least two years.

- Create a website or have one created, preferably one you can upload content to and add to without the help of a webmaster.

- Create a blog.

- Create a Facebook page.

- Set up Twitter, LinkedIn, Google, and Instagram accounts.

- Create Google Alerts for the keywords you've identified.

- Set up a Hootsuite or Tweetdeck account to track mentions of your site and the key words you've identified.

- Create a YouTube account and start developing content ideas for YouTube.

- Add a mailing list signup and management function for sending emails to your website

- Do Search Engine Optimization/SEO.

A typical platform site will include the following tab menu bar at the top:

HOME | ABOUT | MEDIA | WORK/SAMPLES | SERVICES |
ENDORSEMENTS | EVENTS| CONTACT

The tab menu won't actually have entries for "work" and "samples." If you're a writer, those two words will be replaced by "WRITINGS;" if an artist, by "WORKS" or "GALLERY;" and if a consultant, by "PROJECTS." You can also use "kudos" or "blurbs," or some other creative formulation, instead of the word "endorsements."

That's a beginning. But it's not enough. If someone creates a site that lists all they've done and all that's been said about them, they're simply creating another 1990s-style static brochure website. To make your platform website truly bottom-up, you need to build connection, community, and stickiness into it. The following sections will tell you how.

Why and How

If you're doing something you want other people to know about, you need a blog. Millions of people blog. Blogging has become a vital, dynamic form of citizen journalism, and it has the power to make a difference. I started my own blog in early 2003. It grew to become one of the top Google-search-ranked progressive news and opinion sites and a major source of my income.

As a podcast host and community blog publisher, I'm invited twice a year, along with 100-125 other media people, to the National Publicity Summit where aspiring radio show and media-coverage guests pitch me. It's a lot like speed dating. An assistant with a timer makes sure the media-coverage seekers who line up at my booth each get two-and-a-half minutes to make a pitch telling why we should have them on as guests. I always ask them if they have a blog, and it's amazing how many do not. Of course, creating a platform is part of what the conference coaches encourage them to do.

You can start your own blog with your own website and URL. Or blog on a much higher-traffic community blog site, which usually has much higher readership. The advantage of having your own blog site is that it puts you in total control of headlining, content, message and branding.

Tips on Becoming a Blogger:

- Make a list of what you want the blog to do for you.

- Choose a topic you know and are passionate about and that you'll want to keep writing about.

- Pick a content management system. Search "create your own website." Assess the different options and choose one to set up your blog.

- Post new blog entries at least a few times a week.

- Share your content using social media

- Have guests blog on your site, then ask them to share the content with their followers. You both enhance your outreach.

- Create Search Engine Optimized great article titles.

- Integrate the blog with your platform.

- Consider cross-posting to a community blog compatible with your content—ones like OpEdNews, *The Huffington Post*, Daily Kos, Medium, or others.

Remember that blogging is a two-way, many-to-many conversation, not a lecture. That makes the comment section a key blog element. As you write, anticipate that commenters will help enhance your article. I often speak directly to the commenters in my own postings, inviting them to add their information, knowledge, and perspective.

Why Does Blogging Have Power to Influence?

You don't have to be famous to create a blog that reaches far and wide. There are some simple things anyone can do to greatly enhance the likelihood your words will reach the people you want them to reach.

My blog, OpEdNews.com, has grown to reach 150,000-800,000+ unique visitors a month, with up to 2.6 million page views per month. The site has over 100,000 registered members, over 23,000 newsletter subscribers, and over 100,000 articles published since 2005.

Setting up a blog requires a Content Management System (CMS). A CMS is the software that enables your blog website to post, store, archive, and display content: articles, comments, members, member profiles. OpEdNews uses a custom-built CMS but most blogs use blogging-platform CMS's that are available free, such as Blogger, WordPress, Drupal, Joomla, and their variations. The CMS makes your content easy to access and puts it on the web in a way that, hopefully, optimizes it for search engines (SEO).

This book doesn't directly cover SEO. But it will, hopefully, help you better understand how bottom-up considerations can affect your search rank. Google considers hundreds of factors in their full-search algorithm. Do a search on "Google search algorithm" or "improving Google search results" to learn more.

TAPPING THE BOTTOM-UP POWERS OF TWITTER, FACEBOOK, AND INSTAGRAM:

Users who approach Facebook, Twitter, and Instagram solely with traditional top-down thinking see them only as sites to tweet or to share with their followers, even if they have very few followers. It doesn't have to be that way. You can reach far more people than the number of followers you have, and you can use Facebook, Twitter, and Instagram prospectively to gather bottom-up information.

Interview with Twitter and Square Inventor Jack Dorsey

When I met Jack Dorsey after he'd participated in a panel at Personal Democracy Forum, I said, 'I want to get an idea of your philosophy and how this ties into how we're moving toward a more bottom-up world.'

Dorsey replied, "I've always been attracted to very simple, simple systems, specifically minimizing the artifacts—the conceptual artifacts around the interaction. When you do that, Twitter's innovation is constraining the size of the canvas. You're presented with a huge wall and a canvas and you approach that; you're asked to make a mark. When you go up to that canvas you are composing yourself. You are retracting yourself. You are thinking. And that kills a lot of the momentum of some of the thoughts. That medium is still required. But having a simpler approach—minimizing the canvas size so that any mark on that canvas is interesting and in some way beautiful—is, I think, the biggest thing. And I think we can have that approach everywhere.

"That's where simplicity comes in for me, and I think that's where the bottom-up-ness comes in. When you make something simple, when you take away all that conceptual debris around it, then people get creative. They can be more off the cuff. They can be more immediate, because that's the way things are moving these days."

I interjected, "Bottom-up is a kind of 'we' thing, a participatory thing. How does that fit in?"

Dorsey answered, "That's the thing. If people are creating more, if they're communicating more and they're sharing more, and it's easy to do that, then it sparks more interaction. It exposes all these trends about what's happening in their world."

I observed, "That's the kind of thing hashtags are helping with." (Hashtags are like keywords for Twitter.)

Dorsey replied, "Exactly… It provides a general awareness, a general context of what's going on in the surrounding that you care about, be it the smallest social network you can have, which is a one-to-one relationship, or a city, and making it approachable—making it something that people can engage in. And that's really the biggest thing, 'How do people engage in this technology?'"

I asked, "So what's your dream and your vision of the 'big simple?'"

"The big simple simple!" Dorsey replied, chuckling. "Simple to me is utility. Simple to me is the electricity system. It's the water system. It's something that you don't think about anymore, that just blurs into the background and that you just use on a day-to-day basis. I think it requires simple, clever policies. I think it requires getting rid of all this debris around technology. We have so much abstraction in everything we use. The more we remove that abstraction, the more genuine communication we can have and the more we can do faster."

I commented, "It's been said that Michelangelo would go to a stone quarry, find a stone, and then he'd see what he would have to take away to create a work of art. It's kind of what you're describing."

"That's right," Jack replied. "It's the editorial process. It's saying NO. It's taking things away from things and really providing an editorial voice. Every person, every leader that I really respect, in terms of what they've done—Steve Jobs, for instance—has had a very strong editorial voice. And that is the function of anyone leading any particular movement, be it very small or be it very large. Where are we focusing? What are we saying NO to? And what are we getting rid of so that we can expose what's really important and expose it immediately."

I asked Dorsey about enabling content site users to share on Twitter. He replied, "Yes, yes. It provides that more immediate voice, where you can just mix in a stream that's real-time. And I think there's such a desire for real time right now—and just a lot of movement. People want to see things moving and they want to participate in real time, because it feels good, because you see an immediate reaction. You can see your impact on what you are talking about and what you're doing."

Since our interview was shortly after Iran's green revolution, I asked him about his impressions of the role of Twitter in Iran. He answered, "With anything, we're just enabling usage. So people are using it various ways in Iran. People are using it in Iraq. People are using it to talk about Michael Jackson. People are using it to build new companies and to build movements. And it's the company's challenge, and the technology's challenge, but more so our challenge as a people, to really sustain these concepts, so that we have something that's open enough so that you can really build all these things: that it's not focused on any particular solution, because any particular solution rules out anything else. And people are going to approach the technology in completely different ways—ways that we never expected them to approach. That's where it's going."

I'd say the same is true for the bottom-up revolution.

TWO BOTTOM-UP APPROACHES TO TWITTER

"I used to think having all the answers was 'smart'—now I am learning that asking the right questions is much smarter."

—@CHRISSAAD (TWEET), FORMER HEAD OF PRODUCT AT
UBER DEVELOPER PLATFORM

Reach Thousands of Twitter Users Who Don't Follow You.

Even if you only have a handful of followers you can still reach thousands of people, even hundreds of thousands, by using hashtags. A hashtag is a tag or keyword that has the # sign before it, which you add to tweets so more people will find them. A hashtag for antiwar would be

"#antiwar." When YOU use hashtags, you can reach people who track that hashtag. The trick is to identify hashtags that are relevant to the content and message you want to blast out. You do that in several ways:

- Tweetdeck and Hootsuite are apps which help you automate tracking specific hashtags and who's tweeting them on a daily basis.

- Use Twitter search to find hashtags that describe your topic. If your topic is Divorce, hashtags might include #divorce, #alimony, #Custody #ChildSupport, #divorceAttorney.

- Click on one of the relevant hashtags. It will show you a stream of recent tweets. Note what other hashtags are being used, and see who's tweeting with them, and who it is they're following. Then follow them and set up the other hashtags in your Twitter tracking app (Hootsuite, Tweetdeck).

- Check trending tags. Research events related to your topic: conferences, TV coverage, Sports, Oscars, debates, breaking news. They will often have hashtags associated with them that you can piggyback onto. Trending tags can have 100K tweets, even 500K. Trending tags usually only offer opportunities lasting minutes or hours. Trends are listed on the top left side of the Twitter home page.

- Now that you've identified relevant hashtags, including trending hashtags, include one, two, or three hashtags to go with your tweet.

- The hashtags will help you reach people who do not follow you but who follow the hashtags.

How often should you tweet? Social media expert Jeff Bullas sends out 100 or more tweets a day. He does it using tools which automate the process. He can load up a batch of ten or twelve at the beginning of the week and they are sent automatically. Conclusion: don't be shy with your tweeting.

Put Your Ear to the Ground to Tap the Wisdom of Twitter from the Bottom Up.

Here's another way to access the resources of hundreds, thousands, or even millions of people—numbers that go way beyond the followers you have or the people you follow:

- Use the set of instructions on the previous pages to identify relevant hashtags.

- Then go to each hashtag to see what's being posted.

- To get a feel for who is talking about a particular subject, mouse over their Twitter handle to see more about them and how many followers they have. Follow the interesting ones.

- Follow a lot of people. You're allowed to follow up to 5000 people. I encourage you to follow 4500 to 4800 if you have under 5000 followers because when people look at your profile to consider following you, they'll see that you are generous with your follows.

- Check out other hashtags being used to discuss the topic.

- Look to see which tweets are being liked and retweeted the most. See who originally tweeted them since they have become leaders on the topic. Follow them, and check what else they've tweeted and what other hashtags they're using.

- Tweet questions to the hashtag. You may be surprised how generous people are in helping you.

- Set up automated hashtag tracking on Tweetdeck or Hootsuite—for your name, issues, passions, hobbies, brands, competitors' names, companies, etc.

It's a powerful way to find out early what's happening moment to moment. If a plane crashes, if there's a shooting or breaking news, Twitter is the place journalists go to get info sooner.

A Bottom-Up Facebook Strategy to Reach Beyond Your Friends and Followers

You can reach thousands, even hundreds of thousands of Facebook group members to share your content with. Some groups have tens of millions of members.

Find Facebook groups devoted to the topic or cause your content covers. Say you have an article on divorce. Here are the steps to take:

- Type into Facebook's search field a word, for example, "divorce."

- Hit enter. A menu bar will appear at the top of the page.

- Click on the groups tab.

- Look for relevant groups, particularly those with a lot of members.

- Join the groups.

- Repeat for related words like "alimony" and "custody."

- Create a list of the names of the groups you join. I use a spreadsheet, and list the names in order of their size of membership. Activist Stephen Fox opens up a second Facebook tab, then scrolls down to easily access the list of over 1000 Facebook groups he's joined. Fox advises that everyone join at least a thousand.

- As soon as your memberships are approved, check out the groups.

Steps to Sharing with a Group:

- Submit the URL for your content as a status posting on your time-line, or use a sharing icon on your blog.

- On Facebook, click on the share button below the content.

- Click on share again in the drop down menu.

- Click on the top option in the next dropdown menu.

- Click on "Share with a group" option in the drop-down menu.

- Type in a key word that's in the name of some of your groups. Groups that have that word will show up in a drop-down menu. Click on the one you want. Usually, you'll only need to use one or, at most, two key words to get to the group name you're looking for.

- Click on the POST button at the bottom of the box you've been working in.

NOTE: *Facebook occasionally changes this process*

That's it. You've posted to a group. Sometimes, I create a new column in my spreadsheet for content items I'm submitting. For one of my topics, there are over 30 different groups totaling close to a million members.

WIKIPEDIA AND WIKIMEDIA: RESOURCES AND MAKING A WIKIPEDIA PAGE HAPPEN

WIKIPEDIA is a bottom-up curated and created encyclopedia. It is a part of the Wikimedia community, which has created and offers a variety of additional free projects. These include:

- **WIKIMEDIA COMMONS**, a photo-sharing and free image resource

- **WIKIQUOTES**, a site that researches quotations and their sources

- **WIKTIONARY**, a free dictionary used by many cultures to preserve and document their languages

- **WIKIVOYAGE**, a site that helps acquaint travelers with the places they plan to visit

Wikimedia allows free re-use of most Wikimedia content. In an interview I conducted with Katherine Maher, Wikimedia's executive director, she explained: "We use a form of licensing for Wikipedia which is creative commons. [It] essentially says that when you contribute to Wikipedia, you are donating your contribution to the world and anybody can use a Wikipedia article or image on Wikipedia as long as they attribute it back to the creator, but they don't have to pay licensing fees or royalty fees."

Getting down to the nitty-gritty, with platform in mind, I asked her, "How does one create a Wikipedia page for somebody who does not have a page, and what are the criteria?"

First, Maher advised that people should not create their own page. She explained, "Wikipedia is expected to be neutral, and it's pretty hard to be neutral about oneself." Then she added that for people or things to qualify for Wikipedia pages, they must be notable. "What notability tends to mean is, 'Has this person or this place or this event or phenomenon been documented over time in a variety of reliable mainstream sources of information?'… Whether it's the news, academic journals or published books. Once you've got that, then you want to say, 'Can I write this in a way that is verifiable?'… '[Can I] source it back to an original source or document, or a secondary source or document?' Then you want to make sure that it's accurate. So, verifiability, accuracy and neutrality, those are the things that editors look at."

I pursued more details, asking, "How does one become a beginning Wikipedian?"

Maher advised, "The very first thing I would suggest people do is choose an article that you are interested in, preferably not about yourself or your employer. If you're a birdwatcher, perhaps an article about birds, or if you are really into sports, perhaps you want to choose your favorite sports team. If you go to that article, you will see at the top of the page there are a couple different buttons. One says 'talk,' one says 'edit,' and one says 'history.'"

Maher points out that most people read the article part of Wikipedia. But click the TALK tab and you see what editors are saying and asking about the article. She explained that they "can have conversations with each other on that talk page and you will see lots of conversations happening about, 'What should an article include? What should an article not include? What is considered a reliable source of information for a particular statement or fact? If there's a controversy, how do you want to address the controversy?'"

She continued, "Spend some time just reading and browsing and understanding what people are talking about. What do they care about? Who are the people that care about this article? You'll find people tend to edit in the areas that they're passionate about . . . and that's a good way to get to know them.

"Once you've familiarized yourself with the talk page, click on edit. The Wikipedia article will reload and it will now be editable and you can make that change. The best way to do it is with a citation to an original source, let's say it's [an] article [on] CNN. Then you can hit save and that's it. You've edited your first article. There's no waiting, there's no sort of approval process in most articles. It just goes straight to publish."

As a Wikipedia beginner, there are a few places where you can get help. Maher suggests: "When you create your account, go to the 'tea house' and sign up and say, 'Hi, I'm a new editor and I'm here to learn,' and a volunteer mentor will come work with you. Another way is you can write a draft article and submit it for review by a more experienced Wikipedian... They'll come back and be able to say, 'This looks great but I would add this,' or 'This may need to be changed,' or 'This looks perfect. Go ahead and publish.'"

Wikipedia also has a top-down side. Powerful players employ people as Wikipedia editors to vigilantly control certain Wikipedia pages—typically ones about famous politicians, corporations, or controversial issues. For example, the Monsanto page reads like a love letter to Monsanto. If an ideologue editor wants to, he can cause Wikipedia pages to be removed entirely. Those editors are breaking Wikipedia rules, but it happens routinely. Bottom line: Wikipedia is great for noncontroversial topics, but can be skewed for sensitive ones.

One good way to get a Wikipedia page going is to partner up with another person who needs one but is not directly connected to you. Help each other make the other's page happen. Wikipedia frowns on hiring people to create your own page on Wikipedia for you. You could hire someone to, offline, edit your information and do proper formatting, which you could then properly submit for review to Wikipedians.

BOTTOM-UP SEARCH AND RESEARCH: FINDING INFORMATION AND ANSWERS

Search Engines

Search algorithms are at least partially bottom-up-based. When you do a search, the results at the top probably have more sites linking to them. That means more people are using them. You can tap this aspect of the internet to get bottom-up answers. More on this below.

Bulletin/Discussion Boards

There are gazillions of bulletin boards discussing just about any topic. Just search for your keyword combined with the words "bulletin board." Then search the board and ask it questions, or start a conversation, including links to your site.

Listserv Groups or Listserves

Listserv groups are similar to bulletin boards, but they also offer email functions. You can sign up for a listserv group that will email you comments made by another member of the group as soon as they are made. You can set up your membership to receive digests of accumulated comments either once a day, once a week, or for every 25 emails. Or, you can opt to go to the site to view listserv messages. I belong to over forty listservs, including one I created to discuss bottom-up ideas.

Blog for Answers

On your own blog, or on community blogs, you can post a blog, diary, or article with questions for blog visitors to respond to. I've written some articles that explore some of the ideas for this book, asking for people to comment and make suggestions on where to look for more information.

LINKEDIN.COM: GOING BEYOND YOUR RICH UNCLE'S CONNECTIONS

LinkedIn, another social networking site with hundreds of millions of members, is more business-focused than Facebook or Twitter. Like

Facebook, LinkedIn has millions of groups you can join. LinkedIn is also great for posting questions.

I asked Wayne Breitbarth, author of *The Power Formula for LinkedIn Success,* to describe bottom-up ways to approach LinkedIn. He replied, "LinkedIn allows individuals to leverage their experiences and relationships to increase their professional effectiveness." He attributes the power of LinkedIn to "connection visibility—how you can use keywords in the advanced search feature to find friends of your friend, friends who might be able to help you." Breitbarth gave an example, "I'd love to meet that person. I don't know them, but my friend Joe Smith does. I'm gonna reach out to Joe Smith and say, 'I'd love to have an introduction, a cup of coffee, and email introduction.' The number one power on LinkedIn is finding people you want to meet that maybe one of your good friends know."

Breitbarth advised, "Some of the biggest mistakes people make on LinkedIn is to not think about the leverage that their existing friends have in helping them accomplish their business. I have a really good network of people that I know, love, and care about that would help me if I call them. That's the treasure that people underestimate."

LinkedIn centers around creating a profile. Breitbarth advises. "Two things are going on in your profile that you have to manage and think about: keywords and story." It's important to identify the key words searchers might use that will lead to them finding you, "Make sure that those words are lots of places on your profile." He adds, "Story is also critical on profile—telling your story well so that when people read it, they go, 'Man, I'm gonna call him. He would be perfect to work with.'"

Breitbarth suggests that the general strategy people should be employing for LinkedIn is "Ask the question, 'Who do you want to meet?' The second strategy is, 'Does my profile show how I could be strategically aligned with the people I want to be strategically aligned with?'"

Breitbarth added, "recommendations are among the most powerful tools on LinkedIn. Recommendations are the only thing on your profile you didn't write. It's the outside verification that you are that good."

"Are there ways to reach more people than you are connected to?" I asked Breitbarth. He answered that there are two ways: first, by engaging in conversations in LinkedIn's more than 2.5 million groups; and, second, by "publishing" articles on LinkedIn.

Breitbarth continued, "Groups are a great way to find connections, but groups are also a great way for you to communicate what it is you do. I have gotten so many consulting gigs from LinkedIn by sharing my weekly blog posts in all kinds of groups."

A FEW EXAMPLES OF BOTTOM-UP ANSWER-FINDING
Example 1: Googling God

Wikipedia can't answer all our questions. About ten years ago, I decided to Google the different names of God to see which one had the most hits. I started with "Jesus"—and, already, I had a problem. Jesus is also a popular given name. The same is true of Mohamed. So if we go with just the single name, we'll pick up other people with the name, too, who are most likely named after "the" Jesus or "the" Mohamed.

Here are some numbers:

Jesus:	33,800,000
Mohamed	7,110,000
Buddha	5,720,000
Krishna	4,970,000
Vishnu	1,270,000

And here are some stats I dug up on the number of adherents to different faiths from adherents.com:

Christianity:	2.1 billion
Islam:	1.5 billion
Secular/Nonreligious/Agnostic/Atheist:	1.1 billion

Hinduism:	900 million
Chinese traditional religion:	394 million
Buddhism:	376 million
Indigenous:	300 million

There were a few things that didn't jibe in these stats. It struck me that, although Christianity has only 40 percent more followers than Islam, "Jesus" had almost 400 percent more hits than Mohamed. I took a closer look, doing searches for Islam, Koran, etc., and discovered that "Mohamed," which is the way I found the US press tends to spell the name of the Prophet of Islam, is not by any means the most popular spelling.

So I tried some other spellings.

Mahomet	355,000
Mohamet	310,000
Muhammed	3,190,000
Mohammed	6,400,000
Muhammad	9,060,000

Then, bingo!!

Mohammad	61,900,000

The crowd reveals the way the Prophet's name is spelled by the most people and why the numbers didn't add up when we compared the names of the respective founders of Christianity and Islam.

Example 2: Searching for an Accurate Quotation
I received an email that included a quotation attributed to Rudyard Kipling.

The individual has always had to struggle to keep from being overwhelmed by the tribe. **To be own man is hard business.** *If you try it, you will* *be lonely often, and sometimes frightened. But no price is too high to pay for the privilege of owning yourself.*

I liked the quote, but one phrase seemed incomplete: "*To be own man…*" So I Googled the first line of the quote and found that it was attributed to both Kipling and Nietzsche.

Next, I took the same first line and added the word Kipling to the search, and came up with 24,000 hits. Then I used Nietzschze with the first line and came up with 48,000 hits.

Bottom-up, crowd-sourced verdict? It's by Nietzsche. But that may not be enough for top-down situations, like book publishing or some websites, where more specific criteria are required.

How can you use this bottom-up question approach? Want to find out which designer is more popular? Try doing Google searches with the designer names. Or go a step further and use a superlative like "hot," "in style," or "off-the-shelves." See how the different designers' search stats compare to each other.

Want to find out which brand has more recognition? Search the brand names. There are also other criteria for comparison. One brand may have a good name and another a bad one. So add "good," "bad," "great," "stinks," etc. to the search for the brand name. And try the same approaches on Twitter.

Google Trends

I had considered strictly using the hyphenated form of the word bottom-up for this book. But I applied a bottom-up research approach, searching Google Trends, which looks at the numbers of people who have used a particular search term over time, to determine which term is the more widely used. The graph below clearly shows that the unhyphenated form is far more popular and has generated a steadily increasing trend of interest. Consider using Google Trends for product, website, or brand-naming research.

I was going to use the unhyphenated form of bottom-up throughout the book, based on my Google Trends research. But my editor pointed out that there are rules of spelling, that when bottom-up is used as an adjective, it is supposed to be hyphenated. To not use it would incur the disdain of people in the book publishing and selling food chain—a top-down reason to include the hyphen. So there are times, as when I talk about "from the bottom up" when the hyphen will be absent, and times when it will be present. This is the kind of balance and compromise that is normal in assessing top-down and bottom-up ways of handling things.

GOOGLE ALERTS: YOUR PERSONALIZED BOTTOM-UP "CLIPPINGS SERVICE"

Before Google Alerts existed, people and organizations would spend hundreds of dollars monthly paying a service to collect magazine and newspaper clippings which mentioned their names or the keywords they were tracking.

Today, anyone can set up no-cost Google Alerts daily emails that report mention of selected names or search terms that appear on the web. Set up alerts for your name, your friends' and relatives' names, your employees' names, your company names and brands, your competitors' names, product names, or names of illnesses, organizations, sports teams, players, artists. The service can be used to aid your job search or even to find coupons.

Congressional staffers use Google Alerts to track their boss's names, their big-name donors, the committees they're on, and the issues they focus on. Savvy corporate social-media staffers track Google Alerts for company officers, competitors' products, brands, and related topics. This is the way most people think of using Google Alerts—to bring information TO them.

You can also employ Google Alerts to REACH people.
This can be especially helpful for getting past screeners blocking access to busy, famous, or powerful people. It puts emails they've asked to see directly into their in-boxes.

When you blog or post an article and mention keywords or names congressional staffers are tracking, it's almost certain they'll get a Google Alerts email that reports what you said about the congressperson or legislation. Staffers will react to that posting very differently than they would to an unsolicited email. Since they set up the Google Alerts, they'll be looking for the reports and be more likely to pay attention to them.

Want to reach a legislator, governor, mayor, or influencer? You'll raise the likelihood of reaching them via Google Alerts notifications by including their name, their legislation, their issue, and the name of a town within their district or state in your article writing. The same is true if you are trying to reach a corporation, customer, or organization. I've had a senate staffer contact me within minutes of my posting an article that mentioned the senator's name. You don't have to be on network TV to influence the decision-makers. You just need to understand how to tap the power of bottom-up. And you don't have to be famous to be published on a site that is indexed by Google Alerts. Just write a letter to the editor or comment on an article.

In summary, when the goal of your online writing is to influence people or make change happen, be sure to include the key words and the names of the people, companies and organizations that the people you're trying to influence will be tracking.

Interview with CraigsList Founder Craig Newmark

I started my interview with Craig Newmark, the founder of CraigsList, by saying to him: "You've become a master of the internet universe, with one of the most influential sites on the web. That's had a huge impact on the future of journalism and newspapers. What have you learned? What philosophies have you developed and where are they taking you?"

Newmark replied, "We can see that people are fundamentally trustworthy and good. There are some bad guys out there, but the percentage is pretty low, and the more you give a voice for everyone else, the [more] good guys you'll see that come out. By doing that, by treating people like we want to be treated, somehow that created a culture of trust on the site."

I asked him about bottom-up matters. He answered, "I have observed also, when I worked for IBM and elsewhere, that in any large organization the rank-[and-file] folks—the people at the bottom of the hierarchy—they're the folks that know what's going on and how to fix it. And what people need is a way to talk about it, to affirm each other, and then to get upper management to commit. I think this decade we're going to see a big redirection of human history where people work together a lot more. There are people who do work against that because it threatens their profit. But I think it's inevitable."

I asked Newmark if he'd thought of doing something like eBay does, giving people ratings.

He replied, "I do think reputation systems, reputation engines, will be a big part of our future, because in real life, online life, a lot of what we do is based on 'Who do you trust?' And trust is based on reputation. But I think we're going to need a system where a number of companies provide reputation databases which are all interchangeable. I can't think of anything really more important overall than trust. We make decisions based on who we trust. And you [see] there's a lot of untrustworthy folks out there who are really good at scamming people. We've got to look out for each other. We have to figure out what you trust and what you don't want to trust."

I asked, "Where do you see things going?" Newmark answered, "The deal is you're helping them help each other. You want a balance of independence and you want a balance of people helping each other out. You want both, and all of that works together really well. I think over the next decade people are going to work together, through the net, way, way more, to the extent where we are going to see a bottom-up change in tremendous amounts—in politics, commerce, just people socializing."

He's right. We're seeing it and it's going to continue.

CROWDSOURCING

Crowdsourcing coordinates, collects, and aggregates ideas, actions, work, and contributions from the crowd, drawing from lots of people, so things can be done better and smarter. Crowdsourcing is used to develop designs for T-shirts, to raise money, to decide how to prioritize headlines on news sites, and to create Wikipedia.

Crowdsourcing can take many forms. When I check out the *New York Times* online, I usually start with the top-down, editor-curated headlines. Next, I go to the "most popular" page, which is based on reader page views. That's an example of crowdsourcing by tracking user behavior. Some of the most widely tapped kinds don't ask the crowd to give anything or take an action. They simply track what people are doing. That's a major source of "Big Data" and what a lot of artificial intelligence programs are built upon.

When I write an article and ask readers to contribute supplemental information in the comments, that's crowdsourcing. There are also websites like 99designs.com that allow you to put out project calls for proposals—for example, for creating a logo-—and people will submit their ideas before getting paid.

CROWDFUNDING

Crowdfunding is a type of crowdsourcing aimed at raising money. It generally involves a person or project posting to a website platform that makes it easy to make a pitch and get donors or supporters to commit money and share the project with friends.

I interviewed David Boyce, then CEO of Fundly.com. He described how Fundly helps nonprofits raise funds,

"We make giving fun, friendly and easy," he said. "And we provide that experience for nonprofits or for individuals to host on their blogs, their Facebook pages on Fundly.com to help raise money for causes they care about."

I asked Boyce about other crowdfunding sites. He answered, "Kickstarter is a great example of a bottom-up initiative to help artists, creative types, inventors, and engineers get their projects funded. Their terms of use specifically prohibit a nonprofit organization from accepting donations with their platform. Fundly is Kickstarter for nonprofits."

Between the different crowdfunding platforms (over 2000 sites, according to Wikipedia) billions of dollars have been raised from millions of people for hundreds of thousands of projects.

"What's an example of what Fundly does?" I asked Boyce. He gave as an example a town in Shutesbury, Massachusetts: "Their library was built 150 years ago, doesn't have running water or any indoor plumbing. It's 900 square feet, it's tiny, they can barely fit in it, and the citizens decided they needed a new library." After explaining that the town had come up with a grant to match public funding, Boyce continued: "They said, 'Alright, we'll go raise money to match that matching grant and that public funding will get us a new library.' So they went to Fundly.com. Their video is super cute. They've got little kids holding up signs saying, 'We need a place to read.' 'We need a place to learn.' You upload some photos, you set a fundraising target, and you go. They sent it out to their Facebook fans and to individuals, who then forwarded it along to their Facebook fans, who forwarded it along to other recipients, and they raised about a quarter of a million dollars so far to help fund this new library."

You don't just sign up and create a page and wait. Boyce explained, "You have to have a cause that people care about, and then you have to get the word out to them. Shutesbury did a video. You don't have to do a video, but videos are super-powerful. What we found, working with established organizations, is the best thing is to get the word out to people who have already signed up to get a newsletter or who have been volunteers. Each donor is also asked to share this campaign with their social circles, at which point they become advocates and, in effect, fundraisers for the campaign. So, if they retweet or share with their Facebook friends or send out emails, you've now turned each of those donors into a fundraiser.

"It's super-powerful to pull your friends into that experience. When you let them know what you're doing for the world, each donor becomes worth more than just the value that she can write on a check. She's worth that plus her social influence. And it's not just a one-time social influence. It's over the lifetime of her relationship with you. And the more friends she pulls in, the more friends they can pull in. So it's almost like you take your number of donors, multiply that by 130, and that becomes your reach.

"That's the difference between donating under the cloak of darkness, putting it in an envelope and hoping it will be anonymous, versus a much more social and inclusive experience that includes all of your friends."

Boyce added that you can also embed a fundraising widget on your website. He says that campaigns by individuals on Fundly are the most viral. "They're generally around very personal circumstances: I was in a car accident. My neighbor had a flood, and we're trying to help them get back on their feet. I'd like to fund chemotherapy for my aunt. My son is going on a humanitarian aid mission to Belize."

Boyce offered an idea of the money that can be raised, saying, "We had one political campaign with over 50-million dollars. Our average raise is two-thousand dollars. . . . For a lot of those that raise two-thousand dollars, it takes them about sixty days." Wikipedia reports the biggest crowdfunding effort raised over $130 million.

I interviewed John Trigonis, author of *Crowdfunding for Filmmaking*, who is also in charge of coaching people in the arts—movie makers, authors, artists, who are doing crowdfunding campaigns on Indiegogo. He advised that in the first few days of a campaign it's very important to get friends and family to fund 30-40 percent of the target goal. He also advises that one should consider crowd funding to be a full time job that usually is much more successful if done as a team effort.

WORK-SOURCING SITES FOR BOTTOM-UP HIRING AND JOB FINDING
Just as governments put projects out for bids, work-sourcing sites make it easy for anyone to find affordable help from hundreds of thousands of skilled people. Fiverr.com offers tens of thousands of solutions for as little as five dollars. I've used Fiverr.com and Upwork.com to find people to help me with specific projects. Here's how it works. You describe the project—what needs to be done, the skills required, and what you want to pay. Usually, within an hour of posting the job, I get ten to fifty people making offers, from all over the world. Tim Ferris's book, *The 4-Hour Work Week: Escape 9-5, Live Anywhere, and Join the New Rich*, inspired me to look into the resources described above.

You can also *get* work by signing up and then bidding on projects. Don't worry that others charge less. People pay more for experience and in-country labor. Other sites include Freelancer.com, 99designs.com, and Amazon's mechanical turk. Use Craigslist.com and Taskrabbit for local jobs.

FINDING CROWDSOURCING IMAGES
Flickr.com, owned by Verizon/Yahoo.com, with billions of images, is a great source for no-fee-for-use images. You can use them if you link back to them and to the person who owns them. I worked with my programmer to build CommonsSearch.com, an image search tool which searches Flickr, Wikipedia, Google, YouTube, Twitter, and more for photos with Creative Commons or another no-fee-for-use permission. The image selected is automatically added to the content WITH a link back, connecting the image to the source it came from. The site works because of Application Programming Interfaces (APIs) which allow one

website to tap and interact with the database of another website. APIs are major enablers of connectivity between websites.

You can also use Flickr to find images of events, as, or right after they happen. If there's a protest, fashion show, or hurricane, plug in keywords, and you'll find an incredible array of images—more than you'll see on the news services. Often, too, you'll see the images from Flickr on the news.

People connect using images on Instagram. On Pinterest, people "pin" images from web pages, to save and share them. My daughter used to collect hundreds of pages from magazines—designs, furniture, clothing, whatever. She later switched to Pinterest and used it to help plan her wedding. Now, Pinterest is one of the biggest social-networking sites.

MEMBERSHIP SITES

A Canadian mom with five kids started a membership site for people passionate about scrapbooking. Now she has a thousand members paying $20 a month. Her costs might run one or two thousand dollars a month.

I asked an expert, Ryan Lee, his take on membership sites as seen from a bottom-up perspective. He answered, "It's about connecting, community, relationships."

"What's involved in creating a successful membership site?" I asked. "You don't have to be a tech whiz, to know all the techie stuff," Lee replied. "You just have to know where to find people who could do it for you."

Actually, because a lot of the tech already exists, you don't have to build sites from scratch anymore. Off-the-shelf web software can be customized for you. You can hire someone to do it relatively inexpensively using Guru.com, Fiverr.com, Upwork.com, or other outsourcing sites.

Lee says that people come to a paid membership site for information, then stay for connection, for community. Encouragingly, he added, "It's as simple as having a discussion forum where people will go and ask questions and interact."

"But," I asked, "How can a fee-based membership site compete with Facebook or LinkedIn, where there are free pages or groups?"

Lee answered, "If you position yourself as the expert, then people will pay money to have more access—better access to you. And don't forget, there's something about exclusivity, about paying for something and not being in the general public…and feeling like it's a private group. You can do it if you're not an expert, too. Then, you operate as the producer, and bring in experts to provide the content."

Getting started with creating a membership site is pretty simple. First, you register a domain name for around $15 and find a company to host your website for five or ten dollars a month. You then select a Content Management System (CMS). Most people use Word Press, though Lee noted that there are other plug-ins, like Wishlist Member and DigitalAccessPass, for registering and processing member fees. I had my own membership system coded for OpEdNews, with four levels of membership. I recommend that you offer a free level, even if your monetization model is based on paid memberships. It's a way to start building a relationship with people, before they decide they're willing to invest in your site.

Lee points out that the cost of a membership site start-up is a tiny fraction of the cost of a more traditional retail store start-up. Membership sites, he points out, "are businesses you can start from your home, from your kitchen table… You're looking at, higher-end, a couple of hundred bucks for everything all in."

"After they set up the basic membership site, then what do people do?" I asked. Lee replied, "They start adding content and they start marketing. Go to Facebook, set up a fan page, start joining like-minded people and groups, start interacting with them, start answering questions, start posting, start driving traffic… You can do that with LinkedIn as well. You write articles, get people excited about it, and then start selling. It's as simple as that."

"What do you sell?" I asked. Lee offered, as an example, a member site for dealing with divorce. "You're writing about different strategies, tips about surviving after divorce. Maybe one week you upload an interview you did with a woman who survived divorce and is now thriving and built a multimillion-dollar business. The next week you offer one legal tip from an attorney. Maybe the next week you say, 'Hey, here's a cool resource I saw that helps you find nannies for your kids if you're out finding a job.' So you just add this content that they can't find anywhere else. And build a community forum in there where people can talk and interact with each other and form bonds."

To help stimulate discussion, Lee suggested checking out current news and writing about it from the angle of the membership site. He elaborated, "And I'm not talking about writing 75-page theses. I'm talking about writing two or three paragraphs or putting up a quick video. If you don't like writing, then do a short little 2- or 3-minute video update. Get a Mac or a little webcam and upload it. Half of my content updates are just simple videos. Have someone interview you. You could do a live workshop. Record the whole thing with a video, and now you can chop that up into little 4 to 5-minute clips, and you'll have months and months of content for a membership site." He noted, too—and I've done this—that you can take the video and then transcribe it (find transcriptionists on Upwork.com) for more content.

My last question to Ryan was: "What's the biggest mistake people make?"

He answered, "First, trying to do everything yourself. Another is focusing on your weaknesses and saying, 'I can't do it.' The trick is to find people to get the job done."

I suggest checking out Tim Ferris's book, *The 4-Hour Work Week*, to get an idea how to outsource your work, so you don't have to do it all.

In short: be interdependent, cooperative, and build community—core dimensions of bottom-up.

CHAPTER 5

Bottom-Up Revolution

APPROACHES TO POWER, GOVERNMENT, POLITICS, DIPLOMACY, AND ACTIVISM

I was a Bernie Sanders supporter…in 2008 and wishing he'd run for president. I first met him in 2003 or 2004 when he was a congressman. So I have very strong feelings about how the Democratic Party handled his candidacy. Before he even announced he would run, a huge percentage of superdelegates had announced that they were supporting Hillary Clinton. Superdelegates and political party endorsements of primary candidates are the authoritarian, undemocratic antithesis of bottom-up.

This chapter explores how the bottom-up revolution is massively resetting power balances and affecting politics, diplomacy, government, activism, and revolutionary change. That said, top-down laws and regulations are essential. Nature has natural laws that are essential for keeping healthy balance in organisms and ecosystems. We also need centralized, top-down regulations to protect people, justice, transparency, freedoms, ecology, the economy, and health and safety.

The way to make big change happen is not to try to make a big change to the old system but rather to replace it with something better so the old system collapses. History has taught us that bottom-up, small, decentralized, local community-based actions, projects, and revolutions eventually compete with and supplant the big stuff—transnational corporations, globalization—just as tiny mammals replaced giant dinosaurs.

"Never doubt that a small group of thoughtful, committed citizens can change the world. Indeed, it is the only thing that ever has."
THIS QUOTE IS OFTEN ATTRIBUTED TO MARGARET MEAD, THOUGH NO ONE HAS CONFIRMED IT. STILL IT HAS BEEN USED THOUSANDS OF TIMES AND SEEMS TO BE A TRUISM WORTH SHARING.

POWER IN MOVIES, BOOKS, AND ENTERTAINMENT

Mike Medavoy, Oscar-winning producer for *One Flew Over the Cuckoo's Nest, Apocalypse Now, Arthur, Terminator, Tootsie, Silence of the Lambs,* and *Sleepless in Seattle,* co-authored *American Idol After Iraq: Competing for Hearts and Minds in the Global Media Age.* The book explores the powerful influence of the American film and entertainment industries on international relations. Billions love Americans because of their stories and music, instead of hating America for its corporate predations and many wars.

Medavoy's book looks at how arts and entertainment reap the USA incredible 'soft power.' Joseph Nye, described by Wikipedia as the most influential scholar in American foreign policy and the chairman of the North American branch of the Trilateral Commission, wrote in his introduction to Medavoy's book, "In the Information Age, success is not merely the result of whose army wins, but also whose story wins." Story is a form of exercising soft power. Nye says, "Soft power (the ability to affect others to obtain the outcomes one wants through attraction, rather than coercion or payments) often takes longer to show effects, but is often a more effective instrument." Soft power feels a lot more bottom-up than hard, coercive, or money power.

Medavoy's inspiring, touching movies have helped build America's soft power. In our interview, Medavoy told me about "the power of storytellers over the American narrative," saying, "The most powerful American message in modern times is transmitted through our Hollywood films, TV shows, and popular music, the message of liberty that each individual can write his or her own narrative if they can work hard."

POWER DIFFUSION: DIFFUSING POWER TO THE PEOPLE

Joseph Nye characterizes in his books, *Soft Power* and *The Future of Power*, the different kinds of power and how they are changing. I started an interview with him by requesting that he define soft power, smart power, and power diffusion.

He replied, "Power is simply the ability to affect others to get to the things you want, and you can do that in three ways: You can threaten people with coercion, so-called 'sticks.' You can pay them, so-called 'carrots,' or you can attract them and persuade them to want what you want, and if they want what you want, you can save a lot on carrots and sticks! So, soft power is the ability to get what you want through attraction and persuasion rather than coercion and payment. Unfortunately, the world as it is, that's not always enough, and often you need to use the hard power of coercion and payment. And the ability to figure out how to combine hard and soft power, so that they don't undercut each other but reinforce each other, is what I call 'smart power.'"

Nye says the world is going through a huge shift of "Power Diffusion," in which the shift of power is going away from all governments to nongovernmental actors.

I said to Nye, "Your book basically describes how diffusion is something that every power has to consider, and that it gives power to people, or groups, or nations that really didn't have access to it before."

Nye answered, "That's right. Power diffusion is a market product of the Information Revolution, and that is basically the enormous drop in the cost of computing over the last quarter century. If the cost of an automobile had gone down as rapidly, you could buy a car for five bucks. Any time something drops as dramatically in price as that, the barriers to entry go down. People aren't priced out of the action anymore. That means that there are a lot more actors who can play on the world stage. It doesn't mean the governments are out of the picture, it just means the stage they're on is a lot more crowded than it used to be."

I asked Nye to talk about the differences in the use of hard and soft power—and budgets for each.

Nye replied, "Usually we think about hard power as being associated with coercion, which would be the use of military force, and that often is quite expensive. Soft power can grow out of attraction, as I mentioned, and so when you have broadcast or public diplomacy to try to create a story or narrative that attracts other people, that often costs a lot less to do. The United States spends on its public diplomacy budget something like $1.5 billion a year, and that's about what either Britain or France spend on similar purposes. So the American government has a giant in the Pentagon and a pygmy in the State Department, and it's very hard for the two to work effectively together because of disparities in size."

Putting it in plain English, soft power, which is done through the arts, education, science, and through the state department, is budgeted at a tiny, tiny fraction of the military budget. That's crazy, old, top-down thinking.

Nye counsels, "It may be that in an Information Age, you have to think about power as leadership, and how can you attract people to work with you to get things done. That has more to do with soft power. But in the American political discourse, we don't think so much about soft power. We think much more about hard power. We sort of have this cultural icon of the Lone Ranger riding into the city and shooting up the bad guys. But that doesn't always work. For example, if you are trying to deal with climate change, who do you shoot? If you're trying to deal with cyberattacks, how do you respond militarily when you don't know where the attack came from? So, we are going to have to learn to use soft power to organize networks of cooperation with others to deal with these kinds of problems; and unfortunately, our vocabulary, the way we think about power, is very old-fashioned."

BOTTOM-UP DIPLOMACY AND LEADERSHIP

Anne Marie Slaughter is author of *The Chessboard and the Web: Strategies of Connection in a Dangerous World,* the first woman to serve as Director of Policy Planning for the US State Department and former Dean of Princeton's Woodrow Wilson School of Public and International Affairs. I started our interview remarking that former Secretary of State Madeline Albright assured me there are many ways bottom-up approaches are applied to diplomacy. I noted that she'd written in a *Foreign Affairs* article, "In this world the measure of power is connectedness. Business is networked. Every CEO advice manual published in the past decade has focused on the shift from the vertical world of hierarchy to the horizontal world of networks." I asked her what she meant.

Slaughter replied, "We are in a world in which hierarchies are getting flattened: by technology, by transport, by the ability of folks at the bottom to no longer have to wait to see what people want them to read, to wait to be told to organize politically through hierarchical campaigns. They are now in a position to participate actively and to create networks with each other—and that flattens out traditional hierarchies all over the world. Just about every organization under the sun has seen the transition from 'Command and Control Hierarchies' to networks that can't be commanded or controlled. You must work within them very differently. I think any organization that is trying to operate in the traditional hierarchical way is in for trouble. Even the US Military has recognized the importance of devolving responsibility outward to people in the field, giving them much more ability to act on their own, and to respond and to initiate activity and information back through structures that are more horizontal than they used to be. We're definitely in a networked world."

Slaughter described how soft power and bottom-up thinking are changing diplomacy. "It isn't just about government officials meeting with government officials anymore. It is about government engaging with society in all sorts to different ways, and equally about society engaging with society. So, we talk about health diplomacy—that is, doctors and medical groups and emergency responders engaging with their counterparts around the world, or about educational and science diplomacy—that's scientists, universities, colleges, and research institutes engaging with their counterparts around the world."

I pointed out to Slaughter how university history departments were replacing top-down professors with bottom-up faculty and asked if a similar process was happening in the State Department. She replied that if you looked over a period of thirty years, you'd see "a steady shift from engaging only with the officials of the foreign government, to more and more engagement with society. Diplomats and young foreign service officers, are naturally looking for whom they can connect to in society. They naturally think much more bottom-up than top-down, and so it is not a question of retiring and hiring new people who are doing bottom-up diplomacy in the way a history department does. It is naturally occurring generationally."

"Why?" I asked. She explained, "The young people are 'Digital Natives,' and the technology that we are now surrounded with is all about connection! That's why I said *'The measure of power in a networked world is how connected you are, and, equally importantly, how many different worlds you connect to.'* Now, we think about this web of connections. In the Cold War, the classic image of states was billiard balls—opaque, hard, impenetrable, and that bumped into each other. Or when a superpower slammed into them, they all scattered. That really was the image that we have used to teach international relations for fifty years, these billiard ball states. Today, governments are more and more open, and they're embedded in a whole web of social actors, who are themselves engaging with lots of other people across lots of borders: corporations, foundations, universities, nongovernmental organizations, civic groups, and high school groups—any number of social actors. Now, the idea of a billiard ball makes no sense. What you are talking about is governments as kind of 'central nodes,' embedded in this much, much wider and denser web of social and economic networks around the world."

Slaughter had said, "We live in a very different world now. We don't start from separation. We start from connection." I asked how that changes the way that diplomacy is done. She replied, "This is a very deep, important point that is very hard for anybody older than 40 to get. If you start from separation, as my generation did, you have this image of all these individuals out there who are what we used to call 'Atomized Individuals,' these separate little entities (again, think of the billiard ball image). If you start from connection, you start assuming a dense web of relations with other people."

I noted that the top-down people in power also have access to the same bottom-up technologies, and they're also learning how to use them.

"This has been true of all technology over the centuries," Slaughter answered, "Books, when they were first created, were critical to causing the Reformation. Martin Luther's theses against the Catholic Church— they were able to spread that information because of the invention of the printing press. But guess what? The governments and the established authorities then catch up! You have a counter-reformation. You can do that right through the invention of the Xerox machine. It was absolutely essential in the former Soviet Union to be able to disseminate opposition literature, called *Samizdat*, that they were able to circulate because you could suddenly copy it very quickly. But at the same time, of course, it made it much easier for the government too."

Slaughter says the technologies of liberation and the technologies of repression are often the same. "The technology, in itself, is neutral. It is a question of how it is used. You can use it to connect to people, to spread dissident ideas, and to organize protests. You can also use it to send out false information, to deceive protesters, to trap them. There is no way to have the technology and be able to use it for one purpose and not have it to be also available to the other purpose. The best we can do is to do everything we can to support the ways in which it is being used progressively to keep it one step ahead of the ways it's being used oppressively."

I observed that just the act of using bottom-up tools modifies the way people's brains function. So, even if an authoritarian regime blocks the internet, even if a nation blocks Google or Facebook but still allows citizens to access home-grown versions, the bottom-up technologies change the way the citizens think and look at things.

Slaughter answered, "You're exactly right. One of the most important and exciting dimensions of an interconnected world, of a network, is that we are social animals; our brains are built to be connected to others—we grow and develop that way. That experience of knowing that you are not alone, that others think like you, that you are capable of mobilizing others, is politically incendiary and very important for bottom-up politics, for bottom-up social activism. Now you are able to be connected just by getting on whatever social media tools you have—and that will change your brain, and it will change your sense of your own possibility."

I asked how that affects diplomacy in the State Department. Slaughter replied, "We have to really retool how we do diplomacy in a world of connections! The starting point is that we're going to increasingly think of our embassies not as communications outposts, which is really what they were originally. Now, increasingly, they're becoming platforms for convening and connecting Americans in the government, but way beyond the government, with their counterparts in that foreign country, and indeed for connecting different groups in that country themselves."

I asked how things look as we move to this less hierarchical, more networked, more bottom-up world. Slaughter replied. "These changes are changing our sense of possibility in the world. The most positive change is that we face foreign policy problems that cannot be solved by governments alone." She listed the proliferation of nuclear weapons, the spread of violent extremism and terrorists, global criminal networks, global economic stability, global pandemics, climate change, resource scarcity, and individual conflicts from Israel to India, concluding, "Most of those problems can never be solved just by governments. Take climate change or global disease or the health of the global economy. Those are issues that depend on the healthcare, or the use of energy, or the economic productivity of individuals in every country in the world. We're going to have to be able to mobilize those individuals. That's going to require connecting to all the different groups and catalysts that mobilize human behavior, which again, is citizen diplomacy, science diplomacy, health diplomacy, education diplomacy; every part of our society is going to have to be engaged in connecting to their counterparts abroad and working to solve these problems.

"The most positive vision I have of where our foreign policy is going is that government will be increasingly a platform, catalyst, and steward for making connections, mobilizing action, and monitoring what happens, or working with others who will monitor what happens, in ways that mean all of us are going to be engaged in solving global problems." Slaughter gave an example: "To help strengthen education, say, in an African country. You could mobilize your own local public library to create a network of public libraries, say, in your state, and then connect that network of public libraries to public libraries or to educational authorities in a particular country. I think we're going to be developing the tools and the skills—and the mindset, which is very important—the mindset necessary to do that."

Delving further into the transition to bottom-up diplomacy, I interviewed Carne Ross, former UK diplomat and author of the book, *The Leaderless Revolution: How Ordinary People Will Take Power and Change Politics in the 21st Century*, saying to him, "You told Bill Moyers, 'We're almost at a level of paradigm shift. Governments will not provide the answer, no matter how well meaning they may be.' And you've talked in your book about the failure of government to be able to deal with complexity, and the inability of government to satisfy the pact that's supposed to exist between citizen and government."

Ross replied, "I think we're at a moment in history where we will look back at it and realize that a particular model of how we govern our affairs together became outdated. Governments working nationally or cooperating internationally are not really solving our problems. Globalization is producing problems that are of a transnational nature. Boundary-less, border-less problems like climate change, global economic volatility, and inequality have become a global problem in almost every country. And the solutions to these problems are actually to a large extent out of the hands of national governments. They have lost the power to affect these things in their own circumstances. [Politicians] don't seem to be in control. So, the question then is, 'What would be better? What would be effective?'"

Ross says, "Government is becoming slowly less powerful. We need to examine alternatives. We shouldn't overthrow the current system, but seek to replace it by building bottom-up systems, from the ground up, and these will be more effective in arbitrating our affairs." He suggests that the basic premise of government, which promises to give us order, is actually producing the opposite—disorder, explaining: "In a complex system order cannot come from the top-down. It cannot be delivered by authority; in fact, authority from the top-down is the worst thing to try to create order, to try to change the system. Order is created from the bottom up by the combined actions of billions of individuals."

Ross added, "The government's attempt to simplify things is very dangerous because it's saying the world is in one form, when in fact it's in another, and that leads to mistaken policies. Governments' worst error is that they disempower the people who have real power and real ability to change things, which is us: the individual."

Ross recapitulates Paulo Freire's emphasis on the need for education. "Education reverses the infantilizing and ignorance that authority encourages." And he explores how government can dis-empower people so that they depend on it and let it take over, declaring, "Government says the individual cannot be trusted, that without top-down authority there will only be chaos.' And by saying that, they make us feel that we don't have the power to change things, that they have some kind of superior knowledge that we don't have. And that's not actually true. It has contributed to a kind of apathy and ignorance of the public, which we all suffer, me included. Namely that we think, 'What can I do?' 'Why should I even bother learning about this problem?' I think once you actually take the responsibility to try to address the problem yourself, inevitably you're going to educate yourself about it, particularly the things that most concern you. Find that thing and let that be the thing that you try to solve directly, not by asking others or government to solve it, but do it yourself."

BOTTOM-UP AND TOP-DOWN WAR AND WEAPONS

There are top-down war and weapon delusions we could be avoiding. One is the value of nuclear weapons. Ward Wilson, author of *Five Myths About Nuclear Weapons*, argues that nuclear weapons were not the reason the US won World War II, nor do they work as deterrents against war. I asked him who benefits from nuclear weapons. He replied, "The US spends at least $85 billion a year on nuclear weapons. That's an industry that can ante up a lot of lobbying money." I asked who would benefit if nuclear weapon spending was ended. Ward answered that Army generals detest nuclear weapons, but Air Force and submarine officers like them.

An idea came to me. *Nuclear weapons are the ultimate top-down weapon.* One person makes a decision, makes a call, or pushes a button, and *voila*. The fantasy is that the nuke will take care of everything. Why is it a fantasy? Because nobody uses nukes. They build, maintain and talk about using them, but never do.

It's the nuke or daisy cutter or cruise missile fantasy psychology that one person can wipe out an army or an enemy. I have friends who have literally said to me, in response to the Iran/Israel, North Korea, or Iraq situation, "They should just nuke the bastards." This meme, "nuke the bastards," has become a common knee-jerk reflex for a lot of people. No messy battles. No soldiers' lives risked. Send out a lone plane or launch a missile and clean up the problem. What a top-down fantasy! The reality is, as David Swanson writes in his book, *War Is a Lie,* the reasons and justifications for going into war ALWAYS depend on lies and deceptions.

Donald Rumsfeld assumed the US Military's massive top-down "hard" power could speedily succeed in Iraq. The top-down approach totally failed. Eventually the military leadership figured out that a bottom-up, soft power approach was required. The answer was to implement grassroots programs—building alliances, connections, and trust to earn the loyalty of the locals,—to invest in people connections rather than weapons. Building schools and bridges worked a lot better than blowing them up.

". . . conflicts are only solved from the bottom up. Conflicts are not solved from the top-down. They are solved on the ground by the people."

—US REP (PA-D) DWIGHT EVANS

Wouldn't it be nice if the military started seeing bottom-up, soft power plows—construction, teachers and healers—as the their most effective "weapons" instead of reflexively thinking that nukes, missiles, bunker-busters and squadrons, flotillas and battalions are the answer?

Jeremy Heimans on New Power

Jeremy Heimans cofounded Purpose.com and Avaaz.org, which has forty million members in 194 countries. I asked him to differentiate Old Power and New Power, which I think is bottom-up power. Heimans replied, "Old Power's held like a currency, something that you hoard, you gather. New Power is flowing like a current, something you channel. New Power is most powerful when it surges, like water or electricity. An Old Power model tends to rely on something that it has that others don't—some exclusivity and some control. Old Power downloads. New Power uploads. The values that tend to be associated with New Power are really a product of the intersection of wide spread connectivity with this sense of increased human agency that these new models unleash."

Heimans' Purpose website says, "We believe that lasting change doesn't come from the top-down. It comes when people, acting together, have a sense of their own agency." Heimans added, "The kind of fuel for New Power is participation and people's sense of their own power is agency. Think about what it's like to be a young person today compared to even twenty years ago. Your sense of agency is vastly greater. You have the potential to be a producer and creator of your own content. There are teenagers all over the world who command followings of tens of millions of people, larger even than traditional media institutions with far greater resources that have been around for a hundred years. You have the ability to jump over certain institutional barriers. Crowdfunding is giving people a sense that they don't need big institutions. They have their hands on what we would call the means of participation. If you grow up in that kind of world, your values are going to change, you're going to feel more powerful."

BOTTOM-UP TOOLS AS SOURCES OF LIBERATION AND POWER

Some of the people I cite in this chapter have said that the bottom-up revolution, that is, digital technology and social media, have changed the way new generations think about their power, their agency, and their relationship to authority and change. When I brought up these ideas to NYU Professor Clay Shirky, author of the brilliant book *Here Comes Everybody: The Power of Organizing Without Organizations*, he said, "These tools matter—the internet, mobile phones, the applications built on top of them, matter—not just because they change the way people can coordinate with one another…they also matter because they let people imagine that their lives are different from the lives of their parents, from the lives of previous generations. And it lets them imagine that they can do things that previous generations couldn't do… People have a different sense of themselves and what is possible. They simply aren't as cowed or as limited by the actions of the state as they would have been before they started to use these tools."

Shirky went on to tell me later in our interview: "This stuff is just getting started," because the other sort of operating thesis behind his book [*Here Comes Everybody*] is, these tools don't get socially interesting until they get technologically boring. It's not the moment a shiny new tool shows up that changes the world. The moment a tool changes the world is when your mom takes it for granted. Because that's really the time when the internet is becoming invisible, the way the telephone has become invisible, right, which is just "It's always there. We take it for granted. And when it's really essential, that's the point at which it starts to really change society: not just for a handful of techies and early adopters, but for everybody."

That's very similar to what Twitter inventor Jack Dorsey told me: "something that you don't think about anymore, that just blurs into the background and that you just use on a day-to-day basis." The bottom-up revolution is happening because the technologies are becoming the background, the natural, reflexive way we function—with a power unimagined just twenty years ago.

OVERCOMING OPPRESSION FROM THE BOTTOM UP: FREIRE'S PEDAGOGY OF THE OPPRESSED

Paulo Freire's 1978 classic book *Pedagogy of the Oppressed*, with sales of over a million copies, has literally led to "Freirian" departments of education at universities. Freire proposes that both oppressed people and their oppressors are dehumanized victims, but that only the oppressed, not the oppressors, can rescue both the oppressed and the oppressors. The oppressed may actually fear freedom, they've internalized the message of their oppression so much, so they must free themselves. Outsiders can help, but outsiders cannot top-down swoop in and liberate the oppressed. They must empower, inspire, and awaken the oppressed to take their liberation into their own hands. Just as is the case with the hero's journey, to really change people have to go through a "profound rebirth" and they must take on a "new form of existence."

Rosabeth Moss Kanter offers a similar take in her book, *The Change Makers; Innovation & Entrepreneurship in the American Corporation*, which suggests that people see change as a threat when it is done to them but as an opportunity when it is done by them.

PATTERNS OF REVOLUTIONS

The bottom-up revolution contributed to the Arab Spring and Occupy Wall Street and will continue to play a major role in new emerging revolutions. John Foran, UC Santa Barbara professor and author of *The Future of Revolutions: Thinking Radical Change in the Age of Globalization,* told me that revolution "requires three key elements: political change, economic change, and mass participation," adding, "In the study of revolutions, there are three or four big questions: what caused it; how did it come about; who made it and why were they involved; what's been the outcome, the results of the revolution; and what are the future prospects?"

Foran believes that there are no purely economic-, ideological- or idea-driven revolutions, but, he says, "A combination of factors working together can bring about a revolution. Most revolutions are not inspired by attractive visions of the future," but rather, "from a widely shared conviction that the status quo was simply unendurable; the development of a political culture of opposition or resistance and judgments that social arrangements are unfair, are unjust—eliciting emotions of anger."

Foran says that organized, armed insurgents have made some revolutions, as in China under Mao; in Cuba; and in Nicaragua. Foran says that dictatorships are more vulnerable to revolutions. He cites the Mexican, Cuban, Iranian, and the original 1911 Chinese revolutions, explaining, when power is concentrated in a single figure and things aren't going well, that crystallizes the anger of an opposition.

Ironically, functioning democratic systems, the opposite of dictatorships, are also vulnerable to revolution. In those systems, revolutionary parties can actually become elected to office. He cites Hugo Chavez in Venezuela and Evo Morales in Bolivia as examples.

Foran gives an example of a very different kind of revolution—the Zapatista revolution in Mexico, a response to devastating globalization trade policies. "On January 1st 1994, the moment that NAFTA goes into effect, the Zapatistas take over six towns including the capital of Chiapas. They overwhelm the small military garrisons there and they take control of these towns. The world wakes up to the Zapatistas having defeated the Mexican army and controlling their own towns in Chiapas." Foran adds, "The Zapatistas are an ongoing revolution, a work in progress. Zapatista communities are poor, but they're self-sufficient. Politically, they're extremely participatory and democratic. Leaders are changed every month or so. And everybody in the community ultimately has a turn to be a member of the council." That's as bottom-up as it gets.

Foran adds, "We have the global justice movement that is a sort of coalition of forces for peace, for a climate treaty, for labor rights, for women's rights, for indigenous rights found in every country of the world and meeting on a regular basis at the World Social Forum, coming together as a network. The Zapatistas are very much a part of that. There is a kind of worldwide social movement, which is also bottom-up, but which also is aimed at global dimensions of radical social change. What you see then is revolutions or radical social change movements from both below the nation state, as the Zapatistas, and above it, as the Global Justice Movement, kind of making new kinds of revolutions that are no longer armed and guerilla in nature."

"You never change things by fighting the existing reality. To change something, build a new model that makes the existing model obsolete."
FREQUENTLY ATTRIBUTED TO R. BUCKMINSTER FULLER BUT NO SOURCE
FOUND

Malcolm Gladwell reports, in his book *David and Goliath: Underdogs, Misfits, and the Art of Battling Giants,* how political researcher Ivan Arreguín-Toft analyzed conflicts over the past 200 years where one opponent was at least ten times more powerful than the other. Almost a third of the underdogs won. Gladwell points out that David, wearing heavy armor, prepared to face Goliath, for a conventional battle of swords. But David realized he couldn't even walk in the armor. So, he picked up five stones. Gladwell offers a hopeful perspective. He described how Arreguín-Toft asked the question of what happened when underdogs accepted their weakness and picked an alternative, non-conventional approach. Re-analyzing his data, these underdogs' percentage of winning jumped from 28.5 to 63.6. Underdogs lose when they play by the big dogs rules, but they can win when they make their own rules and use alternative strategies.

I spoke with complexity physicist Yaneer Bar-Yam about making big changes happen. We agreed that the way to do it is to start locally. You don't take on the big Goliath. For example, Canadian single-payer health care started in one province. It wasn't implemented nationwide. The same was true for legalization of gay marriage. And every person working for change counts. Even the smallest act can make a difference.

Evil thrives best in darkness. Secrecy, opacity, discretion, and confidentiality are top-down tools used to build, consolidate, and preserve top-down power, control, domination, and exploitation. They are used to hide hypocrisy, corruption, injustice, deception, and criminal actions. Transparency, openness, and the free sharing and release of information are associated with bottom-up democracy, cooperation, justice and fairness. They enable anyone to see *connections*—between people, corporations, legislation, government, and media.

A powerful advocacy movement for transparency and openness is making big changes. It's advocating for expiration dates on state secrets, and tougher rules requiring release and standardization of information, building massive databases showing connections between corporate donors and politicians, and pushing for laws that put data online in readily accessible ways that can be mashed with other software and websites.

Transparency and FOIA requests, which enable access to information by and for all, are WEAPONS in the bottom-up revolution. When transparency and FOIA request efforts fail, sometimes only whistleblowers bring light and truth.

While governments should be open and transparent, individuals should have the right to privacy. You may have nothing to hide, but your spouse, sibling, parent, cousin, or adult child might have secrets, and if their privacy is violated YOU could be the victim of blackmail or coercion based on their secrets.

I asked Ellen Miller, co-founder and former director of the Sunlight Foundation, what transparency is, why it's important, and how transparency, power, and democracy are connected. Miller replied, "Sunlight took its name from Justice Brandeis's very famous quote that sunlight is said to be the best of disinfectants," and so in any society, anywhere around the world where information, data, and access to process is kept secret, there is always the potential for corruption. There's always a place where the powerful make decisions out of the watchful eye of the public. The powerful like that opaqueness. Therefore, the more open we make government and its work and the data it collects, the more powerful citizens become because we have access to information.

"The challenge is to create a cultural transformation inside government where the default is openness and open data and open access to process rather than a closed one. Power resides in the information, and so those who are in power want to hold it close and those who are out of power want it open so they have more access to decisions and to participating in decisions and understanding how decisions were made. Those who are in power want to stay in power. They know that controlling the flow of information is absolutely one way to do that and so that has been the default of most governments." She emphasizes, "We have to get everything put in to law so that it cannot just be voluntary efforts on government, on behalf of government."

THE MASTER OF FOIA (FREEDOM OF INFORMATION ACT) REQUESTS

You don't have to be a newspaper or big organization to investigate the government. Any person or organization can use the FOIA law to request information. I asked Jim Lesar, a full-time FOIA attorney, about FOIA basics.

Lesar noted that before 1967 when FOIA came into existence, "There had been no effective means of getting access to government information. Giving people the right to have government information was revolutionary. Secondly, any person in the world was conferred the right to get information held by a US Government agency."

FOIA is basically a collection of laws that give you the right to ask for information that the government has somewhere, i.e., records. You can't ask about government's behavior, except as that behavior is contained in a government document. Lesar advised, "So you have to formulate a strategy that will enable you to pinpoint the records that might help you answer that question." And that way, you can attempt to get at what is known by the government, what is recorded in its records. The government wants to restrict the searches that it is required to make. Legally it must search for records if it's a reasonably described request for records.

I asked Lesar for some tips on making successful FOIA requests. He answered, "First, describe the search you want carefully. Agencies do not like large volume requests and they try to narrow down the scope of your request. There's a benefit to that in that they process the shorter requests faster. They're required by law to provide a response within twenty working days."

Lesar described how to find an attorney to work on a FOIA request: "Find an attorney and see what sort of arrangement you can make. If the attorney is confident enough of ultimately succeeding, he may be willing to take it on a contingency or a partial contingency."

If you want to do a FOIA request, any person in the world can simply do a search for the agency you want paired with the word FOIA. For example, search "FDA FOIA request" to submit a FOIA request to the FDA. Other resources for FOIA requests include MuckRock.com and GovernmentAttic.org. And I would be remiss not to mention investigative journalist Jason Leopold (@JasonLeopold), whom the Poynter. org characterizes as a "FOIA terrorist."

WHISTLEBLOWING AND WHISTLEBLOWERS

"If it is of such a nature that it requires you to be the agent of injustice to another, then, I say, break the law. Let your life be a counter friction to stop the machine."
—HENRY DAVID THOREAU, "CIVIL DISOBEDIENCE"

What happens when the government or corporations keep secrets that FOIA requests and transparency regulations fail to reveal? Sometimes it takes a courageous soul who sees wrongdoing, and can't allow it to persist, to come forward as a whistleblower. Whistleblowers are right at the top of my bottom-up hero list: Ed Snowden, Chelsea Manning, and some whistleblowers I've had the honor of meeting: Daniel Ellsberg, Bill Binney, Thomas Drake, John Kiriakou, Jesselyn Radack, Wendell Potter, Robert McClean, Kirk Wiebe, Sibel Edmonds, Coleen Rowley, Marsha Coleman Adebayo, Jeffrey Wigand, Christopher Pyle, Michael McCray. and Jim Murtagh.

To become a whistleblower means you try to get your supervisor, even several layers of supervisors, to call out the bad behavior or policy. When they don't, the person doing the whistleblowing puts his or her life on the line. Corporations and governments hate whistleblowers. They do all they can to literally destroy the lives of whistleblowers, prosecuting them (costing them over a million dollars in legal fees), taking away their security clearance, firing them, rifling through their homes, and taking their computers. Excerpts from one of my interviews with Daniel Ellsberg, below, offer a flavor of the experience.

Daniel Ellsberg, Most Dangerous Man Alive

An American hero—my hero—Pentagon Papers whistleblower Daniel Ellsberg, author of *The Doomsday Machine; Confessions of a Nuclear War Planner,* is the subject of the movie titled *The Most Dangerous Man in America*, a description given to him by former Secretary of State Henry Kissinger. I asked Ellsberg, "Why do you think that they thought you were so dangerous?"

He replied, "I had copied some documents, actually copies of studies that I had been involved in from the Nixon administration. But they didn't know exactly what I had. And it could have been anything. They knew they had a lot of secrets that had to be kept from the American public—things, by the way, that weren't secret from our adversaries, because they involved threats of escalation, even threats of nuclear war. So Hanoi and Moscow and China were all very well aware of these threats.

"But it was very important [to Nixon and Kissinger]for the American people not to get upset by the thought that we might be heading toward a nuclear war if those threats were carried out. That's what made me dangerous, that I might have put out documents that went beyond the Pentagon and made it more difficult for him [Nixon] to carry out an expansion of the war in Vietnam."

I observed, "What you learned with the Pentagon Papers was that the whole Vietnam War was built upon a fabric of lies and deceptions and that everybody who had decision-making powers knew that and just lied to the American people."

Ellsberg acknowledged, "That's true in every case. And I didn't have to talk to the public. So I wasn't called on to lie. But I did keep my mouth shut. I was called on to do that. And I did it, knowing that the President and the Secretary of Defense and everybody else were deceiving the public with virtually everything they said. I was not the one to expose that to Congress or the public for years. My advice to people, now, is: 'Don't do what I did. Don't wait till more bombs have fallen and thousands and thousands more have died, as I did, before you tell the truth with documents to the press and not only to Congress.'"

"You've called for people in government to come out and become whistle blowers," I said to Ellsberg.

"I call for it on every occasion that I have a chance, including on this program, anybody in the reach of your radio," he replied. "If they know that the public is being deceived or lied to, they should consider now, not in their memoirs and not years from now, as unfortunately I did, giving that information, with documents to demonstrate the lies, and perhaps save an untold number of lives.

"They'll do that at the cost of their career if they put out enough to be identified. If they leak orally a page or two, they probably will get away with it. And that's the prudent way for them to do it. But to be more effective, I think it's worth putting out 1,000 pages, 2,000 pages, with documents, which is likely to get you identified and means you will not just lose your clearance and your access and your career, but you might be prosecuted. You might go to prison. And you might save hundreds and thousands of lives."

Why Protest Matters

Ellsberg's Randy Keller story is very bottom-up inspiring. Ellsberg attended a talk by Randy Keller, who was preparing to go to jail because of his actions protesting the Vietnam War. "Keller inspired you to release the Pentagon Papers. Is that accurate?" I asked Ellsberg. He replied, "Very much so. Yes. He continues to inspire me with his life. His activism took the form of deliberately courting prison by refusing to cooperate with a war that he knew was wrong, and I knew was wrong; and his example forced me to ask myself, well, since I agree with him, what could I do, now that I am prepared to go to prison, and I was prepared because of his example."

You never know when your activism, when a principled decision you make, especially one that involves civil disobedience that leads to arrest (not necessarily whistleblowing) can set off a chain of decisions and events which change the world. One person, Randy Keller, inspired Ellsberg. You could be the next person to inspire someone to do something huge. Small acts matter. (see SmallActs.org)

BOTTOM-UP POLITICS

The Biggest Demonstration in the History of the World

I asked climate change activist Bill McKibben of 350.org how he organized and coordinated what CNN described as the most widespread day of political action in the planet's history on any issue, with 5200 separate demonstrations in 181 countries, leading to 117 nations supporting 350.org's goal to raise awareness of global warming and commit to reduce emissions of carbon dioxide. He modestly replied, "We barely did it.

It was like having a potluck supper. Mostly, it was people all over the world coming up with their own thing." They shared social media and rented jumbotrons in Times Square to display the tens of thousands of pictures that were coming in from the thousands of simultaneous demonstrations going on. "What worked was having a good hard number to go at, instead of a vague slogan. If we picked some slogan instead for the crusade it would be a lot harder because everybody around the world speaks different languages, but Arabic numerals happily cross linguistic boundaries easily."

"Media-wise," McKibben related, "the biggest part of it was making sure that everybody in those 5200 communities was in touch with their local newspaper, radio, reporter, TV station...then the sheer weight, the tide of that would cause it to get a lot of notice further up the media food chain. The whole thing was extremely bottom-up. We're very decentralized. The world needs to be decentralized as we enter a new economic and energy. We need local food, local energy, and local politics. We have to knit it all together in a way that we can accomplish global change." He added, "We've never asked anybody for money. We're far more interested in getting people to sign up to work, to take action, because that's what we think is key." He described how part of putting together the demonstrations was the inclusion of artists and musicians, faith communities, and college campuses. "Technology doesn't substitute for getting actual people on the ground in actual places, and that's really been our strength."

INTERVIEW WITH BERNIE SANDERS' CAMPAIGN MANAGER JEFF WEAVER

I pointed out to Jeff Weaver, Bernie Sanders' 2016 presidential campaign manager and Sanders' longtime senior political advisor who authored the book, *How Bernie Won: Inside the Revolution That's Taking Back Our Country—and Where We Go from Here*, that Sanders always said at rallies that change doesn't happen from the top down—it happens from the bottom up. And I asked how that philosophy was applied to the campaign. Weaver replied that there was such a fast explosion of support for Sanders that out of necessity they had to use a "distributed approach" and encourage local Sander's supporters to "self-organize." The campaign had to trust local supporters.

Weaver added, "One of the most effective political tools out there is people talking to their neighbors about why they're supporting one candidate or another. Good old-fashioned neighbor-to-neighbor conversations really are the single most effective tool, and we relied on that extensively throughout the campaign."

Weaver observed, "The Democratic party and its candidates are failing to connect with voters in huge swaths of the country and many communities." He cited Politico's Kenneth Vogel, who says the Koch brothers operate a network of organizations that has "an infrastructure that rivals that of the Republican National Committee." Weaver observed that "the Koch brothers understand what the DNC used to understand—that you have to be on the ground year-in and year-out to be successful electorally."

He added, "The Democratic party can no longer just be a fundraising vehicle for presidential aspirants. It must invest in building permanent grassroots infrastructure… That infrastructure needs to be everywhere… We had an extensive people-to-people system set up, a very well-established grassroots network and distributed organizing that was really helping to carry the campaign, and that created the tremendous turnout at all of the events that Bernie was holding."

Weaver described what he meant by distributed organizing, saying, "We developed a lot of tools on the campaign trail that are web tools. For instance, you could just sit in your living room with your computer and bring up a list of names on Bernie's campaign site. You were trained about what to say, and there was a script to use when you called people. If you were, say, living in California, which is at the end of the process, and were told there were a lot of volunteers in California, you could make the decsion to call into people from the next state that was on the events calendar—Michigan or Illinois or whatever rally was coming up next and participate as a volunteer in that area without actually being there.

"So, you could make get-out-the vote calls even if you were not in the state in which you were located, and in this way you could mobilize a large grassroots national network to have impact in a state even if it was not your state of residence. Another way we used a really bottom-up approach to political organizing was with peer-to-peer texting, which means huge numbers of volunteers individually text people who live in the targeted geographic area.

"Bernie said at every speech 'change always happens from the bottom up, not from the top down' and what he wanted the campaign to do, beyond, obviously, winning the nomination—which was the primary goal, was to inspire and empower people. A lot of times people feel down about politics because they feel like there's a lot of stuff happening in Washington DC or in their state capitol or somewhere else they don't feel connected to. They don't really feel that political leaders often are speaking to the realities of their life, and what's happening in their community. And so they become separated from it. And Bernie really wanted to get people engaged and to understand that they can in fact make a difference, whether they participate in politics locally or on the state level or in national politics and congressional elections, people can get involved. They can in fact change the direction of the country. But it really takes this mass, organic sort of grassroots uprising—and I think you're really seeing a lot of that now.

"Bernie is also a big proponent of public financing of elections, and the reason he supports that position, which he articulates quite often, is that he wants us to be in a situation where somebody can run for office based on the merits of their ideas and not just on whether they have a lot of money themselves or have a sufficient number of friends to put together the financing for their campaign—which is all too often the reality.

"Bottom-up is successful when people recognize the commonality of their interest and work together to bring everybody up. And I talk about this as the challenge of the Democratic party—about how you build that type of coalition… the issues that people point out that are of a concern to them are incredibly similar. People want to have a decent economic standing for their family. They want their children to have a good education. They don't want to be without health insurance. They want to live with social dignity. It is incredible to realize this—what I call the common aspirations of people in this country."

Elections and Voting

Citizens United opened the gates for huge flows of top-down money to enter and corrupt politics. Elections should be funded by small donations by the people. Voting should be encouraged, not repressed. When a person reaches voting age she should be automatically registered to vote. Voting day should be a holiday. All votes should be cast on verifiable, re-countable paper ballots. You can't verifiably recount digital tabulations, but you can hack electronic voting machines. Elections should use instant-run-off or related approaches where voters select their first, second, and third choice so voters are not stuck voting for the lesser of two evils or candidates that the two major parties force down their throats. Primaries should be open to all voters, and the idea of super voters, that some politicians are more important than other voters, should be done away with, as the abomination to democracy that it is.

I asked Marta Steele, one of my go-to experts on elections, one of OpEdNews's senior editors, and author of the book *Grassroots, Geeks, Pros, and Pols*, to describe how elections are bottom-up or top-down. She answered, "Think about the old-fashioned New Hampshire meetups where neighbors shared beer and good times while voting and counting ballots. Primary caucuses have some bottom-up characteristics. Candidates come to address people and capture their support, and the paper ballots are cast and counted right there.

"The hand-counted paper-ballot is far and away the most bottom-up of methods with we-the-people carrying out all steps of the process in a totally nonpartisan way. Electronic systems of any description are top-down, benefiting big money. The more people involved directly in the processes, the more bottom-up the system. The trend toward using independent commissions instead of state legislators to redistrict and avoid gerrymandering steers the process away from partisan interests and is thus bottom-up. Then there's the obviously top-down electoral college system as opposed to the popular vote."

MOVE THE CENTER TO MAKE CHANGE HAPPEN

I asked Naomi Klein to plug some of her ideas into the bottom-up versus top-down way of looking at things. She replied, "It's not about how you vote for or who you trust. It's about being a political adult and realizing that political change isn't handed down from above; it's demanded from below. What I've been saying to people is, move the center. Go out there and say some really radical things, and fight for them and organize. Move the center, because that's how America got The New Deal, not because FDR handed it down from above, but because people were organizing in trade unions, in neighborhood groups. That's how things like rent control were won.

"That's how Social Security was won. It was in that interplay between a very, very mobilized, radicalized base and a politician who was willing to listen. But more importantly, FDR was able to sell The New Deal as a compromise because people were so radical that he was able to say to the elite, look, we're on the verge of revolution, we're on the verge of socialism. We need to give them something. And the New Deal, as we know, wasn't just one policy. They had to deepen it and sweeten the pot, more and more, because people were so radical. That's the kind of spirit that we need to return to."

SPEAKING TRUTH TO POWER: INTERRUPTING THE MOST POWERFUL PERSON IN THE WORLD

Medea Benjamin, co-founder of Code Pink, interrupted President Barack Obama. She told me she interrupts powerful people about once a month. I asked her how to do it, with a series of questions. Her first response was, "The most important thing is to have the ability to be in that space, then figure out if it seems appropriate or not to speak out."

How do you get into events like that? Try to get an invitation, try to register, or try to represent a media organization. Sometimes, just walk in.

How do you prepare? What do you wear? Do you bring signs? Wear nondescript clothes, sturdy shoes, no political pins or identifying items. Take a cloth sign with a short message and big letters. Medea hid hers under her clothing, in case anyone looked in her purse, until she got in.

What do you take with you? Driver's license, money, and a fully charged phone.

Do you need to go with other people? Have someone waiting outside, ready to bail you out. Sometimes we have multiple people in the room.

What about seating strategy? Be as inconspicuous as possible. Sit in the middle of an aisle so it's harder to pull you out. Be in direct sight of your target.

For a camera person, what's the best position? Have a person in the front of the room, on the side, with a camera. They should also be gutsy and feel like they own the room so that when the interaction starts they can get up close and walk where they need to walk.

What is your mental mindset? Breathe deep. Think about why you're doing it, think about what is motivating you. You have to be passionate about these issues, and then you have to go with your gut; and if your gut tells you, 'This doesn't feel right,' then just don't do it.

What's the first action? Stand up and project; you don't want to sound, as they say, 'shrill.' Speak loudly, but don't scream. Make first words respectful. Don't waste words. Get out your main point very quickly. You don't know how much time you'll have.

When Security people come at you? They'll come at you after just a few words. Don't go limp and have to be carried out, but don't go very easily: Grab on to furniture, bannisters, and so forth.

What to do once they start moving you? Do what you can do to slow it down. Stay really calm, but threaten to scream. They want to avoid that—the bigger the target the more they want to avoid being seen as shutting down free speech. Keep talking as they take you out. Use every second you have. But don't scare them—don't make them think you're going to do any harm to anybody. If they think you might want to do harm, it could get dangerous.

What do you do AFTERWARD? Put out a press release so that the press knows where they can find and interview you and so you can tell your side of the story. It's important to write your side of the story.

How do you assess success? If the media picks it up, and it starts to get out, and what gets out is the message that you had. If there is a great photo taken, that gets spread around. Getting a meeting based on the action. Seeing a change in the policy you're protesting. The ultimate success is getting movement on the issue that you're trying to affect.

HORIZONTALISM, OCCUPY, WALKING WITH QUESTIONS, AND EVERYDAY REVOLUTIONS

Marina Sitrin is the author of the books *Horizontalism: Voices of Popular Power in Argentina* and *They Can't Represent Us*. When I was at the six different Occupy Wall Street locales I visited and reported on, the concept of horizontalism repeatedly came up, and almost always, it was Marina Sitrin and her books associated with it. I asked Sitrin to explain Horizontalism.

She replied, "It's a relationship, one that's ever-changing, one that people form with each other in a way that is direct. Later people came to call it *Direct Democracy*. Anti-hierarchy is part of what it's about. It's about people speaking for themselves, listening to one another actively, not having power over each other, and creating relationships where they can voice what they feel and think and then together come up with ideas. So, it's a relationship-based concept. We don't want to have power over one another, but to create power with each other, so we all have an equal distribution of power.

I said to Sitrin, "The Politics of Walking, which you describe in your book, beautifully explains why Occupy Wall Street didn't start with a list of goals." She replied, "The Zapatistas were known for saying, '*Caminando preguntándonos*:' walking, we ask questions. There's a very famous Mayan story told in indigenous communities in Mexico called The Story of Questions. It's a story of two Gods and how they're attached physically like Siamese twins. They learned that they can't walk without first talking to each other. They must communicate to walk, and they must figure out where they are going and how they're going where they're going. And there's this walking, asking questions. The only way to move forward is through asking." Sitrin also described a core belief of the Zapatistas as operating "collectively" and "from below and to the left." The Zapatistas talk about unity and building a "new structure from below."

Sitrin went into further details on the idea of walking, asking questions. "The idea is to break from concepts of needing to have an ultimate goal: 'This is where we are going and this is The Path.' But as we are moving together, we figure out where we are going and that necessarily things have to change because we're talking to one another, and as we start moving in one direction, whatever that is, we might change our minds a little bit, or the situation changes, and the world changes, and so where we're going and how we're getting there, needs to change. It's a very sharp critique against political parties, which have The Agenda, The Goal, 'This is The Path, and this is what you must do to win,' and winning has already been defined before you even start walking. And this says, no, that you can't have any kind of ultimately decided [destination]."

In his book, *WTF: What's the Future and Why It's Up to Us*, venture capitalist and tech publisher, conference organizer, and online education pioneer Tim O'Reilly makes a similar comparison to the rigidity of political decision-making, but he's referring to artificial intelligence driven algorithms, which in their own way also engage in walking and asking questions because big data is used to continuously update and modify algorithms based on bottom-up collective intelligence big data input.

I pointed out to Marina Sitrin that Occupy's choice not to state demands drove top-down-thinking, authoritarianism-needing people crazy. Sitrin added, "There's no blueprint. We have to create it together because we don't know and we're only going to find out as we meet each other and talk to each other. Then we're going to change as we know each other, as situations change, so it's that kind of walking, questioning idea. Entire [Zapatista] communities of thousands of people in Chiapas, Mexico [are] self-governing themselves with this concept, making decisions with this spirit of not having the answer, but figuring it out together."

Sitrin also commented on how top-down decision-making and power is baked into some societal structures. She explained "It's not just power over another person. We actually make structures where that power is in place in a way that's not democratically decided—not just 'You have power over me,' but 'That power was decided in a way [where] I had no decision-making in how that was going to happen,' and then there's some kind of structure to it. We live in a society where all of it is vertical: as far as your workplace, how decisions are made, and everything from how often a bus runs to your work hours, job descriptions, things like that. It's very rare that you have any participation in those decisions, and even if you do, it's not meaningful participation." The solution, she suggests, is rethinking power: "In a lot of other languages, power is a verb. And so it's to have power with or it's something you make and you do together. It's active; it's not something you wield. It's creating a power together."

I asked Marina to discuss Todos Somos—"we are all," as in "we are all Chelsea Manning," and "we are all Trayvon Martin." She explained, "It's related to not just seeing ourselves in the other, but really being the other. It's not just, 'oh I feel solidarity with,' it's more than just feeling solidarity. It's that who you are is linked with that other person and so then, we all are. It's that everything is interrelated and how other people are treated is also directly affecting us in a kind of concrete way and then, also, a more philosophical way."

I call that connection consciousness.

BOTTOM-UP APPROACHES TO CHANGE

Paul Hawken, in his landmark book *Blessed Unrest*, says there are hundreds of thousands of small, social and eco-justice advocacy organizations trying to make change happen. We need those small groups. If we consider biomimicry—application of biology to human endeavors, the higher functioning, most versatile life forms have many parts that work together. It is time and necessary for groups promoting change to come together to consciously decide to find common ground and ways to share strengths and resources, cooperate, and develop interdependent networks and ways to help each other. There is a "body politic." We need a "body activic."

Yaneer Bar-yam, Director of the New England Complex System Institute, argues that operating as a collective is essential for dealing with the complex systems that so densely populate all aspects of our world today.

We have millions of organizations, probably hundreds or thousands near you, when you include activists, churches, unions, and local service organizations. Their effectiveness can be greatly increased if they can create a "container," or connector catalyzer, that coordinates the efforts of the leaders and of the "long tail"—the less active member resources. There are reasons to hope that the bottom-up connection revolution has the potential to make new, higher level collective cooperation possible, like the generative social impact networks described in Chapter Two.

There are impediments to making this happen: turf and control issues, trust issues, leader ego issues, resistance to new approaches and technologies, failure to engage enough groups, and failure to build strong communication and resource sharing infrastructure. But we can make this happen, even though we don't know what it will look like, even without—yet—having the billions in resources that transnational corporate forces have. We must build with what resources we have, to create competing visions. I say visions because, as a bottom-up entity our vision cannot and will not be singular. It will be more like the compound lens vision of a honeybee. As Marina Sitrin says, we'll do it "walking while talking." Sitrin cites a quote:

"Alice laughed. 'There's no use trying,' she said, 'One can't believe impossible things!' 'I dare say you haven't had much practice!' said the queen. 'When I was your age I always did it for half an hour a day. Why sometimes I've believed as many as six impossible things before breakfast.'"

—LEWIS CARROLL, *THROUGH THE LOOKING GLASS*

People want and need to do good things and help others. The coalitions, networks, and projects I'm describing will evolve organically. We just need to decide it is an idea worth putting energy into and then work together. Perhaps someone or some organization or coalition will develop a new kind of company or incubator organization (or this may already exist) that helps nurture, incubate, nest, and make such organizations stronger, more bottom-up, and sustainable.

Joe Trippi was the first manager of a national online campaign—Howard Dean's Democratic presidential primary run. He's a consultant to campaigns and corporations. While the wisdom he shared with me applies to politics and power, it also applies very directly to business and branding, not just candidate branding. So check out his section in Chapter Eight.

Why the Internet Hasn't Transformed Politics
Micah Sifry is the co-founder and editorial director of Personal Democracy Forum, my favorite bottom-up conference. It explores what Sifry calls technology for the public good. He's the author or co-editor of numerous books including *The Big Disconnect: Why the Internet Hasn't Transformed Politics Yet.* I asked Sifry to describe his idea of bottom-up. He offered a very different reply, "The part about that that I've stopped using is the 'up.' To me, it's where this authority

comes from. Just the fact that lots of people participate by, say, sharing a piece of content or donating to a cause, doesn't necessarily mean that they have power, because the thing that's aggregating their power may be controlled somewhere else."

Sifry argues that some websites and organizations are not as bottom-up as they seem. Facebook has over a billion users and lots of bottom-up technology. But it's controlled by a very central, top-down group of people. He says, "MoveOn has a giant email list, but most of the power to focus that list is in the hands of the people who work for MoveOn. There's very little lateral conversation between the members. I refer to this as big email, where using the tools has not necessarily changed the power dynamic as much as people might imagine."

Sifry says, "Architecture is politics and coders are legislators." Citing Google, Twitter, and Facebook, he explains that "There are all sorts of political choices baked into the design of those platforms in terms of how they work. For example, Facebook now is automatically throttling what you see in your newsfeed." That means they control and program what you see from your friends and what your friends see from you.

He cites SeeClickFix.com as a great positive example. It's where people can post local reports of non-emergency problems they want their city to fix. "When you put a report in on SeeClickFix, it not only goes to the relevant city agencies, but it also stays visible on a map where other people can read what you've written, comment, and see how long it's taking for that problem to be addressed and solved. And one thing that's very interesting about SeeClickFix's architecture is that when a resident posts a problem, a city worker or other residents can comment, and the city worker may write, 'Okay, we fixed this. That pothole has been filled.' But it's up to the resident who posted the original trouble report to confirm that it's fixed. The ultimate power on SeeClickFix has been architected to sit in the hands of the residents who report problems, not the city bureaucrats, whose job it is to fix them. You've shifted the power in an important, very good way. So, the question of the control of our platforms, that we rely on so heavily now for sharing information, is absolutely vital."

Sifry observes, "The internet is particularly good only at 'stop' and not all that good at 'go,' whether it's social media, hashtag activism, email lists, whatever: stop that execution, stop Mubarak from being the dictator of Egypt anymore. The internet's good for coordination around something we already agreed about. But if when we don't agree and we have to first figure out how to agree about something? Let's create a new political party; let's write a piece of legislation together. Agreeing becomes much harder because we are drowning in the ease of self-expression. We have a surplus of talk and we don't have good listening tools."

I asked Sifry about thin and thick engagement and email. He told me, "When you try to use it (email) in any sort of group activity to coordinate something, it breaks." Sifry says that big email lists are mostly one-way, what's referred to as 'passive democratic engagement' or 'thin engagement.' Email list recipients become disengaged and stop clicking on those emails and unsubscribe from those lists. They do not have a very strong kind of engagement. That's why it's about 'thin engagement.' He characterizes 'thick engagement' as "meaningful ongoing engagement between two people who know each other and have, actually, some sense of obligation to each other."

Email and petitions have led to a new kind of mindset that's faster but 'thinner.' Sifry says, "Lots of people criticize 'clicktivism' where the people who sign petitions think they're doing something when they're not actually doing anything. And the targets of all this email pressure, all those petitions, are tuning out too. Members of Congress are being swamped by this kind of communication. They don't take e-petitions very seriously because they can see how easy they are to generate."

Do petitions work at all? 50,000 signatures might not faze a US senator, but, Sifry differentiated, "They work best at a local level, when the mayor or the city council member in the small town gets 200 to 300 email petitions from people in their town, yeah boy, that has an impact." Sifry emphasized that petitions can influence businesses and corporations more.

Communities Are Organic, Living Systems Best Treated with a Bottom-Up Approach

"The universe is full of magical things, patiently waiting for our wits to sharpen."
—EDEN PHILLPOTTS, *A SHADOW PASSES* (1918)

Cormac Russell is Managing Director of Nurture Development, the leading Asset-Based Community Development (ABCD) organization in Europe. His community organization work is based on a simple, bottom-up idea, "Start with what is strong, not what's wrong, and liberate what's strong to address what's wrong, and to make what's strong even stronger."

Russell says, "The solution to the most intractable problems we face starts from the grassroots, from inside out, and it starts with the belief that there is no two-tiered society where one group of people with all of the problems are rescued by another group with all the solutions, there is no them and us. There is only us. The only change that is truly sustainable is community-driven change." He says the top-down obsession with the "professional" or "expert" approach to looking at problems and diagnosing what is wrong has caused huge harms to millions of people.

He identifies four kinds of harm:

1. First, people become defined not by their strengths, capacities, or gifts but by their deficiency—what's wrong with them.

2. Money, which is intended to go to those who need the help, goes not to the needing people, but to those paid to provide the services to those who need help.

3. In the face of professionalism, expertise, technocracy, active citizenship, the power to take action at the grassroots level retreats, and personal and community agency is surrendered to top-down outsiders.

4. Entire communities defined as deficient come to believe that the only way things will happen is if some outside professional with the right program and right money comes in to rescue them.

Professionals castrate, disempower, and take away the agency from communities.

It's essential to teach, starting in primary school, about how professionals can take away power and agency. And professionals must also learn how to help without disempowering clients.

Russell says that connectors, who he calls "unsung heroes," hold the community together and play a key role in making community magic happen. He brings connectors together to identify resources, "the hidden treasures that exist in the community, and come up with new ideas." He says, "They can connect not just with other people but they can also connect with the economy, with the culture and with the environment and that that creates incredible power and collective efficacy." See more on community in Chapter Nine.

"If you've come to help me, you are wasting your time. But if you've come because your liberation is bound up with mine, then let us work together."
—LILLA WATSON, INDIGENOUS AUSTRALIAN ACTIVIST FROM SPEECH AT THE 1985 UNITED NATIONS DECADE FOR WOMEN CONFERENCE IN NAIROBI

CONSCIOUS EATING: YOUR LIFESTYLE CAN BE POWERFUL BOTTOM-UP GRASSROOTS ACTIVISM

You don't always have to vote in a voting booth to make changes happen. You can vote with your wallet and lifestyle. When enough people do something, or develop a practice collectively, a tipping point can be reached, and big changes happen even faster. Conscious eating is one example. When you eat consciously, you are aware of several things:

1. Meat production inflicts a much bigger footprint on the environment than production of plant-based food, including pollution from animal waste, and drugs that leak into rivers and streams.

2. The exploitation of millions of acres to grow food for animals in the meat production cycle destroys biohabitats.

3. Removing meat from the diet makes people healthier. That affects prescription drug use, health care costs, restaurant marketing, and school lunch programs.

4. Eating organic food often means buying from small, local growers.

When you eat consciously, keeping meat to a minimum and buying organic products, here are some of the bottom-up effects:

- You effectively boycott packaged, processed food with additives and chemicals in it, produced by billion-dollar transnational food companies.

- When you start going local for food, you stop supporting globalization and its devastating effects on communities.

- You stop supporting top-down Big Agra, which engages in monoculture, growing one plant, often corn, soybeans, wheat, or rice. Some nations grow one crop, which is highly inefficient and bad for the soil.

- When you eat little or no meat, you reduce your risk for the big diseases of heart disease, cancer, and diabetes. Add regular exercise, and you can often do with less or no prescription drugs.

- When you avoid meat and or buy organic you stop supporting Monsanto with its GMOs, the genetically modified animal feed plants that tolerate insecticides and weed killers.

If you look at every meal as an opportunity to take a stand, you can become a part of a powerful bottom-up, grassroots movement, which starts with what you have on the end of your fork. The same idea can apply to other aspects of your life: the products you buy, the materials you use, and the entertainment you consume. Divestment programs and consumer boycotts helped to bring down South African Apartheid. Never underestimate the power of conscious action.

Anthony Flaccavento, author of *Building a Healthy Economy from the*

Bottom Up, explores the idea of "food citizens," the millions of people who frequent farmers' markets, food co-ops, CSAs, who eat organic and who are vegan or vegetarian. There are at least five million food citizens, and they could become the core for a political movement that takes a stand and makes a huge difference.

TOP-DOWN INJUSTICE

I spoke to attorney Glenn Greenwald, one of the journalists who brought Edward Snowden to the world's attention, about his book *With Liberty and Justice for Some*. He described how there are different standards for top-down elites:

"If we look at the last decade, what we see is very serious and egregious crimes committed by the most powerful political and financial elites in the country. And yet none of these crimes have provoked meaningful investigations of any kind, let alone prosecutions. And at the very same time that we've created this kind of shield of immunity for elites, we have built up the world's largest prison system and one of the harshest and most merciless systems of punishment for ordinary Americans. This kind of two-tiered justice system where you receive total immunity if you are an elite and commit crimes but extremely harsh and merciless punishment if you are an ordinary American, is really the antithesis of what the rule of law was intended to be."

I asked Glenn if this is a partisan issue. He replied, "It is very much a bipartisan mentality that shields political elites."

BOTTOM-UP JUSTICE: RESTORATIVE AND UNITIVE VS. PUNITIVE

Sylvia Clute, author of *Beyond Vengeance, Beyond Duality: A Call for a Compassionate Revolution*, at one point as a trial attorney realized that she and the legal system were making people's relationships worse. She began working with restorative justice, which she describes as "the model for dealing with breakdowns or crime that seeks healing restoration and reconciliation instead of merely punishment, vengeance, and retribution." She said "I distinguish between punitive justice, which is that model that seeks retribution and revenge, from unitive justice, the model that seeks healing, restoration, and reconciliation. They're seeking healing, understanding of what happened, and getting at the root cause of what happened so it doesn't continue to occur; and they're seeking accountability, holding the person who committed the wrong accountable in a way that's meaningful to the person that they harmed."

The unitive model of justice has its moral roots in the golden rule, something that's found in one form or another in all of the major religious traditions. The punitive model of justice has its moral roots in proportional revenge: an eye for an eye, a tooth for a tooth. That means that you are to answer harm with harm, but the restraint is that you're only to inflict as much harm as what's inflicted on you. That's actually what our scales of justice represent.

Unitive justice is all about inclusiveness and punitive justice is about separation. She explained, "In the unitive, restorative justice conferencing model you would bring together the victim and the offender and supporters of theirs. When a crime is committed, the whole community suffers; it's a breach in the fabric of the community. So with the assistance of a trained facilitator, people in the circle in a spirit of respectfulness, truthfulness, and honesty—but not projecting guilt, shame, or judgment—each speak their truth, so it is inclusive." Unitive justice, which brings in people inclusively and looks at the whole, is really a bottom-up, local, community-oriented, and family-oriented process.

CONSERVATIVE AND LIBERAL | BOTTOM-UP AND TOP-DOWN

"We who live in free market societies believe that growth, prosperity and, ultimately, human fulfillment are created from the bottom up, not the government down. Only when the human spirit is allowed to invent and create, only when individuals are given a personal stake in deciding economic policies and benefiting from their success—only then can societies remain economically alive, dynamic, prosperous, progressive, and free."

—RONALD REAGAN, REMARKS AT THE ANNUAL MEETING OF THE BOARDS OF GOVERNORS OF THE WORLD BANK GROUP AND INTERNATIONAL MONETARY FUND SEPTEMBER 29, 1981

While I'm a lefty, and perceive bottom-up as progressive, many conservatives have told me they think that conservatism is more bottom-up than liberalism or progressivism. I'm attempting here to explore both sides. A few things are clear. It's not simple. There's plenty of hypocrisy to go around. Many of the main issues and values of conservatives and liberals have changed over the years and when it comes to bottom-up and top-down thinking, neither side is purely one or the other.

Wikipedia says the central tenets of conservatism include tradition, human imperfection, organic society, hierarchy and authority, and property rights.

Corey Robin, author of *The Reactionary Mind* and professor of political science at Brooklyn College and the Graduate Center of the City University of New York, argues that conservatives basically value power and resist having it taken away, including protecting hierarchy, and privilege. Robin emphasizes that workers, slaves, and wives have been treated by the law and the courts as property, owned by powerful men. He points out that until 1980 in every state in the US, a husband could legally rape his wife, because her agreement to marry made it legal. And until not too long ago, workers were treated by the legal system as indentured servants. From Robin's perspective, those aspects of conservativism are all about protecting top-down dimensions of culture and civilization. Robin argues that conservatism is literally the opposition to agency of subordinate classes, with the belief that some people deserve power more than others. James Scott wrote a whole book about how people of subordinate classes use secretive or hidden ways of resistance, *Weapons of the Weak: Everyday Forms of Peasant Resistance.*

It's pretty obvious that religion plays a primary role in many aspects of modern conservativism. My go-to expert on early biblical history, former Catholic priest, Michael Rivage-Seul, observed that in early biblical times women did not have the right to even testify in court, and that patriarchy is still a major part of conservativism.

Rivage-Seul points out that Jesus was a radical who resisted the colonizing government he lived under and stood for justice for the colonized oppressed. Christianity was radically changed, around 320 AD, when Roman emperor Constantine convened the Council of Nicea to produce a bible that worked for Imperial Rome. That meant that many passages unfriendly to empire were either thrown out or rewritten. Today's bible is the bible written to serve the needs of the very top-down Roman Empire. Rivage-Seul argues that the modern study of ancient biblical era sources shows that in some cases, Jesus' and his apostles' words were changed to say the opposite of what they taught.

Conservatives embrace religion and God to define many of their principles. While religion can be bottom-up, as I discuss in Chapter Nine, the conservative vision of religion tends to manifest as a more top-down version, which supports a patriarchal, heteronormative model in which the man is the family leader, and the woman is the passive, obedient housekeeper. Progressives are more likely to be either atheist, agnostic, or disconnected from established, hierarchical churches, and they attend church far less often.

Grassroots activism is a core bottom-up behavior. Conservatives have pointed out that it took a bottom-up grass roots approach to start the Tea Party. And progressives point to the bottom-up Occupy Wall Street's influence in shaping the last decade's political conversation. But conservatives say that George Soros funded Occupy Wall Street and progressives say the Koch Brothers funded the start of the Tea Party.

To further approach the question of bottom-up and top-down connections to liberal and conservative perspectives I referenced Paul Kengor's book, *11 Principles of a Reagan Conservative.* Kengor lists eleven Reagan conservative principles.

- Limited Government

- Freedom

- Family

- Faith

- Belief in the individual

- Sanctity and Dignity of Human Life

- American Exceptionalism

- The Founders' Wisdom and Vision

- Lower Taxes

- Peace Through Strength

- Anti-communism.

I'll start with anti-bigness, which I believe is a bottom-up property or value. Conservatives oppose big government. Liberals are willing to enable big government in order to create a world with room for everyone, except for big military budgets. Conservatives win the bottom-up question for big government opposition, but they love big military (strength through power), and they've rarely seen an intelligence agency they didn't like. Of course, most Democrats also like big military and intelligence agencies.

Bottom-up values include strong support for the family. Progressives see that as applying to any configuration of the family—a gay family, a father as a homemaker, or a single-parent household. Conservatives interpret the bible to define the family as a man and a woman in a patriarchal unit, with the man in charge. (Though the great hero kings of ancient Israel had harems—not exactly the family model most associate with the Judeo-Christian tradition.) This is often tied with extreme forms of Christianity, Islam, and Judaism. Liberals, if they embrace religion at all, tend to embrace more tolerant ones. One conservative colleague whom I respect found this book to be "brilliant," but he suggested that I remove the discussion of patriarchy. Rivage-Seul pointed out that Jesus' mother was unmarried at the time of his conception. And let's not forget that for most of humanity's existence, people lived not in family units, but in bottom-up, communal, hunter-gatherer bands.

"Sanctity and dignity of human life," is usually conservative code for anti-abortion. Rivage-Seul points out that Jesus never talked about abortion. Jesus talked about treating people with dignity, about protecting all forms of life, and Rivage-Seul observes that conservatives ignore resisting war, capital punishment, providing health-care for all, poverty, and treating the poor in a way that gives them dignity.

Conservatives in general don't like regulations, except ones that impose their religious beliefs, like "right to life" on others. Both conservatives and most corporate Democrats support trade deals and regulations that protect big corporations.

Libertarians are another breed of conservative. They tend to be liberal on social issues, conservative on economics, taxes, government, and regulations. For example, they believe that through natural economic wisdom and supply and demand, the "free market" will sort things out. That might work in an ideal situation. But the problem is, there is no such thing as a truly pure free market. All markets are part of complex systems. Systems, by their nature, must have regulations.

I commissioned a poll using Zogby polling, related to biofeedback, to explore respondents' interest in self-responsibility for health. The poll showed that conservatives were more inclined to a bottom-up approach, wanting to take responsibility for their own health with diet and self discipline, while liberals preferred a more top-down way, having doctors and the health care system prescribing drugs and surgery.

Conservatives prefer localization, which is bottom-up, while liberals prefer centralization, which is top-down. Yet conservatives have passed or attempted to pass legislation preventing states or cities from passing gun regulation or GMO labeling.

Conservatives and liberals both support freedom but in different ways. Conservatives lean towards liberty—freedom to be an individual, freedom from any kind of external controls, regulations, or influences. Progressives lean toward social justice interpretations of freedom— emphasizing collective freedom and fairness for all.

Conservatives tend to see the idea of collective aything as a manifestation of communism, opposition to which is a core conservative principle. Progressives seek and value bottom-up, collective, cooperative action and society, though not as communism.

Conservatives see communism as evil, anti-god, anti-religion, and a threat to the freedom of the individual. They see distribution of wealth, including taxation beyond the bare minimum needed to pay for the most basic government services, as parasitic or communistic. And conservatives, while they oppose welfare or handouts that help the poor, contradictory to the teachings of Jesus, do seem to love authorizing billions in welfare for corporations. (Centrist Democrats seem to vote for that too.)

But Rivage-Seul points out, that in the New Testament, ACTS 2:43-46 says,

> "And all who shared the faith owned everything in common; they sold their goods and possessions and distributed the proceeds among themselves according to what each one needed. Each day, with one heart, they regularly went to the Temple but met in their houses for the breaking of bread; they shared their food gladly and generously"

Sure sounds like a bottom-up, communal approach to me.

My hope is that by getting people of all ideologies to view the world through a more bottom-up metaphorical filter they will find common ground and shared interest. I doubt that will work for those with the most wealth and power. But it could make a difference for the 90% or even 99% of the rest of the world who can't afford to buy $100 million dollar paintings, homes or yachts.

CHAPTER 6

Bottom-Up Journalism, Media, Arts, and Entertainment

Basically the bottom-up revolution has disrupted and evolved the arts, entertainment, media, and journalism to a point that the old top-down approaches are obsolete or completely dead. Now all of these fields are embracing and thriving in a renaissance, using new bottom-up ways to re-imagine a new vision from bottom-up perspectives.

TOP-DOWN THREATS TO OUR MEDIA, CULTURAL COMMONS, AND THE INTERNET

Antonio Lopez, author of *The Media Ecosystem*, describes the cultural commons as the "things that are important to our cultural survival: how to grow, how to have rituals, how to do political activity." He warns that our cultural commons have been colonized, saying, "There is a process of privatization that has increasingly tried to wall off these aspects that we normally would share, the things that we need in order to grow and to survive. If unchecked, corporate media's power to shape our collective imagination inhibits our ability to envision alternatives beyond a colonial model." Lopez says five or six mega-corporations are privatizing the planetary commons and the space of ideas, "at the expense of the public good and living systems…essentially controlling the majority of the media that is out there."

Lopez told me, prophetically, before the 2016 election, "The internet is also being colonized; it is being divided up by these various services such as Facebook and Google. These services are helpful for us and we can use them, but only up to a point. The privatization of this public space is a threat to democracy because the potential is that they could censor without official backing of the government." Lopez concludes, "If you want to have a democracy, you need to have people who are educated, who talk about things. You need public spaces, places where people can gather and share ideas."

BOTTOM-UP IS CHANGING THE MEDIA

I asked journalist and attorney Larry Atkins, author of *Skewed: A Critical Thinker's Guide to Media Bias*, to give his take on bottom-up journalism. He replied, "Bottom-up journalism has exploded over the last twenty years due to the internet, cell phones, and social media. This type of citizen journalism has allowed anyone and everyone to have a voice and express their opinion without going through the gatekeeper of the mainstream media. In the past, it was hard for the average person to express their opinion to a large audience. Many bloggers and website operators have cultivated huge audiences and influenced public dialogue. Citizen journalists have broken stories and documented events as they happen live, such as during the Arab Spring, the Boston Marathon bombing, and the plane crash in the Hudson River. Bloggers have increased respect as they are cited in news stories, appear as expert guests on television programs, and get access to press conferences, sports events, and political conventions. This democratization of news delivery has been a positive development because it gives everyone a chance to participate in democracy and voice their opinion to a large audience. They often shed light on topics and issues that the mainstream media fail to cover."

Rory O'Connor, author of *Friends, Followers and the Future: How Social Media Are Changing Politics, Threatening Big Brands and Killing Traditional Media*, says, "This is potentially one of the most exciting and opportunity rich periods in the entire history of journalism." He explained that "social media are profoundly revolutionizing the creation, aggregation, and distribution of all kinds of news and information in exciting ways that have never happened before. Twitter has tremendous utility for recreating journalism."

I replied that when I get any inkling that news is breaking, I'll go to Twitter first, because you'll get the biggest, fullest picture there, as well as information very often not presented in the mainstream media.

Rory agreed. "You're going to get it there first now, and that's a huge shift and a democratization. The essential moment in the history of what we are talking about was on January 14, 2009 when the first report of the miraculous rescue of more than 150 passengers from a US Airways jet floating in the Hudson River came by a Twitter feed along with a picture of the jet. This jet went down in the Hudson River, literally opposite the global headquarters of the *Associated Press*, the *New York Times*, and several major broadcast networks. Yet, how did we find out about it? A fellow who happened to be on a tourist boat on the Hudson saw it, snapped a picture, and immediately tweeted the news to the rest of the world. This is what the *Associated Press* and *Reuters* used to do, and now Twitter and the Twitter news network do it."

Given that now anyone can become a journalist or news source, Rory explained the role of bottom-up news filters: "We need filters and short-cuts to help us to find credible news and information. So, you'll be able to have an amalgam of filters: some brands, some machines, some friends and followers, some trusted curators and aggregators that you know over time have been basically giving you good reliable news and information."

Bottom-Up Assessment and Filtering of the News

Most online major newspapers now offer a list of the "most popular" articles. Some offer most viewed. I took the idea when designing my flagship site, OpEdNews.com and let the reader select different kinds of "most popular:" most viewed, most commented upon, most email-forwarded, most highly rated, most shared.

Then there are sites like Reddit or Digg where people submit articles to be shared. Members, if they like an article, click on a button to raise its ranking. The crowd-sourced filtering raises some interesting content you might not ordinarily see.

Daily Kos considers "recommends" as a factor in selecting its top reads for any time. Editors also play a top-down role. At OpEdNews.com, managing and senior editors have headlining privileges. The headlining control panel shows the current number of page views and comments for each article. Community participation is a factor in headlining too, so editors also consider author comments and articles submitted in the past three months. The final decision is top-down, but bottom-up factors are considered. Or readers can go to our popularity pages and strictly use the bottom-up listings that are algorithmically guided based on reader behavior.

Sometimes the most comprehensive way to get the bottom-up-sourced news is to view the links your friends on Facebook or the people you follow on Twitter share. Or you can check trends on Twitter or do searches for keywords or hash tags.

Google News aggregates articles from thousands of sources so you can create your own news collection system using Google News Alerts, as I discuss in Chapter Four. Also, you can use RSS (really simple syndication) feeds and an RSS feed reader, like Feedly, to collect "feeds" from your favorite sources. Most news sites offer it for the whole site. Some offer it for authors or for categories.

Twitter lets you create groups of people for different topics, so you can have your own sets of information sources. Tweetdeck and Hootsuite offer tools, which work with Twitter so you can see tweets related to specific keywords or hashtags.

Bottom line: you no longer need to solely depend on editors to decide what you see and where.

ART AS A BOTTOM-UP CULTURAL DRIVER

The Urban Arts Space of Ohio State University describes, in its mission, *"Art tells a story in a way words cannot. It embodies culture, it is transformative, it links the community to its own people and history."*

Arlene Goldbard, author of *The Culture of Possibility: Art, Artists and the Future,* describes culture as "everything that's not nature in the world that we human beings occupy; our languages, our systems of belief, the built environment and the things that we create under the rubric of art."

Goldbard refers to the idea of "social connective tissue," art and culture being essential elements of that tissue. She advocates for public sector promotion of active cultural participation as a means of making creative work happen, to preserve multiple cultures in the community, and to engage people in beautifying their own neighborhoods

Chicagoans Margo Rush and Reba Blick operate such a program, called Art Van Go Go. It brings art and cultural experiences to Chicago area communities underserved due to lack of funding. I observed them working with mothers and their children who had, until very recently, been homeless, living under Chicago's viaducts. It was unbelievable to see the changes these young women, who had just moved into their first home, went through as they participated in a project of painting flower pots and filling them with plants. It was such a simple thing. For some, the plants were the first houseplants they'd ever owned. These were VERY tough young mothers, ages seventeen to nineteen, who had been homeless with their children, who'd been afraid to sleep with their eyes closed for fear they'd get raped. When they started doing the art, the transformation in their attitude was amazing. Rush observed that the art gave them a chance to have fun, add beauty to their new home, and to share in creating art with their children. Art is incredibly powerful—even the simplest exercises.

Goldbard offers a vision of art playing a role in waking people up: "I want to focus people's attention on re-reading reality, on seeing a different version than the consensus reality of the dominant media and understanding that that mainstream story is neither the only story nor necessarily the truest one."

I observed that consensus reality seems very top-down. Goldbard replied, "If you're embedded in the consensus reality. So, for example, you have these kind of default settings in your mind. 'These people are experts, they know so much more than me, what do I have to say about this subject?'"

I asked how we can wake people up so they free themselves from "consensus reality?" Goldbard replied, "People tend to realize that when a challenge is brought home to them, in the form of stories that engage not just their mind, but their body, their feelings, their spirit at the same time."

Goldbard says, "The capacities and skills that we need to face the future, and develop a future that we want to bring into being, are intrinsic to artistic practice." She detailed "imagination, especially social imagination, empathy, the capacity to create a moment in which we feel something of who the other is and what the other is experiencing. Improvisation, resourcefulness, resilience—all of these capacities are very much the core capacities of art makers in all forms. Those, I argue, are the skills that everyone in this society needs now. It's the capacity to look at what's in front of us. Imagine a different reality. Re-purpose the broken pieces of the old reality in order to bring it into being. And we could all learn from our participation in art, from our art making, how to develop those skills and capacities."

BUILDING COMMUNITIES, NOT AUDIENCES

The arts play a major role in national and local economies. According to Doug Borwick's book *Building Communities, Not Audiences: The Future of the Arts in the United States,* there are 104,000 nonprofit arts and cultural organizations that generate $166.2 billion in economic activity. That's bigger than the movie business, and video game businesses. In addition, for every dollar spent by art organizations, three to seven dollars in the local economy is generated." But the arts are in trouble. The old, top-down model of sell-tickets-to-an-audience does not offer a sustainable future.

Borwick describes a very bottom-up approach to thinking about the future of the arts, audiences, and the communities they serve. He states, "When I say, 'Building communities, not audiences,' I'm talking about focusing your attention on relationship building in your community and the support (whether it's audiences or attendees at galleries and museums) which grows out of that. So the arts organization is changing its way of thinking about its relationship with the community."

In his foreword to Borwick's book, Rocco Landesmen, the Chair of the National Endowment for the Arts, says, "Cultural organizations should be like living cells with permeable membranes that exist to organize and protect the art, but that let the art out into the community and let the community into the art, which creates a two-way relationship between the arts and the community."

Borwick offers a more bottom-up, more sustainable arts infrastructure model, advising, "It's in the enlightened self-interest of arts organizations to be presenting art that touches the lives and makes use of the materials that are closer to a broader range of the population, sort of a cultural democratization. When people outside of an arts organization are primarily thought of as audience or ticket buyer, it sets up a separation, a 'them' and 'us' that is, I think, fundamentally not healthy. I am talking about a re-imagining of that relationship, so that going back to the permeable membrane, it's a two-way transaction. It's not, 'I have the wisdom, I have the culture, I have the aesthetic sensibility, and here is what you should like.' It's that the art that is created comes out of a deep understanding of the needs, interests, and nature of the community in which the arts organization exists.'"

Since the old audience approach to funding the arts is failing, I asked Borwick what does work to support local arts. He answered, "The advances in social media, the advances in online giving, and the capacity to manage online giving, I think, present a real substantial hope if those organizations position themselves as being vital in the lives of people that they are trying to reach." There are new models and approaches emerging. Borwick cited the partnering of smaller arts organizations with fiscal sponsors—larger, registered nonprofit organizations for "individuals and for small collections of people who want to do art in communities, but don't want to bother with the strictures of creating a not-for-profit or 501c3 organization."

"There are some really interesting things going on in museum work, where you have what they're calling Crowd-Sourced Curating, with communities helping museums figure out 'Okay, what's going to be in this exhibition?' There is a phenomenon called pop-up museums, where an idea is put forth about 'Okay, what kinds of things could we gather together?' And people in the community bring them, and that then becomes, for a brief period of time, a little museum in a community."

I suggested that we're beginning to see art that is being created not by individuals, but by groups or communities. The future of art could be that it's created by communities, by the shifting collections of people, and even that the art itself, because it could be digital, could be organically evolving and changing from day-to-day rather than something frozen in stone, metal, or oil on canvas. Borwick responded, "Because of the advances in technology, you're absolutely right that we're going to be seeing more and more collective creativity."

Art Van Go Go was brought in to facilitate art programming for teens at a Chicago Southside drop-in center and developed a mural project. These were angry, homeless teens, leading frighteningly tumultuous lives, who didn't feel like doing a mural. They were mourning the loss of a fellow drop-in center attendee, Chris, who'd just been murdered. Rush and Blick pivoted to focus the mural on Chris. The teens became animated, talking about other people they'd recently lost. The mural became a collective memorial that helped them to explore the deaths and violence in their lives, bringing some of the hardened teens to tears and creating and deepening a sense of community. The project won a national award from the National Clearinghouse for Families and Youth for the Runaway and Homeless Youth Mural Contest.

I asked Doug how the arts help and offer value to people and communities. He replied, "Economically the arts are good for communities, especially from the standpoint of public education. The arts have so much to offer in terms of how you teach basic concepts, how students remember things, how they initially grasp them, in terms of keeping people in school. You understand history better if you know the culture and the cultural artifacts of a particular era. There's the capacity of the arts to build communities, and by that I mean social capital, better relationships, highlighting needs, or providing opportunities for celebration, opportunities for cross-cultural awareness, and understanding."

Doug gave an example of bridging arts and local culture. "The Houston Grand Opera commissioned small one-act operas about the various immigrant communities in Houston, and they got stories from those immigrant communities, commissioned people to set them to music and perform them in those communities, but then after they did that, they brought them together in a sort of collective presentation, and [that] does a variety of things. It validates the experience of those communities in ways that are really quite profound, but it also lifts the experience of those communities up before the larger city so that the city can have a greater understanding of the diversity of experience and the strength of that diversity in their own city. What I would hope is that as we work towards this democratization of culture, we will understand that it's important to value all kinds of cultural expression and see varieties of cultural expression as material for us, not only to have an aesthetic experience, but to learn more about the cultures that those modes of expression are representative of."

Eric Whitaker's Virtual Choir
A few years ago, a woman sent Eric Whitacre a video she'd created of the soprano part for one of his compositions. That set in motion the idea for a new bottom-up musical art form—a virtual chorus. Whitacre invites

people who are spread throughout the world, and whom he has never met, to participate separately in creating a celestial choir composed of thousands of voices that are merged through YouTube. He recorded a video of himself conducting with a piano background. For his second project, over 25,000 people downloaded, for free, the music to sing their parts for his composition SLEEP. 2052 people from 58 countries eventually uploaded their videos.

Once the thousands of videos are uploaded they must be woven together, then audio synched. Then there's a tying-in with Google Earth, so, when you go to IanWhitacre.com, you can choose to listen to just the singers from one country.

With each new virtual choir project, there have been new technological and artistic approaches. The first time I interviewed him and asked what he wanted to do next. He told me that he didn't want to just make bigger choirs. He wanted it to evolve. He wanted to do a live, real time choir. But there were problems with latency, or lag time and he speculated that he'd have to wait for a technological solution—until something like "iPhone 8, or something like it" would come along. Back then, I observed that the latency added variability, in the way that chaos theory describes. He replied, "I'm not a religious person, but I would call that God, if I were."

Two years later, technology had not come to the rescue, so Whitacre embraced the technological challenge and came up with a creative, artistic solution, explaining, "There's a one second latency, so I've adapted Cloudburst so that it embraces the latency and the performers sing into the latency instead of trying to be exactly together."

I've sung in a few choruses. You drive somewhere, then get on a stage. I love the idea that Whitacre's virtual choir concept allows people to dial in to participate from anywhere in the world, and for the non-real-time ones, at their convenience.

I asked what lessons he'd learned. "People come out of the woodwork and share their disparate talents. It's a kind of crowdsourcing," he replied. "I was stunned by the effort that people exert connecting with others."

I'd say that connection, in so many new ways, is where the magic is. That's why I wrote Chapter Two.

SINGING AND DANCING FROM THE BOTTOM UP—THE HOTTEST TV SHOWS, THE NEWEST STARS

Some of the most popular television programs have been built upon bottom-up ideas. For example, to win *The Voice*, a singing competition, the competitors must win more viewer support than the others, via phone calls, tweets, votes on *The Voice* app and purchases of songs on iTunes. There are dozens of versions of the voice in nations all over the world, and a whole genre of television shows that use bottom-up audience participation to determine winners. Another bottom-up aspect of *The Voice*, one of my favorites, is that the directors always capture and share the joy of the family and friends when a singer succeeds by turning judges' chairs, meaning the judges want the singer on their team. Winning is not just about the winner. Ask any Little League parent.

BOTTOM-UP SPORTS

Dave Zirin writes on the intersection between sports, politics, and justice for edgeofsports.com. I asked him to delve into bottom-up aspects of sports. He replied, "Certainly, there needs to be a project at play that talks about how do we reclaim sports and how do we make sports something that more people have access to in this country? How do we stop the corporate looting that's connected with sports, particularly in terms of public subsidies for stadiums? How do we make sports less sexist, less militaristic? How do we make sure that community centers stay open? I think all of these questions are very real and very connected, not just to sports but to the question of building the kind of bottom-up community where people feel empowered." He added, "The relationship of fans to sports themselves is a very passive relationship. You sit and you watch. I would like to see sports fans try to take a more active role in shaping the teams that are in their local communities."

I asked him how he envisioned that happening. Dave answered, "It already is happening in a lot of places. One way is with fan movements, to make sure that public funds don't go to stadiums. Another thing is, trying to make sure that if public funds do go to stadiums that some sort of fan or public advocate is part of the process of seeing how the profits that are produced get spent. And lastly, I think it is about looking at Green Bay Packers as a model. Their team is owned by fans. There is no owner, [inasmuch] as the owner is the people of Green Bay. I think having fans, using that as a model to say, 'You know what? This is our team more than it is yours.' Saying that very directly to owners, I think would be a very positive development, because right now, sports owners live in a consequence-free universe. This is something I would like very much to see changed."

I asked Dave how the fans owning and operating the team makes it different for Green Bay. Dave replied, "Profoundly different. There's a strong sense of ownership, not just actual ownership, but a spiritual ownership between the city and the team itself. It's a team that's been owned cooperatively since the 1920s. And the NFL immediately wrote into its bylaws that no other team could operate in such a way because they didn't want it to be an example for others. And it's proven to be a very critical revenue source for Green Bay. It's proven to be an incredible point of community cohesion, and I think it's a model worth replicating. We should challenge the NFL to change its bylaws."

GAMES AND GAMIFICATION

The game industry has grown bigger than the movie business. The biggest games are MMORPG: Massive Multi-player Online Role Playing Games. The most popular of them all is Blizzard's *World of Warcraft*, which has had over 100 million accounts created over the lifetime of the game. What makes them bottom-up? The only way you can win is by making alliances and cooperating with other people, who can be spread all over the world. Anyone can be a team leader. Playing these games has become a spectator sport, with some game players building huge fan bases.

The bottom-up connection revolution has begun to wreak huge changes upon media, entertainment, the arts, sports, and games. Some institutions, like those of top-down pro sports have resisted, but overall, I believe we're going to see a lot more change happening in these worlds—changes that will reverberate through our culture in ways that go beyond their direct arenas of influence, just as many of the people interviewed in this chapter have described. Arts, entertainment, and media all affect the way we see the world, and more bottom-up arts will contribute to the deepening and expansion of the bottom-up revolution.

CHAPTER 7

Top-Down and Bottom-Up Economics

GLOBALIZATION BEYOND CAPITALISM

"The credibility of economists has been damaged by our insufficient attention, over the years, to the problems of economic adjustment and by our proclivity toward top-down, rather than bottom-up, policies."

—BEN BERNANKE, FORMER FEDERAL RESERVE CHAIRMAN, NOW
DISTINGUISHED FELLOW IN RESIDENCE, BROOKINGS INSTITUTION,
SPEAKING AT THE EUROPEAN CENTRAL BANK'S FORUM ON CENTRAL
BANKING IN SINTRA, PORTUGAL, JUNE 6, 2017

This chapter covers top-down economic challenges like centralization, big money, globalization, and wealth and ownership inequality. It offers bottom-up alternatives. Be assured. The bottom-up economy is well under way, in the process of replacing the existing, top-down economy. It better be. As Zeitgeist movement founder Peter Joseph says, "We're not going to have a productive future unless we change our economy."

BIG MONEY SHOULD BE BOTTOM-UP

President Obama gave lip service to bottom-up economic ideas, but he only implemented one actual bottom-up program, Cash-for-Clunkers. Rather than top-down handing billions over to banks in bulk, like most funding, the money was bottom-up delivered to individuals

THROUGH banks when they traded in used cars to purchase new cars. Though successful, the approach has not been replicated. Most funding is handled in a very top-down way, with one huge pile of money given to a top-down entity that then engages in what publisher and venture capitalist Tim O'Reilly calls "spray and pray."

Imagine if the trillion-plus dollars the USA expended rescuing banks had been required to be distributed bottom-up, directly to individuals and small businesses, channeling ALL the money into local economies rather than enabling too-big-to-fail banks to grow even bigger. What if we applied the standard of requiring bottom-up delivery channels to individuals and small businesses to a lot more government and business funding initiatives? It could prevent misuse of funds and ensure that the money went to local economies.

BILLIONS TO THE POOR: MICROLENDING AND ENTREPRENEURISM FOR THE POOR

Muhammad Yunus and the Grameen bank he founded in Bangladesh were awarded the Nobel Peace Prize "for their efforts to create economic and social development from below." Yunus started microlending, lending $27 to forty-two very poor people so they could create or expand their businesses. Over 300 million people have received microloans, 97 percent of them women. When he started, he found that banks would not give loans of any amount to poor people because they had no collateral and were not considered to be credit-worthy. He's found that 99 percent pay back their loans. Yunus told me he believes that humans evolved to be entrepreneurs, and that we survived by working together. He differentiates the entrepreneurial mindset from the "get a job" mentality by characterizing "getting a job" as a form of subservience and even told me that civilization created slavery, the early equivalent of jobs.

Compare Yunus's approach to giving billions of dollars to huge agencies that dole out money in the form of food stamps. The latter approach perpetuates a cycle of bare subsistence and does not empower people to become entrepreneurial or to fend for themselves.

CENTRALIZED DISCONNECTION

Top-down banking policies—where centralized credit assessment algorithms and decision-making replaced local community lending—were a major cause of the 2008-2009 financial meltdown, Tufts University economics professor Amar Bhide says. Before centralization, a local banker might know you, your references, your community, and the value of the real estate you were buying, and so could make an informed, LOCAL decision. Banks probably embraced top-down, centralized algorithmic automation of millions of loans as more efficient, more scientific and cost-saving. In reality, it was profoundly more expensive, producing economic disaster.

Scott Baker, author of *America's Not Broke*, told me, "Small banks that made the kinds of decisions you're talking about are going extinct. This is critical because even with just 15 percent of the country's bank assets currently, they provide the majority of small business loans, and 98 percent of all jobs come from small business." Big banks are wiping out the local banks, which support job creation.

Membrane Economic Globalization

Globalization, another form of top-down centralization, creates trade deals, which remove or reduce regulations and import tariffs. Proponents claim globalization is inevitable because it helps trade. Globalization, as it currently exists, is bad for most people, communities, local culture, democracy, justice, nations, nature, and the future.

Every living creature needs a skin to survive. Skin is a smart organ, not just a wrapping. It's a highly complex membrane that allows some things to pass through and exit the body and some things to enter the body. It keeps invasive organisms out and maintains proper chemical balances. Strip away its skin and an organism dies very quickly. Globalization—with dumb, top-down, rigid regulations—flays the skin of nations, not just economically but also culturally, industrially, and locally, drastically disrupting communities.

Helena Norberg-Hodge offers an example in her documentary, *Economics of Happiness*, about Ladakh, Tibet, a happy, beautiful agrarian community where no one experienced joblessness or poverty, and where Buddhists and Muslims got along. Globalization brought Ladakh high unemployment and violent conflict. Globalization routinely brings this kind of destruction of local community and culture. Towns where steel, textile, or furniture industries used to thrive become shadows of their former selves.

The "Terminator's" Parents Already Exist: Psychopathic Predators

Science fiction writers have long described apocalyptic scenarios, like the Arnold Schwarzenegger *Terminator* movies, where human inventions take over the earth, transforming the planet and making it uninhabitable. Those man-made monsters have existed for centuries, enslaving and killing millions and destroying natural resources to meet their needs. Those monsters are transnational corporations.

In his book and movie, *The Corporation*, constitutional scholar Joel Bakan proposes that corporations are guided by laws to act like psychopaths. *The Corporation* explores the factors used as criteria to diagnose psychopathy in people. Corporations fit just about all of them. I mentioned to Bakan that the invention of writing and the printing press massively changed the way humans perceive and think, then asked him how the invention of the corporation has changed us. He replied, "The operating principles, which I described in *The Corporation* as psychopathic, have become the operating principles of our society as a whole."

Psychopaths and narcissists are predators. Globalization is also predatory. Ian Hughes describes in his book, *Disordered Minds: How Dangerous Personalities Are Destroying Democracy,* the "'toxic triangle,' comprising [of] destructive leaders, susceptible followers, and conducive environments," which enables psychopaths to gain power at a national level. We must reinvent globalization so it compassionately smartens nations' economic membranes/skins instead of flaying them, and so it produces cultural and economic environments that prevent psychopaths and psychopathic corporations from gaining power. I believe that soon, big data (collective-intelligence-driven artificial intelligence) will enable creation of trade policies that reflect externalities like energy waste, and effects on local culture and local jobs. But the crafters of such trade deals will have to be motivated to create them.

I asked former US Congress member Alan Grayson for his take on globalization. Grayson replied, "We've seen over and over again that these deals weaken our economy and gut the middle class. We've lost five million manufacturing jobs and roughly ten million other jobs, and the middle class is being destroyed."

THE PROBLEMS WITH GLOBALIZATION

University of Arizona Professor Julian E. Kunnie describes globalization as a recolonization of the world with a concentration of wealth and power held by a tiny monopoly of elites (an oligarchy).

Helena Norberg-Hodge says, "We have these two paths into the future we can choose: either toward economic globalization where businesses are pressured to become bigger and bigger and more global, which is also connected to a speeding up of life, and to a scarcity of jobs and to a bigger environmental impact. Or, if we choose localizing instead of globalizing, we would start diminishing the environmental impact, increasing job opportunities, and very, very importantly, start to rebuild the fabric of our connections to one another and to nature. And there is so much evidence those connections are necessary for our well-being, for our happiness, and for a sense of meaning and purpose in life."

Norberg-Hodge described Ladakh, Tibet before globalization. "The Tibetan people were absolutely the happiest people I had ever encountered. There was this bubbling vital joy in life and humor. I came to realize that this sort of joy and well-being was also connected to a deep sense of self-esteem connected to children having grown up with so many loving arms around them." Norbert-Hodge warns, "Globalization is this expansion of a consumer culture through media and advertising. Children are bombarded with advertising that make them believe that to get the approval and the love of their peer group they must have the latest fashion, the latest gadgets. It's a tragic manipulation of a truly human universal need to be loved and connected, to feel a part of society, especially for young children. This path, instead of leading to love, approval and community, leads to separation, envy, and competition, which fuels the spiral further. We now have, in the West, a real epidemic of depression, and at an earlier and earlier age, self-hatred." She recounts how globalization's arrival in Ladakh "even influenced three-year-olds to feel that their own clothing, their own language, their own food, their own everything, was wrong; and they needed to identify with this commercial culture, which is based on constantly buying new things."

Advocating for local economies instead of globalization, Norbert-Hodge pointed out, "If we are growing food, planting trees, and fishing and mining, all the primary production is on a smaller scale. It means higher productivity per unit of land, of water, and of soil and more employment and less pollution. The local food movement is now demonstrating that when you localize in this way—so that you start building up shorter distance between production and consumption—you're actually stimulating and encouraging markets that encourage diversification. When a farmer is selling in the local farmer's market, there's a demand for diversity. So there is a real win-win strategy for all of us if we can understand the benefits of having many smaller businesses instead of a few giants."

I asked Norbert-Hodge to talk more about how people are "going local" and what people can do. She replied, "We have been promoting localization, particularly starting with food, encouraging the setting up of farmer's markets and CSAs, and also school gardens, so that young children learn more about growing food and city farms, urban gardens, and farming. There is a real new farmer's movement where young people actually are turning toward agriculture and the local food movement. This movement is demonstrating that you get greater productivity from a given piece of land this way. The big myth about industrial agriculture has been that it is more efficient and more productive. We've been told that we need large-scale farms to feed the world. But that is the opposite of the truth. We can't afford the waste of industrial agriculture."

It's time to replace existing trade deals with smarter ones that are designed from the bottom up, with input and influence from and for all people, not just the few hundred corporations and handful of industries that benefit from the existing global trade system.

Centralization worked at the onset of civilization. Farming fed the masses and cities housed them. But in today's world, the varieties of centralization have hypertrophied, leading to massive waste, decreased flexibility, and diminished use of local wisdom, resources, and knowledge. It's time to reassess—to identify top-down thinking and policy problems and excesses, and to fix, heal, and balance them with bottom-up approaches.

Bottom-up vs. Top-Down Capitalism and Regulation
Centralized regulation is different and essential. Friedrich Hayek, Ludwig von Mises, and Milton Friedman's neoliberal economic model proposed that economies work best unfettered, that regulations prevent the natural unfolding of the power of capitalism. Guardian newspaper columnist George Monbiot, author of *Out of the Wreckage,* described to me the message of neoliberalism, which he characterizes as virulent:

> Very rich people are the pioneers, the scouts who blaze the trails that the rest of us should follow. Nothing should be allowed to interfere with that role, so they should be subject to almost no tax, to no regulation, to no democratic constraints. They should be able to behave exactly as they want; and the more extreme their behavior, the better the trail that they will blaze for the rest of us to follow. Their freedom is our captivity. Their freedom must be absolute. Democracy is subordinate to the absolute freedom of the very rich. So their freedom translates into our loss of freedom so [that] they are free from all forms of regulation, from all forms of public protection for the rest of us.

This is the anti-government, anti-regulation approach that Koch brother conservatives and libertarians advocate for—no worker fairness or safety rules, no ecological or climate change rules, no tariffs, no food safety or regulations.

But nature has many rules. Violate them and the ecosystem or organism sickens or dies. The same is true for economic ecosystems. We saw in 2008 what happened when Glass-Steagall regulations were removed. Naomi Klein, in her bestseller, *Shock Doctrine*, described how dictators used Friedman's economic theories to justify elimination of protections and regulations that prevented transnational mega corporations from extractively strip-mining smaller countries' economies. The problem is neoliberalism, protecting the wealthy and corporations, is the main economic model that US Congress members embrace— Democrats and Republicans alike. We need regulations to protect all the people. That's an essential function of government and the reason why neoliberals hate government.

Alternate Approaches to Regulations

Marjorie Kelly, author of *Owning Our Future: The Emerging Ownership Revolution*, offers a useful differentiation between regulations, norms, and design. "If there's a certain behavior that you want to eliminate, let's say that you don't want people to go onto railroad tracks when there's a train coming, you can put up a little sign that says don't cross here. That's like a warning sign. It's weak. You can put down a cross bar and add flashing lights, so that's like regulation, to prevent this behavior. But the best way to prevent accidents is to actually design it out of the system. You can build an overpass so the cars just go over the train tracks. Then there's no possibility of having that kind of accident. That's the best possible solution." That's an example of structural change.

Kelly gave an example demonstrating how it's better to shift norms rather than directly confront established rules, "There were people who built innovative buildings that recycled the water, that used renewable energy. They began to create norms around these. There are the LEEDS standards. And it became, 'Wow, I want to build a platinum LEEDS building that's the highest standard.' And it became this kind of race to the top to put up really cool buildings that met LEEDS standards. Eventually New York City said any new buildings built here need to meet LEEDS certification. So you have best practices, you shift the norm, and then the laws come later. That's a good model of how this can be done."

Tim O'Reilly, in his book *WTF? What's the Future and Why It's Up to Us*, observes that more and more digitally oriented corporations are using algorithms to regulate how data and users are handled. Artificial intelligence and big data come together so that algorithms can be tweaked moment-to-moment, based on how the algorithms perform. O'Reilly points out that it can take years to create government regulations and more years to see if they even work, and there's no tweaking or fine tuning included. O'Reilly observes, "There's a great deal for government to learn from the iterative development processes of modern digital organizations." He did point out to me that governments are starting to use big data to drive policy from moment to moment, for example in the case of congestion pricing to regulate traffic in London.

Beyond the Corporation

David C. Korten, the author of *The Great Turning: From Empire to Earth Community*, *When Corporations Rule the World*, and *The Post Corporate World: Life After Capitalism*, told me in our interview, "We need a positive vision. We need to create economies that function more like healthy ecosystems. And the defining feature of healthy ecosystems is not the kind of brutal competition that we associate with Darwinism. It is indeed cooperation, the fact that ecosystems are involved in continuous mutual beneficial exchange, optimizing the use of resources and energy to sustain life. So, if we begin to think about this in terms of economies, we start to think about what some of us call local living economies."

Beyond Capitalism: Worker Cooperatives

Economist Richard Wolff, author of *Democracy at Work: A Cure for Capitalism*, argues that capitalism can't cope with the problems it itself creates, that our "economic system has completely broken down, cannot be fixed. We maybe really have to consider changing our economic system in a fundamental way."

Wolff offers an example of a living, thriving bottom-up economic alternative to capitalism: the Mondragon cooperative, in existence for over fifty years, with co-op businesses in the USA, Canada, Mexico, China, Russia, and India. With sales exceeding $36 billion, if Mondragon were a publicly held company it would be among the Fortune 100.

Wolff enthusiastically describes it this way: "The Mondragon corporation has 85,000 worker-members, plus another 20,000 people they employ in literally hundreds of corporations—co-ops that are merged under this one corporate roof. They produce everything from electric ignitions for cars to stoves and software programs. They have their own university, their own bank. They're a stunning example of the success of a noncapitalist way of organizing production. For example, there are no external shareholders. Ownership is in the hands of those worker co-op members, the 85,000. Once a year, all the workers in each cooperative enterprise have a meeting and the workers decide by majority vote whether or not to retain all the managers, what to pay them, and what corporate policies to change. The workers democratically, together, decide what to produce, how to produce, where to produce, and what to do with the profits. They have a rule: the maximum distance [in salary] between the highest paid worker and the lowest paid worker cannot be—and that's across the board for all of these roughly hundred thousand people—more than six and a half to one."

Instead of a tiny group of people of major shareholders and board of directors making all the decisions, which is the norm in a capitalist corporation, Mondragon has a collective democratic operation in which the workers collectively function as their own board of directors. Americans like to say that the greatest thing that could happen to them in their working lives is they become their own boss. In Mondragon, 85,000 workers have done exactly that.

Wolff states, "This is a different alternative to capitalism. This is not about the government doing everything, not the idea that the government will take over the enterprises and use planning instead of markets, which has been the conventional notion of the socialist alternative to capitalism. Literally nothing captures it better than your phrase, 'bottom-up,' because it's about what happens right there from the floor of the factory, on the floor of the store, on the floor of the office—how the people on a daily level, every day, reorganize their lives so that they are not always doing what other people tell them—that they are the order givers just as much as they are the order takers. These people have a sense of being masters and mistresses of their own destiny in a way that I think would excite most Americans."

Wolff points out that Mondragon has done very well as a non-capitalist enterprise, competing with capitalist enterprises, saying, "We ought to have in this country a program to provide capital and support for cooperative enterprises, organized, run and owned by collectives of workers. And then let's see how the American people react and choose between them and the capitalist tradition."

Imagine if worker co-operatives were funded with tens of billions of dollars in corporate "welfare" as energy and big Agra corporations receive.

Transitioning from Extractive to Generative Economics

Marjorie Kelly says, "The democratic ideals of liberty, justice, and equality remain our ideals. Where are the corollary ideals in the world economy? We really have an economy designed to serve the few. We need an economy designed to serve the many. We democratized politics and government with the American Revolution and the French Revolution and all of the changes since then, but we've never democratized economics. The distribution of wealth and income should be fair. That's a key moral principle of economic democracy. I think that's the next phase of democracy.

"We have a system that is built for a single purpose, extracting financial wealth, no matter the consequences for anybody else. Financial extraction is really the central aim of our economic system and that's the problem. The system is dismantling and flattening all of the protections that we have managed to build since the '30s." Kelly explains, "Because perpetual growth is programmed into the operating system, or DNA of extractive economics, you can't really change this. If you try to barge right in and say, we're going to change the operating system inside corporations, they're going to fight you off. And it's the most well defended territory and the greatest power that has ever existed in the history of the world. What you have to do is build a system with a different logic at its heart. That's what I call the generative economy, an economy designed to generate the conditions for life, to keep us alive and healthy and to serve all of us."

Kelly says, "Every economy is built on a foundation of ownership, assets, and who owns and controls them. When you see that's the name of the game, then we need to start playing that game, and not just talking about, 'let's try to limit the bad behavior of companies.' We need to own and control the companies. It's really that simple."

Kelly observes that there's a huge churn as companies and jobs are created and destroyed—about 15 percent a year. "A new economy is coming into existence all the time. Record companies are gone, newspaper companies are going. You don't charge in and take over companies or have government take them over. But you begin to think how, over time, could we have an ownership transition." Kelly emphasized that ideally, you create an economic ecosystem. "You don't just have an isolated company out there making an isolated investment, you have a whole system of support. There's a prototype of that in Cleveland, the Evergreen Cooperatives, three employee-owned companies, networked together, one in solar installation, an industrial laundry and a greenhouse growing three football fields worth of lettuce, all owned by employees. They're supported in part by purchases from what we call anchor institutions—large nonprofit hospitals and universities."

When many corporations left Cleveland, Kelly noted, "The Cleveland Foundation looked around in inner city Cleveland and [concluded] 'These huge nonprofit hospitals and universities buy 3 billion dollars' worth of stuff every year, almost none of it locally. What if we researched what they're buying and created some employee owned companies attached to those purchasing streams?' So you have support on the buying end, which is huge. You have employees owning it. The companies are networked together. There's a central holding company that supports them and helps finance them, and there's a foundation that helps start them. You're starting to see the ecosystem that can make these things happen. People have come from all over the world to study Evergreen. We *can* create the systems that support the kind of economy that we want."

MAKING ECONOMIC CHANGE HAPPEN

Gar Alperovitz, co-founder of The Democracy Collaborative, assembled a list of measures on which the United States now ranks lowest, or close to lowest, among advanced affluent nations:

- Inequality: 21st out of 21

- Poverty: 21st out of 21

- Life expectancy: 21st out of 21

- Infant mortality: 21st of 21

- Mental health: 18th out of 20

- Maternity leave: 21st out of 21

- Paid annual leave: 20th out of 20

- Material well-being of children: 19th out of 21

- Overall environmental performance: 20th out of 21

- School dropout rates: 14th out of 16

Alperovitz noted, "We come out near the bottom on almost every one of the important indicators. The long trends are getting worse, which tells you not only that something is wrong, but that politics is not working. It's a systemic problem. The system, the corporate capitalism we live with, is itself generating trends that are no longer countered, balanced, or reversed by other political forces."

Alperovitz gives more details: "Because the old system is failing, because things aren't working, people are doing really interesting things that actually change the ownership of wealth." Alperovitz says there are thousands of new developments that change ownership or build on old ownership structures. There are ten thousand worker-owned companies in the United States and 130 million—that's forty percent of Americans—who are members of some kind of co-op: agricultural, electric, rural, food-group, grocery, hardware, credit unions. "Entirely new models—very sophisticated worker-owned companies, both brick-and-mortar and digitally platformed—are popping up. It is systemic in nature. These various models we're talking about begin to suggest a bottom-up democratization slowly emerging."

Alperovitz believes the needed system changes will develop in a way similar to how the New Deal emerged. It didn't just pop up in 1932. For 20-30 years beforehand, states had been experimenting. People were learning, the discontent was growing, and then the crisis of the Great Depression came along. People took innovations developed at the state level and adopted them at a national level. Alperovitz says, "There are things going on all over the country that are building up quietly, and all of them involve 'Who gets to own wealth?'—which is the basis of any system. This is highly decentralized, very American. It's not like Soviet Union State Socialism. It's very down-home, starting at the bottom, very Democratic. It's beginning to sketch the outlines of a different system, based on, not the 400 people owning more wealth than the bottom 185 million, and not the giant corporations, but different forms of owner-ship building from the bottom up."

Chuck Collins and Wealth Inequality

I asked Chuck Collins, senior scholar at the Institute for Policy Studies, coeditor for inequality.org and author of the book *99 to 1: How Wealth Inequality is Wrecking the World and What We Can Do About It*, to describe the problems that extreme wealth inequality produces.

Collins replied, "It definitely undermines our democracy. As wealth concentrates, it undermines economic stability. There's a lot of research showing that too much inequality is bad for your health. It breaks down social cohesion, community connection. It's pretty much bad for everybody, including the very wealthy. When we become too unequal, there's a breakdown in social solidarity and [loss of] the notion we're in the same boat, and [that] what happens to you matters to me."

I asked Collins to comment on the claim that individuals create great wealth. He replied, "That's one of the reigning myths of our culture, I call it the Great Man Theory of wealth creation. It's like saying 'I did it all alone.' The reality is, if somebody has substantial wealth, they didn't do it alone. They live in a society in which we together have made investments that have created a fertile ground for wealth creation."

I asked Collins how ultra-wealth affects culture. He responded, "We now live in kind of a winner-take-all culture where one Taylor Swift song, one Adele song, is all you hear because huge rewards flow to the top. Our whole concept of culture is warped. Culture is what all of us do. Culture is not celebrities. Culture is the music we make together, the theater we create in our communities, the storytelling, the art, and sports is what all of us do, the games we play, the things that we do to better ourselves and deepen our community ties."

I asked Collins, if we could really create a new system, what would it look like. He answered, "We would remember that the most essential things are our human relationships and connections with others and with nature."

Blockchain

Blockchain is a huge, looming, technological and economic development, with Bitcoin being the first example of it. The basic idea of blockchain is that recording of information is done in a bottom-up, decentralized, distributed way. That means that when a record is changed, it is changed everywhere, making record keeping much more resistant to loss or corruption. New applications of blockchain are being created every day.

CHAPTER 8

Bottom-Up Business

CHANGES IN LEADERSHIP, BANKING, INVESTING, BRANDING, MARKETING, AND MANUFACTURING

Bottom-up thinking, relating, and strategies have irreversibly changed the way we do business. Simply doing business through the bottom-up metaphoric filter can make magic happen, and, like the Heisenberg effect, changes people, organizations, and systems. There are an infinite number of ways bottom-up is changing aspects of business. This chapter offers an incomplete but representative sampling.

People apply bottom-up thinking to investing, marketing, sales, data analysis, management, leadership, and banking—so much that goes beyond social media. We'll touch on a sampling of the applications here. Start by considering that just as bottom-up brain processing involves taking in the basic, raw sensory information, bottom-up business must include a lot of listening and paying attention to customers, workers, and potential companies in which to invest. Top-down investing, for example, looks at markets, industries, and big picture elements. Bottom-up investing looks at the details of companies.

When I first met Don Lafferty, he consulted for major publishers on how to use social media to promote books and authors. Now he helps heating and air conditioning (HVAC) contractors and companies use digital tools to sell more systems. I asked Don for his bottom-up philosophy and how it applies to doing business and marketing.

He replied, "Often, I'm translating how the internet works to corporate types who think their message is what matters. How does bottom-up translate to that? I am always trying to get people to listen better, to really talk to the people they want to be in business with, to their base, and use *their* language. Use the words they use. Don't try to force your language down anybody's throat."

Forcing your language on customers is a top-down idea! I asked Lafferty about other top-down marketing mistakes. Lafferty offered, "This idea that when someone comes to your website, the only thing they want to do is talk to you, that the only option you give them is 'contact us,' or 'call us,' or 'fill in this form and we'll call you.' Ninety-seven percent of the time when people come to your website, they are not interested in talking to anybody. They are on their *buyer's journey*, doing discovery, trying to gather information. People hate talking to sales people. The buying process has changed dramatically. The idea that anyone wants to talk to you is preposterous."

The bottom-up approach is to know your typical customer and have answers on your website to their most common questions. Seth Godin wrote a book on *permission marketing*, where people give you permission to provide them with sales information. That's what *inbound marketing* is based on—attracting people to come to you, rather than sending mailers or doing cold calling. It's a bit like soft power, which attracts, as described in chapter five.

Lafferty described this inbound marketing idea, from the buyer's perspective, as the buyer's journey. "There are certain milestones along those journeys. A good seller provides information we need to make smart decisions along the way. Bottom-up philosophy is stop selling people and start teaching them how to be better buyers. The goodwill comes from when that trust-gap gets closed, when all of a sudden, you are the trusted authority and not the salesperson saying 'call me' or 'let's do this deal.' You just keep feeding people information until they reach that spot on the buyer's journey."

As Lafferty said, "The old corporate messaging rules don't apply." He advises us to speak in customer language and fill that buyer's journey. Understand it first. Interview every person who buys something from you. Know how they got to you, what research they did before they found you. Then publish that information on your website. Use loads of endorsements, which Lafferty characterizes as *social proof*, like case studies and reviews, which he describes as "social trust markers like the Better Business Bureau, Angie's list, Yelp, Google reviews."

Lafferty tells us: "These signals of social proof are often the gap closer in the end. If you have bad reviews or no reviews, all things being equal, people are going to choose the company with better reviews or the higher number of positive reviews. Social proof is taking over. When I build a website today, social proof needs to be among the first things people see."

He also uses video tutorials, Instagram, even Pinterest, using images of workers, happy customers, and finished installations, but he starts with the basics, explaining, "I make sure they have a solid website and really good email marketing practices." He says that a website should offer information, maybe a downloadable digital brochure, in exchange for the potential customer's email. Then, the site should have a collection of auto-responder emails that are sent out to answer common customer questions. He explains how the customer will "go to an HVAC contractor website—they will notoriously not have pricing on there. So we send them an email that says most people want to know what these things cost. Click here to learn more. They click on that link and my Hubspot system is in the background, building a digital dossier on this person. Okay, they've downloaded the brochure; now they've looked at the pricing article. If they look at the pricing article, five minutes later they're going to get an email that says, 'Now that you know a little bit of [what] they cost, here's some example installations we've done in your neighborhood.'"

Lafferty added, "Social media is really just the hook at the end of the line. When you reel the person in and you work to get him to the boat, it's not just a one-and-done proposition. Everybody is bombarded by so much information, if you want to become a trusted source of information, you must be prepared to have follow-up, to establish that 'know-like-and-trust' quotient and establish yourself as the trusted expert, trusted adviser. It's not just a simple 'I got them. They clicked on my thing. I win.' No. It's 'they clicked on my thing, they found fifteen seconds of what they wanted, and I made them a promise for thirty seconds more and then they took that,' and then you made them a promise for five minutes more. And that's how you grow that relationship—in these little bites. Based on the buyer's journey that we're accommodating, there may be three things or maybe eight things that I know a buyer needs to know. I know that if they get past the pricing block, and are still opening the emails, it means I am over the pricing hump. I've only got serious people opening emails now. And even if it takes them a year, they'll pick the phone up and finally say 'Thank you for all the emails you sent. It's really kept us informed of our options and we're ready to buy.'"

Lafferty's company offers a membership site for $37 a month, for which members receive: "A community of sharing for HVAC contractors so that a newbie can come in there and ask us a stupid question and get advice from colleagues that are experts. We do conversation starters every week. We have things that we learn in the commission of the work that we do, that we share for free in that community. If I have a great campaign with one of my paid-for contractors, I'll dump it right in my group and say hey, this is what we did, here's the structure of it, here's the link back to an article in our website and how we did it. Go do it."

Membership sites (also discussed in Chapter Four) are a very bottom-up concept. People join for the community, to connect with and learn from other people. Lafferty agreed, saying, "That's the real gold in it. The idea that a contractor going there to pose a question and a scenario and get half a dozen to 30 different opinions on it is tremendously valuable." Lafferty's organization also offers mastermind or mix groups—face-to-face meetings with 5-10 noncompeting colleagues who meet regularly and share ideas, resources, and advice.

Tracking is an essential part of using social media. Lafferty told me he'd earned more income in the past two years than the prior eight, explaining, "I was undercharging. People didn't really understand how to apply value to the nebulous nature of the social media environment." He explained that by using Hubspot to track end-to-end all the marketing efforts he provided to customers, he was able to measure and show results "and draw a direct line to the dollars earned. Hubspot is essentially a measuring stick for all your marketing." Before that, a client would be charged a fee based on hours, for three months services, say $3500, even if the efforts brought in $700,000 in additional sales. Once Hubspot enabled him to show what he'd earned the customer he was able to "to really justify the amount of money that we were charging. These days, I'm getting a fair share of that $700,000 and the contractor doesn't mind paying me because he knows, that without me, he doesn't even have it."

Lafferty summarized some important bottom-up marketing thinking that applies to both business and politics: "Understand who your audience is. Understand how to pick up markers in social media." This goes back to the listening aspect of social media, not the messaging side. "It's the words of the people that you want to talk to that matter. Write your website content and your emails in words that people use and the concepts that they see the world in, if you want to connect with them. If you have the right messages prepared, and you're really good at the listening side, you can spoon-feed people what they want to hear, if you know who to send it to."

Joe Trippi ran, for Howard Dean, the first internet-based national political campaign. Now he does a mix of nonprofit, political and corporate consulting. I asked Trippi, "What are companies and organizations struggling with?"

"Mostly loss of control," he answered. "They're used to having total control communicating anything about the brand."

Trippi is talking about "peer-to-peer"—the everyday communication between people via smartphones, email, text messaging, and blogs. Trippi pointed out, "It's really easy for peers to inform each other what's good, what's bad, what they like, what's not to like. And the usual top-down P.R. and advertising from a corporation is being disrupted by this bottom-up peer-to-peer communication that's not centralized, that they have very little control [over.] A communications department in a company always knew the reporter at the *Wall Street Journal* and at *P.R. Week*, who you needed to call during the launch of a new product to try to get a favorable review. Peer credibility is increasing; top-down credibility is decreasing."

"In the Dean campaign, one of the things we learned is that it's about, if you think about it from a corporate point of view, forming community around the brand and empowering that community to make the brand stronger. We let people form a community around the Dean campaign, and didn't tell them what to do for Howard Dean. We got their input and asked them how they could make us stronger—make us better. And if you think about that from a corporate side of things, to have that from consumers and to actually help empower them to help make them stronger, is how I think you're going to be able to have peer-to-peer messaging that's positive for the company in the long run. Just in the short time between the Dean campaign and today, the power of this communication change has really accelerated and shifted and put even more power in the consumers' hands, in the hands at the bottom, and [it] has become more disruptive."

Trippi summarized it this way:

If the Internet is creating this army of Davids, you have a choice. You can be Goliath, and your brand can be Goliath; or you could be the slingshot, and your brand could be the slingshot for the army of David. One is going to get clobbered by the army of David. The other one—the slingshot—enables and empowers the army of David. Now, if you think about this, the recording industry was Goliath. Apple decided, "No, we're going to be the slingshot. Hey, you army of Davids, we're going to give you iPods; we're going to give you iTunes." The slingshot . . . That's what this whole thing's about. It's to be a slingshot.

THE SHARING ECONOMY: PLATFORMS AND PEERS-INCORPORATED

I asked, Robin Chase, founder of Buzzcar, and before that Zipcar, and who has been included in *Time Magazine*'s annual list of 100 Most Influential People, to tell me about Zipcar and what made it unique. She replied, "We talked to and related with our customers in a way that was very different. For example, the idea of being passive consumers is really passé. Today we see ourselves much more as work producers and work collaborators."

With traditional car rentals you go to a specific car and walk around together and look over the car to make sure there isn't anything wrong. Same when you return the car. Chase explained, "Zipcar fundamentally changed that, by saying, 'We believe most people are good, and we're going to trust and enable you to do a whole bunch of stuff.'" Chase described how Zipcar let people do their own reservations, do the car walk around, fill the gas tank, and return it in good maintenance.

"When we started in 2000, people thought those things were just ridiculous; you could never trust people to do that. Zipcar is really thinking of our customers as members and as collaborators, co-creators of that service. Without individuals doing their part, Zipcar does not exist. And what we see over this last decade more and more is companies understanding that value of customer insight, comments, interactions, and shaping their products and their service. People are physically helping and making the service, in collaboration with a platform, or company that builds a platform for them."

Chase explained that industrialization standardized things and produced economies of scale to drive prices down. Peers Incorporated is this new collaborative partnership that the internet has enabled, that's giving us the best of both worlds to get economies of scale, while delivering all these things that individuals do much better than companies, including a whole bunch more innovation.

Chase differentiated between peer to peer and Peers Incorporated: "Peer-to-peer makes it sound as though it's just person to person. That leaves out a huge amount of what's actually happening and interesting. We would never say that yard sales are the same thing as eBay, or that craft fairs are the same thing as Etsy. They're fundamentally different because Etsy and eBay have the platform for participation. Transaction costs are completely different, and it has standardized these discreet human interactions. What I'm calling Peers Incorporated is something much more powerful—organizational structure that's giving individuals all the power and the benefits of corporations and institutions."

Chase, the author of *Peers Inc.*, gave an example of the power of Peers Incorporated: "The InterContinental Hotel Group is the largest hotel chain. And after sixty years it had 650,000 rooms in a hundred countries. We know this is a hard thing to do." Then she added the kicker, saying, "We know today that in fact they are not the largest hotel. Airbnb, which is doing very much the same thing, with people renting out rooms by the day; and after four years they had the same number of rooms for rent as The InterContinental Hotel Group. And they had it in two hundred countries."

"So, what took the industrialized model sixty years to do, this connection economy, or peers-incorporated company was able to do in four. This peers-incorporated model delivers incredible speed and high growth that you just can't compete with the other way. The company, institution, or government that is creating this platform for participation has made an investment creating this model where [they] can grow so fast, because it's not something that's done serially. Tens of thousands and hundreds of thousands can simultaneously add their stuff onto the platform."

Talking about dealing with climate change, Chase cited Banny Bannerjee's quote, "'You can't solve exponential problems with linear solutions.' Indeed, you can't solve it by building things out the way the InterContinental Hotel did, day-by-day, brick-by-brick. We don't have that kind of time. I do see this peers-incorporated organization structure delivering exactly what is needed, once you get the platform right. So my call to all of us, and to entrepreneurs and to government and to big companies, is for them to start thinking in terms of platforms for participation. And really going after solving these big intractable problems of energy, transportation, education, water, rain forest destruction, using platforms for participation that will let us solve them [at] a much faster pace. I think it's Bill Joy who's credited with saying that we absolutely know there's more smart people outside the room than there are inside the room. The power is with the people and with lots of them. We definitely have to rely on them."

PLATFORM COOPERATIVISM

Platforms can be really powerful and can make a huge difference. But they can also be exploitive, or as Marjorie Kelly says, extractive. Hundreds of thousands, even millions of workers for Amazon's Mechanical Turk, Uber, Upwork, and the big platforms, as Trebor Scholz lists—Yahoo, Google, Amazon, Apple, Microsoft—are sometimes treated like slaves, working for a few dollars a day, unprotected by national laws. Scholz has a better idea—merging the idea of worker cooperative, (like Mandragon, described in Chapter Seven) which is usually based on a brick-and-mortar business with digital platforms. "Platform cooperativism" is a real thing, with over 300 platform cooperatives already operating. Some countries are starting to support them with legislation and even funding.

Scholz offers the following basic principles: communal ownership of platforms and protocols, income security, and good pay for all the people working for the co-op. People working on the platform should have a role in design and decision making and should know what they are working on (gig or piece-workers often don't). Lots more information is at platformcoop.net.

In my conversation with venture capitalist and publisher Tim O'Reilly, he had a few takes that apply to the problems with big platforms. He told me, "There are two lessons from technology. One is it can help people in power extract more from the system and create more power. Microsoft and Google [fit this description]." O'Reilly suggests we ask the question, "Is it supporting an extractive economy or is it a platform for a rich, diverse, bottom-up economy?" He says, "Companies that win the race to become global-scale platforms have to be a fertile ground for everybody else." He shared one of his tech philosophies with me: "The economy and companies flourish when they use technology to do more to make everybody richer, not when they use technology to just to do the same thing more cheaply. Over the long run I think the companies that do more will win."

BOTTOM-UP LEADERSHIP AND MANAGEMENT

My early exploration of bottom-up manifestations in all spheres led me to the writings of Peter Drucker, often described as the founder of modern management. His work with Japanese companies led him to encourage businesses to assign more trust and responsibility to workers—to see them as valuable assets. The Japanese have a concept, Omikoshi, which encourages workers to take their own lead in getting things done. The term is based on the *mikoshi*, a small prayer palanquin/shrine that a group must work together to carry. Reflecting this mikoshi idea, Drucker said, "The leaders who work most effectively, it seems to me, never say 'I.' And that's not because they have trained themselves not to say 'I.' They don't think 'I.' They think 'we,' they think 'team.' They understand [that] their job [is] to make the team function. They accept responsibility and don't sidestep it, but 'we' gets the credit. This is what creates trust, what enables you to get the task done." Drucker also said, "Rank does not confer privilege or give power. It imposes responsibility." Drucker took his insights from Japanese management and brought it to some of the biggest corporations in America.

Even given my strong advocacy for bottom-up approaches, I still believe that top-down leadership plays an essential role. Bottom-up approaches to leadership look and operate differently, encouraging inclusion, participation, and input into planning and decision-making. They're both valuable and essential.

The bottom-up leader provides vision, focus, and discipline, guided by bottom-up values. Some top-down people might see this as weak or indecisive. Actually, it takes *more* confidence and strength to be a bottom-up leader. The strength is supported by and enhanced by the crowd, i.e., participation of others, but it is absolutely personal leadership based on individual character, passion, determination, and drive.

BEYOND A HIERARCHICAL LEADERSHIP METAPHOR TO AN EMERGENT NETWORK METAPHOR

Peggy Holman, the author of *Engaging Emergence, Turning Upheaval into Opportunity*, and the co-author of *The Change Handbook*, asks, "What does leadership look like in a leaderless movement?" She explains, "the principle that scientists probably talk about the most when they talk about emergence is, 'No one's in charge.' The language comes from, essentially, a hierarchical...mindset. You can just as easily say, 'Everyone is in charge.' That's more along the model of thinking in terms of how things get done horizontally. One of the major transitions that we're in is we're moving from our principle organizing metaphor as hierarchy, and thinking in terms of pack animals, to an organizing metaphor around networks. And there you can think more in terms of flocks of birds or ants or bees, or animals that work in the collective."

Report from a Meeting Led with a Bottom-Up Approach

At the Progressive Democrats of America (PDA) conference, leadership is very much about facilitating and encouraging bottom-up participation to get input and to empower and energize the full power and passion of ALL the attendees. In the first session, all of the approximately 50 participants were asked to introduce themselves and tell what they hoped to get out of the meeting. That's unusual with a national organization with so many attendees. The same process was repeated in breakout and single track sessions. Each person was asked for reports on progress locally, such as ideas on how to improve things and problems with the organization. Reports were recorded, summarized, and then fed back to the group—both feedback and feedforward.

Two people who attended the DNC's platform planning discussions reported that the DNC held planned prewritten presentations—totally top-down. Such hierarchical thinking, leadership, and organizational policy are on their way out. Based on archaic conclusions that it is not feasible to include the "we," the "many," in discussions and decision-making, they fail to tap the wisdom of the crowds.

PDA could do even better. Many events designate a Twitter conference hashtag. Some use a digital projector to display tweets by meeting participants, and they will livestream for remote attendees during presentations. Slido allows people attending or livestream watching a conference to post questions to a speaker. Other Slido users can vote up questions so the crowd helps decide which questions have the highest crowd priority. These bottom-up approaches make conferences accessible to people who can't afford the travel and lodging costs.

BOTTOM-UP KNOWLEDGE MANAGEMENT AND LEADERSHIP

I asked Steve Denning, former director of knowledge management (KM) at the World Bank, to explain knowledge management. He replied, "KM began as a movement to systematically enable the sharing of knowledge from people who knew, to people who needed to know, and in the case of the World Bank, sharing knowledge not just with the staff, but sharing knowledge with people all around the world. It's a powerful concept, but at the time when I was trying to introduce it into the World Bank, I couldn't really get anyone to take it seriously until I stumbled upon the power of storytelling."

KM is used at NASA and at many major corporations. The basic idea is that at a company of any size, some employees possess valuable unrecorded knowledge. Lose that person and you lose essential organizational knowledge. The challenge is retrieving and archiving this wisdom so it's available. Denning discovered the way to do it was to get people telling stories and engaging in narratives describing different problems and the way things got done. "You're using story to access people's wisdom and knowledge."

I asked how KM is a bottom-up process. Denning explained that more important than the information collection was "the connections between human beings, the connections of dialogues and conversations about 'Do you know about this?' 'Have you thought about that?' 'What about this other aspect?' It's in those kinds of conversations that knowledge really starts to come alive. And that is really the bottom-up aspect of this. Traditional management with a command and control bureaucracy are based on efficiency and scalable efficiency, and departments and divisions get in the way of those conversations and dialogues between people who know and people who need to know."

Denning, author of *The Leader's Guide to Radical Management*, and *The Age of Agile: How Smart Companies Are Transforming the Way Work Gets Done*, proposes the better approach to management is to get employees to focus on the customers, as he says, "to focus their efforts not on making money for the company or producing widgets, but on delighting clients, on delighting the people for whom they are doing the work. One of the reasons why traditional management has failed is that it's focused on things, whereas this is focused on people—focused on the people who are doing the work and the people for whom the work is being done."

Denning says, "Any standard management textbook says the purpose of an organization is to produce goods and services to make money for the shareholders. The client or the customer doesn't figure in that. And if you look at the practices of traditional management, they flow from that goal of producing things: goods, services, making money…as opposed to delighting clients, and as opposed to focusing the organization and saying, 'Our goal is to delight the people who do business with us.'"

Denning calls for "small groups, in other words, micro-organizations that exist for a short time, almost fractal-like, manifesting in brief iterations." He says these are very resilient and asserts, "It's a people-centered way of running organizations that we need to shift to—the bottom-up way of running organizations."

With his talk about group iterations, I asked Denning if he had intended to echo chaos theory. He replied, "Absolutely. This is a shift from seeing the world as a linear phenomenon to seeing the world as a complex, chaotic phenomenon. The basic assumption of traditional management is the world can be understood, is predictable, is manageable, and we can put in place systems and processes and manage it. That's certainly not true today. The world is going through this massive flux and change in which the future is not predictable. So what we need is a style of management that recognizes the unpredictability and copes with it in a productive way and treats surprise as a benefit, as opportunity, not as something to be eliminated. Traditional management hates surprises because it upsets the whole linear framework. Linear thinking dominates these big organizations."

BOTTOM-UP MONEY: PUBLIC BANKING

Ellen Brown, author of *The Web of Debt: The Shocking Truth About Our Money System, and How We Can Break Free*, could be the world expert on public banking. Forty percent of the world's assets are in public banks, largely in the countries that escaped the 2008-2009 credit crisis: the BRIC countries Brazil, Russia, India, and China, which have 40 percent of the global population. The United States has had one state-owned public bank since the 1920s, in North Dakota, the only state that escaped the credit crisis.

Brown, founder of the Public Banking Institute, says the public bank of North Dakota pays a substantial dividend to the state and funds all sorts of infrastructure development in the state. They partner with the local banks and allow the local banks to take on products that they otherwise couldn't have taken on. They give very low interest loans, such as a 1 percent loan for start-up farmers, and they fund alternative energy. Brown believes that every state should have one. Even counties and cities can set up their own banks.

Brown also believes that too-big-to-fail banks should be nationalized rather than broken up, including the Federal Reserve banks. Reiterating that 40 percent of banks globally are publicly owned, Brown points out, "China, because it owns the banks, can issue the money and the credit. They can determine where it goes; they don't have this parasitic financial sector that's draining 40 percent of profits away from the whole economy."

Walt McCree, director emeritus of the Public Banking Institute and founder of Public Bank Associates adds more details, saying, "A public bank allows the people's money to be put to work for the people as opposed to having public-approved taxes and revenues being sent off to private banks, primarily the ones on Wall Street. The reason that's so important is that cities, counties, and states are running out of money for infrastructure, and they need affordable credit for small businesses, better schools, and a host of other things. The money is hard to get. They have to go to the bond market, to private banks to borrow the money. And by doing that, the cost of our infrastructure projects and other public needs double because the financing costs, typically, amount to an equal amount of the project itself, which is extraordinary."

McCree compared that to working with a public bank: "Take the North Dakota bank for example. In North Dakota if a municipality wants to build a school, the bank there has a mission to serve the public interest in a variety of ways—to be able to partner with the community banks and credit unions to make things happen. If the municipality wants money for a school, instead of going to the bond market and paying say, 3, 4, 5, 7 percent for the bonds that they would borrow, the public bank of North Dakota would give it to them for 2 percent. Just the spread between 2 percent and 4 percent is enormous. But in addition to the cost of the money, it also saves the cost of the other overhead, which is the underwriters and the insurers, and the bond traders and the market interests.

"In North Dakota that 2 percent would not only be a huge savings, but it would be coming back to the people as revenue into the bank, which would be able to make even more loans. So in North Dakota, [what] that looks like, bottom line, is that people save money, taxes are kept down, but the bank makes money. So in North Dakota, in the last ten, twelve years, the bank has spun off a total of $600 million in revenues. That's nontax revenues, meaning money that comes in to the state treasury without people having to pay more for taxes."

To be clear, a public bank does not do direct business with the public. It only does business with other local banks. For example, a local bank might not ordinarily be able to handle a big loan or a project, let's say, to fund a new wing for a school. It can go to a public bank that has more resources and get the help it needs to finance the school's loan or other kinds of local projects—road building, repairs, or infrastructure.

McCree added, "The public bank helps the community bank do the deal by making it either more cost effective or providing the liquidity that's needed by capital investment to enable the community bank to keep that business at home. Now, what is happening from the bottom-up standpoint, which is so important, is that community banks and credit unions are this part of the sinews of the local business economy. Community banks have been disappearing because big banks have been eating their lunch. We've lost thousands in the last ten years. What happens to our community in the bottom-up scale is that local banks are the places you for go for small business lending, for local mortgages, for a variety of other sorts of community credit needs. When they go away, people don't have any place to go for that. Credit is the lifeblood of the economy. And if people can't get it, they go away. In North Dakota, community banks, the private banks, retain 82 percent of money deposited in the state. In other states it's exactly the opposite. The big banks have 82 percent of the deposited money. The community banks have only 18 percent."

This is going to have a massive effect on big bankers. If this happened nationwide—like it already has in India, China, and Japan—and if 88 percent of the people started going with small local bankers, where the money went back to the community, I'm sure that, for starters, the big banks would spend hundreds of millions of dollars trying to block widespread establishment of public banking. This is a bipartisan issue. Democrats, Republicans, even Tea Party people like public banking. McCree explained that it's very conservative in that we're not giving our money away unnecessarily. It's not Washington, and it's not central power, so it's not centralized control. Retaining local control and self-independence and self-reliance are values shared by both political sides.

McCree says, "We're talking about hundreds of millions and billions of dollars per city, billions of dollars per states. This is huge money that could make the difference between raising taxes, having more money for helping people, for infrastructure, education, for Medicare for all. These are the kind of things that can really make a difference."

This is a major game changer for politics as well. When public banking becomes common in major cities, counties, and states and even at a national level, it will take away a lot of power, money, and lobbying funds from these big banks and finance companies and hedge funds. There's a saying that you don't fight these big powerful people head on. You create something that replaces the system. Public banking does replace the system and when you do that, the old system falls and loses its power.

It can happen very quickly. Once one state adopts public banking, other states will see that states with public banks are attracting business because they can give businesses better treatment, better interest rates, better infrastructure, better education, lower taxes, and more favorable treatment. Public banking could domino and explode, just as policy changes happened after legalization of gay marriage and marijuana.

Instead of providing billions in corporate welfare to transnational corporations, national governments should create and use public banks to provide funding to encourage co-ops. They should fund and support research that explores alternatives to businesses getting bigger and more centralized through mergers and acquisitions. And, to prevent "too-big" institutions and support small businesses, states and nations should create legislation and tax structures that provide incentives for staying small and local and dis-incentives for growing too big.

America Is Not Broke author Scott Baker adds that New York City and New York state each have stocks and bonds worth $180 billion. Even if the extra costs in interest are only two percent more when using big banks instead of public banks, we're still talking billions in extra costs. There are trillions of dollars in union accounts and pension funds in the form of corporate stock ownership, that we the people could be using as sources of power. For example, several funds have pulled funds from the Dakota access pipeline. All that bottom-up power is barely tapped.

HOLACRACY—NONHIERARCHICAL ALTERNATIVE TO TOP-DOWN MANAGEMENT

Brian J. Robertson is the author of the book *Holacracy*, which describes a nonhierarchical, distributed bottom-up approach to running a company which gets rid of the top-down patriarchal, parent-child, industrial, predict-and-control authoritarian model of management, replacing it with one that gives power to the process instead of the people. That results in empowering everyone in the organization. Robertson also works with HolacracyOne, which helps companies transition from a top-down hierarchical corporate structure to becoming a Holacracy. Holacracy is the leading edge of a movement that could change the way we think about leadership, management, and how government and organizations work.

Robertson describes one of Holacracy's main goals is to, "find better approaches to run companies where everyone has a voice and yet we can actually let them use the voice to drive meaningful change."

Robertson states, "We go into companies today and it's like we stepped back into the feudal ages. There are kings, barons, and peasants, and we think we need that. Management hierarchies can provide some clarity, some structure, and some alignment. But we've long since learned there are other ways to make sure we're all cooperating effectively together, without having to have feudal lords. We have a framework of rules that allow us to connect and work together, and to not step all over each other's property.

"We see the same thing in nature. The way the human body works, there's no boss cell that tells the others what to do and directs them. Even if we look at an organ, an organ isn't a boss to its cells. The organ doesn't violate the cell membrane, it doesn't reach in and direct the cell on how to structure itself. Rather, what it does is take a cell that has its own autonomy and it integrates it with other cells and deals with the process flows between cells so that they're woven together into a larger functioning organ. That's how nature scales. That's how nature deals with complexity and creates some phenomenally complex adaptive systems.

"Holacracy is a governance system where there's autonomy at every role. Every role in a company has real power, real leadership rights. Then we have teams that also have autonomy that can self-organize, structure their own work and their own processes. Instead of a management hierarchy of people who have the power to direct other people, Holacracy is more about structuring the work than the people. It breaks them down by having functions that have a lot of autonomy and can self-organize, to get the job done. It actually gives you more structure, more order, more clarity, more alignment than you get with a management hierarchy. It just gets there in a very different way that tends to be a lot more flexible and gives more people more voice."

I asked, "Where do autonomy, individualism, the hero, and the heroic leader fit into Holacracy?"

Robertson replied, "It's often the people who have reached a point where they're no longer tied up in having the status title, and wanting to be the boss that directs everyone. They want what's best for the company and its purpose in the world. It's a lot like the parents' journey, leading our children lives by directing them, which we have to do when they're younger. But good parents aren't trying to direct their kids' lives when they're adults. They recognize their journey is to actually make themselves obsolete. They want their children to outgrow them and to not need a heroic boss leader figure, because they can stand on their own. I think the metaphor applies really well to the CEOs job.

"You don't want an organization that's forever dependent on you being a hero, saving the day. If you want an organization that's going to outgrow you and outlast you like we want for our kids, you need an organization that can stand on its own and ultimately that doesn't need any heroic leader at the helm, because the organization itself is self-sufficient—it has all the processes it needs. It has people throughout that are going to step up and lead their pieces of it. It becomes a self-organizing enterprise when you do that well.

"Our culture idolizes these superhero leaders. And it makes the organization addicted to its CEO. And it's no wonder we see skyrocketing CEO pay when we treat them as these superheroes [without whom] the company couldn't possible survive without them at the helm. Imagine if we did that to our kids. Where would our next generation be if we looked at our children that way? Holacracy invites CEOs into a different relationship with their company. Ironically, the last heroic act of that superhero CEO is often to let go of power into a process that will distribute power and hold it better than the CEO will. Kind of like the last heroic act of a monarch might be to adopt a constitution and allow self-organization in society as opposed to top-down autocratic rule.

"In a company that uses the Holacracy constitution, instead of the ultimate power of the company resting with the CEO who's kind of above the law, with Holacracy, the ultimate power rests in a constitutional process which means a document that everyone can go look at. It gives you a law of the land so that the heroic CEO can release power into something other than just total chaos. The CEO can say, 'This rule-set, this is now the rules of the game, how we're going to organize, and I'm bound by the rules just like everyone else.'"

"There's a lot of talk of empowerment in businesses today, but one of the ironies of it is if you need a heroic leader to empower you, you're kind of in a disempowering system. What Holacracy does is allow those empowering leaders to say, you don't even need leaders to empower you anymore, there's a constitution that protects your basic power in this organization," Robertson concluded.

I asked if the Holacracy model might provide an alternative to government as we know it. Robertson answered "I think Holacracy might have some interesting contributions to make when we look at society as a whole. What Holacracy does is give us purpose-driven organizations, whether they're government organizations or private sector. When you're running a company with Holacracy, power ultimately resides with your purpose, not with your investors, if you have them, not with the executive team, not with anyone else, but ultimately it flows from what are we trying to achieve in the world. Which makes the distinction between for-profit, nonprofit, and governmental a lot less meaningful. It's first and foremost a purpose-driven entity."

Close to 1000 different organizations are using Holacracy in some way. Zappos, a billion-dollar company now owned by Amazon, had 1,500 employees at the time that Holocracy was introduced. They actually offered people who were not interested in working within the Holacracy model a three month or more paid leave, and about 14 percent of the people left. Some left for the three-month advance, but some left because they weren't comfortable without the management structure.

I said to Robertson, "You talk about how people have to relax into embracing the power that they get. And some people, having grown up in patriarchal authoritarian families and culture, have a hard time using the power and accepting it." Robertson replied, "Often when people are used to not owning and leading their authority, they're used to turning to a boss to just kind of make sure it's okay. It's a lot like how kids might look to their parents to make sure, 'Is this okay? Am I on the right path?' And then they have to leave home and grow up and be an adult and make their own life decisions. In a patriarchal system [they] continue looking to someone else to take responsibility for their decisions.

"And Holacracy breaks that. You can see it in early meetings after a company adopts this, where you know someone has a hard decision to make and you'll see their eyes naturally go and look to the boss, looking for the approval or the head nod. They're giving up their power and their autonomy to that boss to lead. The job of the Holacracy coach, at that point, is to jump in and say, 'Wait a minute, let's be clear, the boss has no authority here, there is no boss anymore. You have the burden of leadership, you have to make this decision.' And then you see nervous laughter, and you see squirming in their chairs. *It's uncomfortable to really have to step up and lead and own your authority.* And yet what an awesome blessing when kids leave home and grow up and get to be an adult. As uncomfortable as that transition is, I don't think many of us would want to go back. I like being my own sovereign adult in life. And I see the same shift in organizations once people really own that leadership, very few would want to go back to be sheltered by an overprotective boss."

"Are there massive CEO salaries in Holacracy?" I asked.

Robertson said, "It's really hard to justify massive CEO pay when you have a system where everybody is leading their part, and adding more value and being more entrepreneurial; and there is no superhero leader at the top who's looked at as nearly an infallible single point of success or failure for the whole business."

There's a free Holacracy software program, Glassfrog. Robertson describes, "It basically holds the structure of a company and supports [the] governance process that Holacracy adds. I can log in and see exactly what anyone in my organization is accountable for, what authority they have, so it gives you an unprecedented view into the inner structure and workings of the company."

BOTTOM-UP EMPLOYEES

Currently, most employees work when their employer tells them to—a very top-down way of thinking about employment. But that is changing.

Tim O'Reilly argues, in his book, that Uber has created a new kind of "on-demand worker" that I think is pretty bottom-up. Uber's algorithms allow independent workers to offer their driving services when they feel like it, not when the employer tells them to come in. The algorithm is based on customer demand. Workers are paid more when demand is high and "surge" prices are implemented. So workers can choose to jump into the system when consumer demand exists.

O'Reilly also points out that a growing, already large percentage of the workforce is being programmed to work specific schedules based on "scheduling algorithms," which companies use to avoid paying extra benefits, like health care. The scheduling algorithms allow employers to hire more workers so they no longer need full-time employees. O'Reilly argues that we're using an old, bad map and says we need to make a new map that makes it okay to have a flexible continuum of work.

He said, "In order to support that 21st-century marshaling of workers on demand, as needed, we actually need flexible scheduling that empowers workers to figure out when they want to work. We need portable benefits that mean that you don't have some arbitrary distinction that says 'well if you work full-time all the time for one company you get this big level of social benefit, and if you work part-time and on a contingent basis you get a much smaller social safety net or none at all.' We clearly can track if you work five hours here, an hour here, 20 hours here. Everybody pays in, in proportion to what percentage of your income they provide. We already do that for Social Security. We could do it for other social benefits too." This fix would eliminate a glaring benefit externality loophole—avoiding paying any benefits at all to part-time employees—that employers have been able to evade.

BOTTOM-UP MANUFACTURING: 3D PRINTING

Paul Tinari, author of *The JOOM Destiny: Just On Order Making: How 3D Printing Will Revolutionize Your World* and consultant to NASA, the US Navy, and Fortune 500 corporations, explains 3D printing: "The old way to manufacture was to carve out the part or make a mold.

3D printing uses 'additive' manufacturing. It prints objects layer by layer—only putting down material where the object is. Imagine a printer, and you have to give it toner. The toner is fed into the nozzle, and the laser melts the toner onto the page. In 3D printers, the raw material is sintered metal. The laser melts the metal." Tinari says 3D printouts can be as strong as a conventional casting or molding techniques, are more energy efficient, and produce less waste. He says, "Twenty years ago no one had laser printers in their home. Now everyone does. The same thing is going to be true for 3D printers."

Most examples of 3D printing I've seen have been small pieces of plastic. Tinari suggests there's a much bigger future—that cars, battleship parts, even houses can be built using 3D printing, that in not too many years, 3D printers will be printing out plumbing, electrical fixtures, even furniture. He predicts that there will be millions of downloadable open-source or low cost designs, including printable spare parts. People will find a 3D design, download it, and produce it on their printer or a printer at a local 3D service center. How is this bottom-up? Tinari explains, "The ordinary person, in their own home can design their own product. People are empowered to create stuff. Human creativity is being democratized."

Tinari described how the Navy will use 3D printing. When a naval task force goes out to sea they need to bring along about 20 million spare parts. Absence of a spare part can threaten the mission. 3D printing would allow you to go sea with no spare parts. Now they go to sea with a computer system where all the spare parts are stored so they can print out large parts, even in titanium; for example, a replacement aileron.

Extrapolating, I observed that there's talk of a one-way trip to Mars. They could bring 3D printers and make things that weren't even invented before they left. Thinking of Star Trek's food replicators, I asked about food and 3D printing. Tinari detailed, "Food can be printed just like any other material. You start with a stem cell from an animal and program it to become the target muscle. Eventually it will be a much more efficient way to produce food than farming."

BOTTOM-UP AND TOP-DOWN ENERGY

Most energy is generated using top-down approaches. We drill for gas and oil, process them in multi-billion dollar refineries, and then transport them by potentially ecologically disastrous means—pipelines that leak, rail cars that derail. Coal is burned at massive electricity generation plants. Nuclear energy is produced by multi-billion dollar nuclear plants like those in Fukushima and Chernobyl. The grid today is mostly top-down—a classic one-to-many system.

Bottom-up energy generation does not depend upon a centralized grid, which makes it more resilient. In less developed places, like Africa, where a massive centralized infrastructure is not in place, mini-grids and decentralized energy systems are more affordable and sustainable.

When I asked Jeremy Heimans how New Power will change things, he said, "The emergence of decentralized distributed energy, means people are able to make their own energy using the solar panels on their roofs and sell it back into the grid, so it is a world in which one of the classic Old Power institutions, the utility, becomes less important, and we make and sell our own energy."

Rooftop solar panels are supplying over 20 percent of Germany's energy. Local water power has a long history going back hundreds, if not thousands of years. Wind power can be small and local. Hybrid automobiles generate and then use electricity.

Top-down forces are pushing back against bottom-up energy. For example, big energy companies lobbied successfully to pass an Oklahoma bill, which required people adding solar panels to their homes and connecting them to the grid to pay a fee. Top-down power holders may throw up obstacles, but the bottom-up energy revolution is inevitable.

BOTTOM-UP VERSUS TOP-DOWN FOOD AND FARMING

I got an early start one morning, doing a few hours of farm labor weeding, and squishing beetles on broccoli plants (it's an organic farm.) Afterward I chatted with John, the farmer who runs the CSA (Community Supported Agriculture) farm and asked him how bottom-up thinking applies to farming.

He replied that on Earth, life begins with soil. There is more bio-mass, like bacteria and fungus, in the soil, below the surface, than above, "even including elephants." John explained that organic, small farmers work with the living things below the surface, for fertilizer for growing. Big, top-down, mono-culture—growing one crop, in some cases for a whole nation—are factory farms that kill everything below the surface with things like methyl bromide and then add chemical fertilizers like phosphoric potassium nitrate. Then they spray to kill weeds and bugs. Organic farmers plant ground cover plants. They take the approach that things start below the surface of the soil, and then they add cover plants, then seedlings, then crops. People who are part of the CSA and a few paid workers, usually students or farmers in training, do the planting, weeding, and harvesting. The harvested food goes to local community members with a stake in the farm. This bottom-up approach to farming is small, local, and good for the environment.

The top-down approach harvests with big machines and then moves produce by truck and train thousands of miles away. We need to start asking how we can move the big corporations to start seeing with bottom-up eyes to find bottom-up solutions that are good for the earth and healthier. There's a lot of gasoline in food that's been transported a thousand miles. The eat-local movement—locavore—is growing by leaps and bounds. You can make a difference. Ask local restaurants and grocery stores to carry local food, preferably organic. Or join a local food co-op or CSA.

Bottom-up approaches can be applied to an almost infinite range of business approaches and practices. Hopefully this chapter will get you to see all aspects of your business with new, bottom-up eyes.

CHAPTER 9

Bottom-Up Personal

VALUES, HAPPINESS, CHOICES ABOUT
RELATIONSHIPS, SUCCESS, INTELLIGENCE, HEALTH,
SPIRITUALITY, AND COMMUNITY

Your top-down and bottom-up filters powerfully affect the ways you interact with people and with your community, your feelings, your spirituality, and life experiences. Understanding and balancing them can help you expand your options and choices, enabling you to live a happier, deeper, more meaningful, and connected life.

If you're over-stressed, you can't appreciate the good things that give you a sense of well-being and moments of happiness and positive experience. This means you need to start from the bottom up, maintaining the basics of wellness, like eating right, sleeping well, and being physically fit and relaxed.

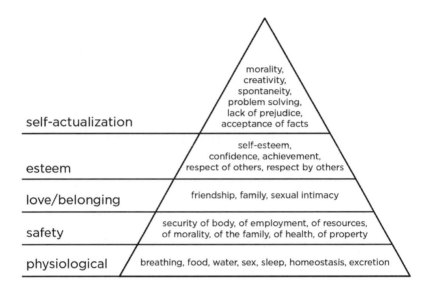

Our Hierarchy of Needs based on Maslow's theory

I spent over 35 years working in the world of stress management, biofeedback, meditation, and behavioral medicine. One of the simplest bottom-up "tools" you can acquire and routinely use is the ability to quiet yourself—mentally, emotionally, and physiologically. That creates a clear, blank slate, so you can paint beautiful pictures for your life. Maslow's hierarchy starts from the basics at the bottom and builds new levels of stability and inner and outer resources that enable you to enjoy your highest potentials for functioning—emotionally, spiritually, creatively, productively.

Top-down approaches to happiness tend to be based on what societies or cultures say should produce happiness—acquiring power, influence, consumer products, passively experienced entertainment, and wealth.

Bottom-up happiness is built upon experiences and the behaviors and ways of seeing, relating, and reacting, which produce them.

A number of years ago, I created a guided relaxation recording with psychiatrist Keith Sedlacek. I discovered that when people with anxiety, stress, or pain simply recalled heartwarming experiences, their physiology, as measured by my biofeedback equipment, would move towards healthier levels, and they started to feel better. Fascinated, I started experimenting, asking clients, students, and workshop participants to remember their "heartwarmers."

Heartwarmers give you a warm glow inside, sometimes a chill, and, sometimes, sweet tears. I've collected thousands of heartwarming and positive experience anecdotes. Most of them involve people experiencing love, closeness, growth, beauty, sharing, insight, or healing. Starting in 1985 I began presenting workshops on Positivity Training and Positive Emotional Self- Regulation Training (before Positive Psychology existed) where I collected thousands of people's positive experience and heartwarmer anecdotes. I put together a list of categories of positive experience—the Kall Positive Experience Inventory, or KPEI.

Not everyone experiences heartwarmers. Researcher Avram Goldstein found that only half the population experienced chills up the back of their necks listening to rousing music. Goldstein also found that Naloxone, the drug that blocks opiates, also blocked the chills up the neck normally experienced by the music listeners. He assumed that there was an endorphin connection to that "frisson" experience.

After six or seven years of studying the phenomenon, collecting data, and reviewing the responses and descriptions I'd accumulated in my work, I developed my Anatomy of Positive Experience model. It is based on the idea that positive experiences and the good feelings associated with them are the basic building blocks of our ability to face adversity, embrace challenges, to love, and be happy. I've presented this idea to at least a thousand psychologists, psychiatrists, and therapists, and literally 99.9 percent agreed. Given that assumption, the next logical step is to build skills for having more, better, deeper, stronger positive experiences and for integrating them into your life. It doesn't get any more bottom-up than this. You build your capacity for happiness, love, and strength by connecting to the world through positive experiences, mostly experiences connected with other people.

POSITIVE EXPERIENCE (PE) ANATOMY

You have the most advanced, and most powerful, multisensory positive experience (PE) system known to exist. But it didn't come with an operating manual. You didn't learn it in school. You can learn how to get the most out of your PE system. Many research studies have proven that you can learn to magnify your enjoyment of the moment and the intensity of your good feelings. Your actions and behaviors may change the shape, size, and functioning of different parts of your brain. The absence of such actions can cause those parts of the brain to atrophy, leading to changes that affect other major parts of the body, so you may lose the capacity for enjoyment and pleasure that came with your "original equipment." If you develop and use your PE skills to make powerful emotional PEs happen, you insure your continued ability to have them.

To understand all the positive states of happiness, positive attitudes, the positive emotions, and self-esteem, it helps to know positive experience anatomy. You can start mastering your PE control system by exploring the details of PE's phases and elements; their biological, behavioral, and social aspects; their integration into your memory and self; and their effects upon perceptions, attitude, and everyday life. The same basic concepts I discussed in depth in Chapter Two on the anatomy of connecting apply to positive experiences. Here is is a brief re-cap.

A Brief Outline of the Anatomy of Positive Experience

1. Be prepared for PEs mentally and physically. Be relaxed and comfortable about feeling and expressing strong positive emotions. Maintain healthy habits, positive attitude, and self-talk so you have robust positive emotional reflexes and lots of bounce and energy to make the most of PE opportunities whenever they appear—either planned or unexpected.

2. Plan, schedule, research, and anticipate PEs—not just on vacations or weekend evenings—but throughout each day of the week. Study your own behavior patterns, your inner and outer resources, and your environment to build a PE knowledge-base that helps

you zoom in on PE opportunities, planned or unexpected, and schedule challenges for fun, pleasure, and good deeds.

3. Recognize, identify, initiate, and embrace your PE opportunities. Sharpen your skills for recognizing positive experience opportunities and initiating them most effectively. Develop a positive attitude that expects to find and seeks out positive experience opportunities.

4. Intensify and prolong the positive experience. Increase its complexity, extend its length, and enrich its sensory, emotional, social, and spiritual content to make the PE more meaningful and memorable.

5. Encode it to memory: Store the PE (in your brain or on paper, audio, video, smart phone, or computer) for integration into your memory, your view of yourself, and your relationship with the world. Do a post PE stretch to etch the experience even more solidly into your memory.

6. Use the PE later: Transplant the feelings to new situations. Clone it, strengthen your self-esteem and positive attitude, face adversity with strength and equanimity, and brighten your happiness.

Embrace, Don't Define.

Jon Kabat Zinn's book *Wherever You Go There You Are* starts the idea rolling. Whatever you have, that's what is, good or bad. So embrace it, because it is part of you and you are part of it anyway. When you face a challenge, you may have a culturally ingrained top-down urge to label and define and categorize or control it. But you can let go of those filtering processors and shift from repelling to attracting, from extracting to interconnecting. It takes practice to start seeing with bottom-up eyes and heart. It's a matter of inhibiting top-down filters and reflexes, and replacing them with their bottom-up counterparts.

BOTTOM-UP PROBLEM SOLVING AND WE THINKING

When you tackle a problem or challenge, your tendency may be to think about what YOU can do. How much time do YOU have. What resources, experience, energy, money, and knowledge do YOU have to bring to the project?

When you take a bottom-up approach, you'll want to also think about how you can tap the rest of the universe. Remember, you are an integral part of the universe. So open your imagination as wide as you can, shifting from an "I" to a "we" mindframe.

If you are planning a project, expand your expectations of how it will be accomplished to include other people. If you don't let people know, they can't help. Use social media and more traditional means to make them aware of the project. Give them an opportunity to opt in, to decide whether or not they want to help.

Some people are raised with a top-down mindset that resists asking for help, to have a goal to be totally self-sufficient, to consider seeking help as dependency or weakness, and to feel ashamed asking for it. The bottom-up world is different. There, people want to help and be helped. They seek out ways to assist others because being cooperative and inter-dependent is the natural way, which gives real satisfaction.

There's an African word, Ubuntu, which offers a bottom-up way of thinking. Ubuntu means that a person is defined by other people and is part of a greater whole, and belongs to a community, even to a world of people. Ubuntu means that when one person is treated badly, we are all diminished. It means that your humanity is irreversibly, deeply, systemically connected to mine.

It can take some practice to let go of the need to be totally self-sufficient. We're all in this together and can help each other. This applies to seeking and accepting help. Open yourself up. Trust.

TRUST

If you are going to open yourself to others' help, it's essential to increase your trust, your faith in people, and your faith in the bottom-up etched into humanity. This isn't easy. Change your comfort level at which you've dealt with the world and let go, maybe even a lot. It has worked for me.

ValaAfshar @ValaAfshar, Chief Digital Evangelist @Salesforce sent out a tweet listing eleven ways to earn trust that makes a lot of sense:

1 don't lie or exaggerate
2 don't speak poorly behind others back
3 deliver on promises
4 do not manipulate
5 share the credit
6 do not point fingers
7 do not spread rumors
8 show vulnerability
9 trust others first
10 give without expecting get
11 share intent

But also know how to recognize and defend against top-down minded predatory psychopaths, sociopaths, and narcissists.

Develop your Radar for Negative Top-down Values and Behavior.

You may want to avoid organizations with excessive top-down characteristics, such as secretive, nontransparent, authoritarian, big, centralized, hierarchical, and closed to feedback. They may be out of balance, archaic, nondemocratic, and nonresponsive. And if you meet somebody who is patriarchal and authoritarian or narcissistic and self-centered, then you might consider whether you want to connect with the person.

Understand People in your Life who Demonstrate Top-down Approaches.

There are people who see and think in top-down ways at your work, in your social, religious, and cultural environments. There are people in your personal life who think using top-down filters that affect their expectations of how you behave. The more you understand the top-down approach to seeing and doing, the more effective you can be at communicating and connecting.

Deal with Top-down Thinking the Workplace.

If you are an employee working for someone born before 1980, that person probably thinks about doing business in a top-down way. That can make it difficult for you to get approval for bottom-up approaches and strategies. These approaches can scare top-down thinkers for a number of reasons:

- Letting go of control

- Delegating or sharing authority

- Opening up to more input, getting feedback

- Becoming more transparent

- Interacting more

- Creating a space for conversation

- Seeking feedback

- Inviting people your organization has relationships with to create content

- Connecting with and supporting the creation of related groups

- Creating a public voice, often in the form of a blog and Facebook and Twitter presences

This is a partial list, but any of these approaches can scare, intimidate, or make top-down thinking people nervous, leading to them saying no to or resist projects that you know will be good for the organization.

There are a few factors that underlie top-down people's resistance:

- Control: People in charge are accustomed to tight control. Bottom-up organizations develop a looser, more relaxed, trusting culture.

- Resistance to cooperation and interdependence.

- Fear of taking responsibility instead of being told what to do.

Engage in some Bottom-up Rethinking of Success, Winning, Leadership, and Being on Top.

From a bottom-up perspective, the top is NOT necessarily desirable. Ego can be valuable. Some amount of self-interest and pride can be motivating. If you ARE so good that you've risen to the top of an endeavor, a bottom-up perspective will lead you to feel a sense of responsibility to bring other people with you, closer to the top or ahead of you, to share the rewards.

Consider extreme accumulation and holding on to domination, things, money or power as an emotional disorder, like hoarding or fecal retention. A healthy member of the human community shares and is fully aware of his multitude of connections, responsibilities, and obligations to others, to community, culture, and ecosystems.

Critics who are advocates for neoliberal economics, individualism, and the self-centered way of existing described by Ayn Rand—may characterize this idea as socialist or communist. But it is bottom-up, systemic, connected, networked, biological, ecological, integral, organic, and sustainable. Elizabeth Warren has said you don't become successful on your own.

The healthy way to become successful and manifest success is to be explicitly and transparently conscious of how you will share your good fortune, acumen, primacy, and wealth as it grows. You don't create your achievements on your own. You become wealthy or powerful because of your wise, creative use of the human, bio-system, cultural, infrastructure, and economic resources at your disposal. Therefore, you have an obligation to share the fruits of your success.

We need a science of tracking the connections—Noam Chomsky described them to me as externalities—which directly or indirectly contribute to successes. Simply tracking those externality costs, like the way Hubspot tracks sales, will reduce some wealth, as they are paid back. But tracking the other success connective factors will assure that, as the successful person benefits, other people who also helped will also benefit. It is fair, intelligent cooperation, connection, sharing, and interdependence. We have a long way to go from our entrenched elite system built upon routine theft of commons resources and externalities. Riane Eisler, in her work advocating for partnership over domination, emphasizes that caring work—parenting, nurturing, and community work are all of great value, but usually left out of most economic considerations. That must change, especially as we move to a future where billions are made jobless by automation and artificial intelligence. Eisler argues that giving a minimum guaranteed income should include a responsibility to perform some kind of meaningful caring work.

Humanity has been better at sharing for most of our existence, than we've been since the onset of civilization and industrialization. Bringing back a level of sharing and no-boundaries connection that exceeds humanity's past levels will be a challenge. But it's do-able and probably essential if earth is to survive, as we know it, especially without wiping out massive swathes of biodiversity. Unfortunately there will be many people who cannot tolerate this new world's values. It could take generations. It brings to mind how Moses kept the Israelites in the desert for two generations, until they were ready to enter the Promised Land, because the old generation, unable to accept the new paradigm, had to die off.

BOTTOM-UP INTELLIGENCE: A NEW CATEGORY AMONG THE KNOWN MULTIPLE INTELLIGENCES?

Years ago Harvard Psychologist Howard Gardner introduced a revolutionary idea—that that there are different kinds of intelligence. I asked him to summarize his model. He replied:

"Thirty years ago I published a book about multiple intelligences called *Frames of Mind.* I was critiquing the notion that there's just a single continuum of smart to average to dumb and if a person is smart in one thing he or she should be smart in everything and if they're not smart in one thing they're going to be dumb in everything, and the Theory of Multiple Intelligences claims that human beings have several rather independent forms of thinking.

"When we talk about intelligence we usually mean people who do well in school, and that's fine, but it's certain kinds of intelligences. It doesn't predict who is going to be good in the workplace, who is going to be entrepreneurial, who is going to be artistic, who is going to be mechanical, etc. That idea has become pretty well known in education now."

I asked him to list the different kinds of intelligence he has identified. He replied, "Linguistic intelligence, logical intelligence, musical intelligence, spatial intelligence, bodily intelligence, and two kinds of humanly related intelligence: inter-understanding of others, and intra-understanding of yourself. Since then I've officially anointed another intelligence which I call the naturalist intelligence, that's the capacity to make significant distinctions in the world of nature between one plant and another, one animal and another, one cloud configuration and so on . . . It's important to say that people have different kinds of minds, they have different strengths, and my list is a good, opening list."

I believe bottom-up intelligence is re-emerging as a new kind of intelligence based on connection consciousness and desire for and tolerance of diversity, differences, justice, fairness, inclusion, sharing, participation, interdependence, empathy, and democracy. Darcia Narvaez describes a kind of social, ecological imagination that I consider to be a kind of intelligence, somewhat related to Gardner's naturalist intelligence. Compared to most Westerners, I'd say that indigenous peoples are geniuses in this form of intelligence.

ARE APPS PRODUCING AN APP GENERATION?

I interviewed Howard Gardner with Katie Davis, who co-authored the book, *The App Generation: How Today's Youth Navigate Identity, Intimacy, and Imagination in a Digital Word.* I've already introduced Dr. Gardner. Katie Davis is assistant professor University of Washington Information School where she teaches the role of Digital Media Technologies in Adolescents' Lives.

I asked Gardner to tell a story which demonstrated the ideas in *The App Generation.* He replied, "Something that made me realize how different it is to grow up today than it was half a century ago is that, nowadays, many kids have never gotten lost. Not only have they got a device that gets carried with them that has many different kinds of maps and routes they can pull up, but many of them have parents who are monitoring where they are and who can get in touch with them at all times—helicopter parents. Doing a contrast with my generation, we used to go away to college or go abroad, and you might contact your parents once a week or once a month. . . Not only do many kids not have the sensation of getting lost or being distanced, but this is also a metaphor for how many kids nowadays think about their lives. Katie and I came up with this notion of the super app. An app is basically a convenient way to get something done online. You want to know where to go and eat or how to get somewhere, or you want to check on the status of something or somebody.

"The tendency now is to see your life as a set of apps, one after another. You have to go to a certain school, take certain courses, have certain majors, have certain internships, and then when you graduate school you have to get a certain kind of job. You can't plan your whole life, at least not yet. Kids are very risk averse, that is, they don't want to stick their neck out unless they're told it's okay to do so. They can be in for a very demoralizing experience when the super app doesn't work out, when the job doesn't work out. So this notion that just as the individual app is quick and efficient and gets you where you want to go, if you think about life like this, this can be very risky in the sense that if you've never faced risk, when finally, something doesn't work out, you really don't know what to do."

Davis added, "We open up our final chapter with a quote from Alfred North Whitehead, the philosopher, who observes that civilization advances by extending the number of operations we can perform without thinking about them. At first that sounds like a good thing. The more we can outsource and automate our tasks the better, right? That makes life a lot easier. But if you take that to its logical conclusion, all of a sudden we've given up a whole lot of our agency. And I think there's a danger if we are outsourcing all of our decisions, all of our actions, and experiences to apps, and having them dictate our course of life for us."

I asked them to describe how "agency" applies to apps.

Davis replied, "I've been thinking a lot about this lately because when I'm looking for a restaurant, either in my neighborhood or when I'm visiting a new place, I rely on Yelp to give me suggestions, and if I'm trying to find my way I use Google Maps, and it's hard to say that that is not a good thing. It makes my decision-making process a lot easier, and I don't really have to think about where I'm going ahead of time, I just sort of allow Google to take me there in the moment. It sounds good, but what am I giving up? Am I losing part of my decision-making capacity and my agency to chart my own path? Because Yelp is not going to give me all of the restaurants in my area, so it's framing my experience in a very specific way, and if I'm not thinking about that, then all of the sudden, if I add apps like that, one on top of the other, my whole experience of my life is being framed in a particular way that I haven't really chosen myself."

Gardner chimed in, "Katie, do you want to say something about App Dependence and App Enablement. It may convey the difference between Yelp as a friend and Yelp as a dictator."

Davis added, "A major tension that we've identified in our book is this distinction between App Enabling and App Dependence. If we can use technology, and apps in particular, as springboards or entry points into our experiences, and then know when to put them away and chart our own path, that is an example of using apps, and more broadly, the technology of today in an enabling way, just to get us going. But if we become dependent and reliant on apps to make our decisions for us, if we look to them first before we look inside ourselves in terms of showing us where we should be going, what sorts of experiences we should be having, who we should be interacting with, then we say that's using apps and technology in an app-dependent way. One is more agential, and the other one you're giving up your agency."

Doctor Gardner raised the issues of empathy and relationships, observing, "When I grew up in the middle of the last century, I had a few good friends and that's all I ever had, but that was enough and we got to know each other very well. Now, people have thousands of friends and they spend a lot of time deciding about adding and then de-friending when they've been insulted in some way or the other. It's totally different when you have to maintain relations with many, many people. It's inevitably going to be superficial. One of the shocking statistics from a Pew study said that a decade or two ago, when people were asked how many people they really felt they could trust when they had a deep, personal, sensitive issue, the mean answer was three. Then, when this was repeated a year ago, the mean answer was two. It's a third less, and it's quite troubling, because what does it mean if you have a thousand friends, so to speak, but there are only two people whom you feel that you can trust? And of course this is what empathy is about, feeling other people's pain and their love and wanting to help and believing that they can help you, and they can be trusted not to post something or drop you right away. So these are things . . . which we say we better pay a lot of attention to. We need to be aware that we're losing things that are important, things that we value."

I responded that I wondered whether apps feed into or worsen attachment disorder. Gardner replied, "On the one hand, we're connected all the time when we connect with many, many people and yet at the same time, Sherry [Turkle], is making the claim that that's not a genuine, deep attachment. It's transactional, the opposite of deep and transformative."

Davis added, "One of our findings [was] that parents [are] increasingly keeping tabs on their kids for longer and longer and more and more throughout young people's lives, at least in Western society. Part of growing up means getting a sense of autonomy from one's parents. But it's very hard to do when your parents are texting you and you start texting your parents at college. There's evidence that young people either text or call their parents on average thirteen times a week. When Howard and I went to college that was a time when we were striking off on our own and didn't have that much contact with our parents."

"You're talking about a loss of individuation," I noted, adding, "One of the biggest parts of becoming an adult is going through, becoming an individual and separating from the parents. The whole Oedipal conflict is a rejection of the parents to become your own self, really."

"I think you're right," Gardner agreed, "It used to be when we talked about identity formation, which takes place in the latter part of adolescence, people would try out different identities. It was called identity exploration and it was seen as being a positive thing because you don't want to have a premature closure on being a certain kind of person in a certain kind of outfit, both physical outfit and more psychological outfit. When the digital media first came to the fore, experts like Sherry Turkle speculated that this would be a time for wonderful identity exploration where in games and communication you could try out many different kinds of things, and end up with a more robust identity because you hadn't just put on the first mask.

"But with the advent of social media, exactly the opposite has happened. There's tremendous pressure to develop your brand, as Katie says, very early, to be a certain kind of person to broadcast that to other people and, of course, it's difficult to change it because you've already kind of made your chess move and you're stuck with it. So, rather than having a full blown integrated identity which makes sense to you and to your surroundings, you may be pushed in to a premature form of identity where individuation is much less pronounced.

"You are more tied in to the relationships you have with family, and not a chance to re-invent yourself as something which makes sense for today and for the life that you're going to be living. The work that Katie and I have done, in what we call, 'The Good Project,' [explores] what it means to be a good worker, a good citizen, a good participant and so on, I am personally very worried that that kind of selflessness, that kind of empathy may be an endangered species, though I would love to be wrong" said Gardner.

"At the end of the day we have to become our own agents and the question is, do we remain in the driver seat when it comes to technology of any sort or do we turn it over willingly or let's say naively to somebody else's notion of what our lives should be."

"Wrapping up," I said, "It sounds like you're talking about app-consciousness, you've got to transcend the apps almost." Gardner answered, "We use the word app-transcending in the book. I take Steve Jobs as my example here, for Steve Jobs probably has more to do with apps than any other person on the planet and yet it's unthinkable that he would ever let his own life be influenced by an app that somebody else created. He created himself and did amazing things."

THE HERO'S JOURNEY OF CHANGE AND REBIRTH: TAPPING BOTTOM-UP POWER

Paulo Freire, author of *Pedagogy of the Oppressed,* tells us that for people to wake up to oppression and begin resisting it, they must go through a rebirth which creates a new form of existence. Freire says they can't stay the way they were.

You can learn a lot studying the patterns of the hero's journey, which I described in detail in Chapter Three. Keep in mind that the hero's journey actually describes how we go through the sometimes-challenging process of personal growth. Overall, it is a rebirth process where you find yourself reinventing yourself from the bottom up.

BOTTOM-UP GROWTH, TRANSFORMATION, TRANSCENDENCE

Most of the important, pivotal, emergent life moments happen when you are bottom-up connected to people or nature. There are many ways to expand your connection consciousness, simultaneously connecting in many ways to all the good you can. It's a kind of unconditional love for nature, family, community, ecosystem, or God, making it even better for you. Or, if you're an atheist, you can love all you can consciously connect with.

In many meditative and other consciousness raising practices, part of the work aims to dissolve boundaries, to be aware of or awaken to a multiplicity of connections. Connection consciousness adds consciousness of relationships and patterns. As you develop your personal connection consciousness, you'll want to be around people who also have connection consciousness, where you'll receive as a part of the ecosystem and network other's empathy, compassion, and love and embrace truth and transparency.

How do you build your connection consciousness? Think about the way you would like to be in terms of connection consciousness. How often would you like to be in face-to-face contact with people, to walk in nature? How much time do you want to spend with family, friends, and community or with top-down jerks?

I know from my 35 years working in the world of positive psychology that connecting is one of the best ways to initiate/begin a positive experience or to intensify or deepen one. Make eye contact, touch, talk, and sing. Make positive sounds—oohs, ahs, etc. When people share good feelings, they are magnified. There's magic in that sharing, as I've observed at my talks and workshops. Here's a thought. At Occupy Wall Street, if someone wanted to talk to the crowd, they'd shout "Mic Check" and other people would echo their words, so the crowd could hear what they were saying through the crowd's echo/magnification chamber. A mic check is used to communicate words. Why not have a crowd or group share positive emotions—enthusiasm, joy, empathy, and happiness—to initiate and participate in different positive emotion sharings.

BOTTOM-UP AND TOP-DOWN RESPONSIBILITY

Western health care has created a top-down, dependent mindset. While drugs produce incredible cures, there is a down side. People now believe their doctor can provide a pill to solve any problem and they feel only a doctor can help them heal. Because of malpractice concerns, doctors now feel the need to take over the full responsibility for the patient's health to defend against lawsuits.

Edward Tenner, in his book *Why Things Bite Back*, cites from Ivan Illich's book, *Medical Nemesis*, "Medical bureaucracy creates ill-health by increasing stress, by multiplying disabling dependence, by generating new, painful needs, by lowering the levels of tolerance for discomfort or pain, by reducing the leeway that people are wont to concede to an individual when he suffers, and by abolishing the right to self-care." That was written in 1976, long before managed care had the temerity to tell doctors that therapy other than pharmaceutical was unacceptable for depression and other disorders. Tenner asks, "Have the public and private insurance plans of the industrial world eroded responsibility and rewarded sickness?"

Self-responsibility approaches to health have many faces, including nutrition, exercise, lifestyle, work style, and thought style. They are barely given lip service by the prevailing medical model. James Gordon, in his book *Manifesto for a New Medicine*, writes, "If anyone had come up with a new drug that doubled the life of women with metastatic breast cancer, every oncologist in America would have had his or her prescription pad ready; when David Spiegel demonstrated that support groups could make this kind of difference, his work hardly made a wave on the surface of orthodox medical practice."

RELIGION AND SPIRITUALITY: BOTTOM-UP AND TOP-DOWN

When people get together and gather to share prayer and faith without a leader, that's bottom-up behavior. When a priest, rabbi, or mullah runs a ceremony in a religious building using prayers in a book that were decreed to be THE prayers to read, that's top-down. When you read prayers that glorify God as a supreme being that speak God's almighty power, that's top-down. Prayers that connect with and respect nature are bottom-up.

I believe that we are all part of God and all one, that our perception of separateness is a matter of lack of connection consciousness. So I seek in MY prayer meditation to, as Ken Wilber describes in his book *No Boundaries*, "remember" that I am connected, as part of the universe, to let go of boundaries in my mind that separate me from everything. Then, I start repeating to myself, a kind of mantra: *I, you, we, all, one*— attempting to forget the artificial separations and boundaries I've created that keep me from being conscious of my connection to everything else in the Universe.

The prayer meditation takes me to all kinds of different states of awareness of oneness and connection:

A beach, where I am conscious of being one of billions of grains of sand.

I visualize myself as one of billions, even trillions of organisms all creating a symphony of breathing together.

Being an animal, like a bird in a flock, or a worm, in an acre of soil with millions of other worms.

Being the sky.

One theme of these meditations seems to be that all the meditations take me to a consciousness that is not about being human. Being a part of everything transcends one species.

Some religions posit that humans are better than all other life forms. I don't believe the founders of those religions would support that. Maslow wrote about how visionary founders of religions often have their teachings distorted by those who institutionalize the faith.

Fritjof Capra told me, "It is very important to distinguish between *spirituality* and *religion*. The original meaning of spirit, from the Latin *spiritus,* means breath and its meaning is the breath of life. The Latin word for soul, *anima*, is also related to breath. So, spirit or soul are really the breath of life, and our spiritual moments are the moments when we feel most alive. This spiritual experience, wherever it happens and whatever culture and whatever historical period, has some very distinct common characteristics: the experience of unity of mind and body, of self and the world, of belonging to a larger world and being integrated in it. Religion is the organization of mystical or spiritual experiences into institutions. And what happened very often in history was that these institutions then became institutions of power where the spiritual core was forgotten. So then we can have religion without spirituality, and this is also what we call fundamentalist religion, where religious texts like the Bible or the Koran or the Buddhist and Hindu texts are interpreted literally, without realizing that these writers who were mystics used metaphors and symbols to express their experience."

There are many religions which claim that they came directly from God. You can't get more top-down than that. But generally, a person who is not famous, not special, not from the elite has originally envisioned and founded those religions. Even Buddha, while he came from wealth, abandoned that wealth to walk the world before bringing the world his teachings. Abraham threw out all the idols—the manifestations of top-down old gods—and replaced them with his one god—a god existing in all people and things—the ultimate bottom-up.

MOST RELIGIONS OFFER BOTTOM-UP OPTIONS

Jews join together, without a rabbi, to form a Chavurah, with congregants fulfilling many of the roles of a full-time rabbi.

Within Islam, Tablighi Jamaat is a bottom-up approach that Wikipedia reports: "Primarily aims at . . . working at the grass roots level, reaching out to Muslims across all social and economic spectra to bring them closer to Islam." A top-down Islamic approach, called a *"Khilafat or Caliphate,"* might be one where there is a supreme cleric, like the Ayatollah in Iran.

Christian Churches have lay persons leading home study and prayer groups. The top-down opposite might be a mega church with a very authoritarian pastor or the Catholic Church, with its infallible Pontiff and incredibly powerful cardinals and bishops. But even the Catholic Church is opening to some of the more bottom-up approaches.

Subsidiarity: Pope Francis basically says the future of freedom requires a spirit of bottom-up.
He didn't say it directly. He used the word "subsidiarity" when he said, in a speech to the US Congress, "Building a future of freedom requires love of the common good and cooperation in a spirit of subsidiarity and

solidarity." Subsidiarity nails the idea of bottom-up. Wikipedia tells us:

> **Subsidiarity** is an organizing principle that matters ought to be handled by the smallest, lowest or least centralized competent authority. Political decisions should be taken at a local level if possible, rather than by a central authority. The *Oxford English Dictionary* defines subsidiarity as the idea that a central authority should have a subsidiary function, performing only those tasks which cannot be performed effectively at a more immediate or local level."

Bottom-Up Christianity

Daniel Fazzina is a minister who answers his calling through his show, Divine Intervention Radio (found at Divineintervention.typepad.com). I asked him to describe bottom-up aspects of religion, spirituality and spiritual experience.

Daniel replied, "When Jesus came, the religious people of his day were what he had a problem with. He was teaching people, 'Look, you don't have to listen to a religious leader in order to have a connection with God. You can have that on your own. You can talk to God directly.' And this whole movement sprung up from the ground up."

There are tens of millions of people practicing in their homes outside of the usual church hierarchy. Even within some churches, they're creating community and this bottom-up religious experience, where the church coordinates and organizes circles of community members praying in each other's homes, for example. Fazzina pointed out, "We've lost our sense of community in many ways. But in the churches, I've found that if you're just going to church once a week on Sunday, and you're just staring at the back of the head of the person in front of you, it's really hard to develop relationships. In a home group fellowship that would meet weekly, people come together, they share food with each other, they share ideas, fellowship, commune, they study the Bible, and pray together. It really provides a sense of community."

Later in our interview, Fazzina said, "We serve a God." That inspired me to challenge him. "I don't think I serve God. I think I'm part of God, and God is part of everything. And so, I have a problem with the word serve. How do you respond to that?" I asked.

Fazzina replied, "Jesus told his disciples, 'If you want to be great, you're going to have to serve one another. You're going to have to love one another.' He got down on His hands and knees, and washed the feet of the disciples, and this was a huge lesson for them, because just before this, they were arguing about who was going to be the greatest when Jesus comes into His Kingdom, into His power, and He was like, 'Look guys, you don't get it. I came not to be served, I came to serve.' Jesus said, 'If you do the least of these things, unto these least of my brothers, you do it unto me.' So, if you're giving food to the hungry, if you're feeding the hungry, if you're clothing the naked, if you're visiting people in prison, Jesus said, 'You're doing that to me,' and that's what I mean by, We serve a God' . . . just loving each other. We're all God's children, so when we serve each other, we're in effect serving God, because we're made in His image. That's what I believe."

Whatever faith you practice, consider exploring the ways it can be lived, explained and experienced from a bottom-up values perspective.

BUILDING BOTTOM-UP COMMUNITY VS. TOP-DOWN MARKET FORCES AND SUBURBIA

John McKnight and Peter Block, co-authors of the book *Abundant Community: Awakening the Power of Families and Neighborhoods,* offer a valuable bottom-up approach to reclaiming community, characterizing two basic ways of living—as a Consumer or as a Citizen.

McKnight explained, "Living life as consumers, we can never be satisfied because there's never enough. That's the purpose of a consumer society, to always get you to think you need more. That kind of dissatisfaction leads to a life that we don't really want to lead. The alternative is a life that is satisfying; and much of the life that is satisfying will come mainly from the things that we do together outside of the market, outside of the world of buying things. We have given too much of our life away to the idea that institutions can provide a good life; and in giving that away, we have vacated the space in which we can make a good life. The good life we can make is very possible because what makes a good life is abundant: It's not scarce like things in the marketplace are.

"A consumer believes that a good life is produced by somebody else, that when they produce it and we buy it, we have a good life. The opposite of that is a citizen—somebody who acts in ways to create with their neighbors a good life. That's how our society was created, by all kinds of groups of people coming together around all kinds of purposes and celebrations and creative activities that made this society. Our society was not made by universities and corporations. It was made by active, productive people, and they are the people that we call citizens. A citizen is somebody who has two powers: the power to envision a future, and the power to join with their neighbors to create that future."

I noted that they say in their book, "People start things and then managers and organizations and companies take over," and that these systems, these companies and academic institutions, and governments, and professionals, they say to us, "You are inadequate, incompetent, problematic or broken. We will fix you. Go back to sleep."

McKnight replied, "Yes, and the citizen says, 'That's nonsense, if I do that we won't have a democracy, we won't have a community and we won't have a satisfying life. So those are all siren songs for how to not be a citizen."

Block added, "When that siren is played, saying, 'I will take over, I will provide. I will raise your child, take care of your elderly, heal your wounds.' The consumer says, 'Thank you very much,' or they complain that you haven't done it well enough. So you get a culture of entitlement. It says, 'Well, you promised me satisfaction, and what you're marketing is dissatisfaction, because every time I purchase something, I need another one.' The economic belief system we have now is 'Grow or die.' Most of our development is trying to export our culture to other places. And it's a colonial process. As soon as you decide to scale matters, then you look for replicability, that somehow we become standardized. We lose our uniqueness. Diversity isn't about race; diversity is about living in a world not of like-minded people. And what it does is it steals our humanity. This is a methodology by which we can restore our humanity."

McKnight added, "There's a pretty clear measure. When a scale is larger with a group of people than the number of people where everybody knows each other's name and uniqueness, beyond that scale, you are beginning to institutionalize things. You will have to assign to somebody else the knowledge about your members and let them become central, and as they become central, the staff develops, the institution grows. Beyond a certain scale, you lose the essential nature of the power of our diversity and relationships, and you begin to see the institution- alization and the market use of relationships."

McKnight described the difference between service and care: "Care is abundant. There is no limit to the care that we can have for each other on our block, but there is a limit on the amount of service that can be brought into our block, because it is produced by a system in an economy of scarcity. So, I can live in a block where we care for our seniors, or I can pay for a service and send them away to be stored in a home. And I don't know of anybody who says, 'Gee, I hope when I grow old that I can be in a nursing home, because they'll really care for me there.' That's service. There's a huge difference, in this sense, between the abundance of care and the scarcity of service."

Block added: "The question is, 'Do I have enough?' Or 'Do I need more?' This is, at every level, a spiritual question. It's a 'things' question. The [consumer's] assumption is, 'I am not enough.' The civilian assump- tion is, 'I have everything, really, that I need, even if I am poor.'"

I noted that their book describes "A consumer is one who has surrendered to others the power to provide what is essential for a full and satisfied life. This act of surrender goes by many names: client, patient, student, audience, fan, shopper—all customers, not citizens. Consumerism is not about shopping, but about the transformation of citizens into consumers." It's about giving up who they are, really. That sounds like Gardner's and Davis's description of loss of agency.

McKnight pointed out, "In the broadest political sense, every tyranny allows people to be a consumer. . . . What you can't do in a tyranny is act together with your neighbors to be the definer, producer of the future and of the society. The real distinction of a democratic society has nothing to do with what you can buy in the marketplace; it has all to do with your power to define and produce the future."

McKnight added, "The consumer systems have become warm and loving, but infantilizing." That's another way that self-responsibility is undermined.

I said to McKnight, you write "Until the 20th century every society in all of history raised its children in villages. The basic idea was that children became effective grownups by being connected with community adults in their productive roles."

John replied, "We have so many neighborhoods where there is no real human economy around the kids. They have to go to a place that's totally manufactured, totally artificial—a mall, to see it. Or in urban neighborhoods where the economy has collapsed, there's nothing at all to see. So the experience of the economy is lost. And that then leads another institution, school and university to say, 'We are the only avenue for you to enter the economy. You need to invest 18 years of your life and then you can enter the economy.'"

They write, "So, if we don't know our neighbors, aren't active in local community life, pay for others to raise our children and service our elders and try to buy our way into a good life, we pay a larger price. We produce, unintentional as it might be, a weak family, a careless community, and a nation that tries hopelessly to revive itself from the top-down."

THE THREE BASIC TOOLS OF THE ABUNDANT COMMUNITY

McKnight and Block offer, "There are three basic tools that we have. They are abundant and they are everywhere and they are the basic building blocks for the recovery of the power of citizens and community. The most important place to begin would be to find out what are those skills, gifts, capacities, and abilities, and what is the willingness of people to share and to teach that?

"The second tool is what we call 'The basic power of association.' Association is the word for a group of citizens. So, every time we connect any of these gifts, knowledge, skills, and abilities to other adults and to young people, we're using our power of association to multiply our gifts and capacities and then to begin to fulfill functions that haven't been fulfilled before. We begin to say, 'This is what we're doing to raise our children.' This is what we're doing to begin to produce as much food as we can locally. We begin to see that those are all possibilities for us when we get connected in all kinds of associational forms.

"The third thing that we have is hospitality—the ability to welcome everybody, all of their gifts and capacities, and to be welcoming to people on the outside, because one downside of small communities is that they can be awfully parochial and exclusionary; and so the third capacity we have locally is the welcoming of strangers. A really powerful community is one that says, 'Hey, come on in, we want to show you who we are.' A weak community is one that is the reverse, that says, 'Hey! We don't want you to come in here, we're fearful of you.'"

Those are the three abundant capacities that exist in every community, the three building blocks. They are simple: you don't need grants, you don't need technical assistance to begin to move in that direction, and the steps that you can take when you recognize those three abundant capacities are outlined on our website, at "How to Begin."

Their book describes connectors, the people who actually make the connections and identify the gifts of the members of the community. McKnight fleshed the idea out; ". . . there is no block that doesn't have people with connective capacities. So in a sense, the way you really get things moving is to recognize those people's special skill . . . to begin to encourage, authorize, incentivize them, to take their natural talent and apply it to the connective tissue in the local neighborhood; the gifts, skills, capacities, and abilities and teaching knowledge of the local people. Once the connector helps us identify that there are four people on this block who are musicians or have musical talents, and lets them know that they can start a band. There are six people here who have gardens and twelve people who want to learn how to garden. Then you're creating, out of the connector, connected people around common interests that will make a difference in the satisfaction in our lives. We can see possibilities by connecting that we never saw before. The ready-made connector begins that process. It multiplies itself."

"What if you're not connected to a community?" I asked. "How do you get started?" The answer, they replied, is to find a neighbor and start talking, connecting to other neighbors. "Emphasis on children is often one of the best beginnings," McKnight advised.

BOTTOM-UP AND TOP-DOWN HEALTH CARE

There are top-down and bottom-up ways of approaching health.

McKnight offers a powerful perspective on health care. "In terms of our health, that system, what we buy from doctors and hospitals, probably accounts for 10–15 percent of our health status. 85 to 90 percent of what keeps us well and keeps us with a life lived as long as we ought to be alive has to do with what we do, how we live our daily lives together; how we design our physical environment, how we use our land. Those are the things that make the big difference in terms of health."

I asked Fritjof Capra about the systems approach to health and health care. He referred to Descartes' mechanistic approach, saying, "Descartes said a healthy body is like a well-functioning clock and an unhealthy body is like a clock that doesn't work. A certain piece is faulty and has to be fixed or replaced. That's been the approach of mechanistic medicine; to concentrate on small parts of the body; forgetting the whole over the parts. The systems view of health sees health, in terms of processes and relationships, as a state of dynamic balance that involves various parts of the organism and the relationship of the entire organism to its social and natural environment. When you see health as an experience of well-being, as a consequence of the organism's functioning in a balanced way, then that also includes the self-organization of the organism and its ability to find a path back to a balanced way when it has become unbalanced. This notion is present in many traditional systems of health, the notion of natural healing forces; that the organism can heal itself and the idea that the doctor or therapist is an assistant or an attendant to these natural healing forces. The root meaning of 'therapist' [is] the Greek verb '*therapeuein*' to assist or attend."

When he refers to traditional forms of healing, he's talking about nonscientific, indigenous kinds.

Physician Rishi Manchanda describes a related bottom-up health approach, Upstream Medicine. His Ted Talk discusses "upstream" things that affect your health, like a water polluting factory, mold in your walls, environment-related allergies. The treatment might be moving to a new location or stopping the water pollution, or suing a landlord to fix moldy walls. The "upstreamist" idea is to create systems that find patterns and identify and prevent the sources of problems, not just treat the symptoms.

TOP-DOWN AND BOTTOM-UP PSYCHIATRY

Bonnie Burstow, author of *Psychiatry and the Business of Madness* and associate professor at the University of Toronto, sees psychiatry as a very top-down field, saying, "The history of people taking control over the so-called mad has been one tyranny after another. The entire direction of putting things in the hands of the state, as opposed to empowering the community to solve problems together, is a gross misstep."

Burstow told me how, in the early history of psychiatry, "there was dunking people in cold water, rotating people in chairs, opium, bleeding. There was also genital mutilation. Don't forget they thought madness was being caused by masturbation. It's horrible, but no more horrible than what we have now. The reality is if you go back, that happened to very few people. Whereas now people are brain damaged for life, massively, by huge, huge numbers. If you go to nursing homes, I would say that 90 percent of senior citizens are on psychiatric drugs after a certain age. Antipsychotics and antidepressants are the most major drugs."

She argues that there's no biological basis for any of the psychiatric drugs in use and claims psychiatric drugs not only don't work, but longitudinal studies have shown that people who get off the drugs do better than those who stay on, and people who never take them do best because psychiatric drugs often cause long-term or permanent brain imbalances or irreversible brain damage.

A 2014 study found almost 80 million people in the US take psychiatric medications—almost seven million take antipsychotics and over eight million children, five million of them on ADD drugs. Some nations don't even use an ADD diagnosis. Thom Hartmann, author of *Attention Deficit Disorder: A Different Perception*, sees ADD as a difference, not a disorder, that ADD-ers are like hunters in a farmer's world, that fidgeting or mind-wandering kids are okay.

John Taylor Gatto, a revolutionary educator who won teacher of the year for New York City and New York State talks about how a lot of education is about dumbing down the brain, preparing obedient workers and soldiers. Between education and psychiatry, and let's throw in the boob tube, addictive video games, alcohol, and recreational drugs, it's almost like this dumbing down or mental impairment seems to be a systematic, intentional goal of consumer culture.

Burstow says, "When you dumb down, as you put it, people are more controlled and more orderly. But even more significant for the psychiatric empire, you have grown your field—more and more absolute repeat customers." She's referring to the mega-billion dollar pharmaceutical industry, which she suggests is part of the political system. She argues, "The fact that the state is involved with it, this is particularly problematic. The state funds psychiatry. The state, beyond funding psychiatry is the foundation of psychiatry's power. Psychiatry can lock people up on the basis of putative mental illnesses because the state says it can. Psychiatry is underpinned by the laws of the state."

And it gets worse. In some authoritarian nations, psychiatry is used to control, even institutionalize dissidents. Burstow says, "In fact all of psychiatry ultimately is political. Psychiatry is a regime of ruling that captures people up in its net in country after country, and which is empowered by the state in country after country."

Burstow advocates instead of prescribing psychiatric medications, to help people with community support and cooperation. Studies have shown that countries that take the community approach have better success. But, she opines, "It's done less and less in other cultures because psychiatry is colonizing those other cultures bit by bit by bit." And worse, she adds, "The World Bank and the International Monetary Fund, both push psychiatry," and, if "you're in desperate need of money, they'll only give you money if you take up the mental health template of the West." I just read a tweet claiming that the group lobbying the most bills in Congress is the Pharma industry.

I asked Burstow to talk about cultures that deal with mental illness through community support, such as indigenous cultures. She answered, "There's a problem, and the elder is consulted, and other people are consulted, and then there is a circle and people come around in a circle and try to figure out together what's going on here—what are everyone's needs here and how do we solve this? To me those are humane, decent ways of attending to the conundrums within a community." She's not proposing something that's been untested and untried. It's the way it was before psychiatry, for most of human existence.

I spent a couple years working in an inpatient unit and outpatient emergency facility, where people would be brought in hallucinating and delusional, some literally wiping their excrement on the walls. Drugs and electroshock helped them. Unfortunately for much of the world, families and communities no longer have the resources to use the social support approach Burstow advocates. But as we return to bottom-up psychiatry, psychiatric medicating of such huge proportions of the population should not be on the table.

Next, let's talk about child rearing and education. Darcia Narvaez, who I've mentioned numerous times, has written several books on child-rearing that could be characterized as bottom-up approaches. They focus on healthy attachment, meaning strong deep relationships and respecting the child, not engaging in domination. Her blog Moral Landscapes is well worth getting to know if you are a parent or grandparent.

Education, for most people, is top-down and patriarchal and has been characterized as designed to prepare students to be docile, unquestioning soldiers and factory workers. Paulo Freire, in his best-selling revolutionary book, *Pedagogy of the Oppressed*, says liberation is done by education which enables people to become more fully human, but Freire makes it clear that there are different kinds of education and only unoppressive education can work. Freire characterizes oppressive education as the "banking model," in which information is deposited into the student—that is, by didactic memorization. Sounds very top-down to me.

Freire characterizes good education as teaching people how to think, how to ask questions, and how to engage with ideas and each other.

True liberating education is bottom-up and involves teaching how to think, how to ask questions, how to see for one's self, and how to engage in conversations in order to tap the power of dialogue. A bottom-up approach treats students and teachers as equals and aims to empower free spirits who ask questions and challenge top-down rules as part of their responsibility. And it deeply involves parents, who in today's top-down culture have handed much of their parental responsibility over to schools.

Darcia Narvaez offers her vision of child rearing, parenting, and the idea of a human nest, and she discusses her issues with how it is done today:

"How does one group come to believe and act as if they alone should live on the earth? In early life, when neurobiological, social, and moral foundations are being established, the continuum of feeling one with Life, with mothers and others, bonded to the fabric of life and embedded in natural processes, is critical. No other animal intentionally breaks that continuum, introducing toxic stress. In modern societies like the USA, there is a massive break, intentional detachment between mother and child, often forced by laws and authorities, beginning with hospital birth practices.

"What happens with a broken continuum? Do this to other animals, even separating a newborn from its mother for an hour a day after birth, and you get abnormality later. This is the result of the toxic stress of breaking the continuum of a species-typical upbringing.

"Like all animals, humans have an evolved nest for their young. It's much more intensive and lengthy. Humans are more sensitive than other animals because they are massively influenced by their postnatal experience, more epigenetically shaped than their hominid cousins. The evolved nest includes soothing birth, extensive breastfeeding, responsive care, plenty of affection (and no punishment), multiple adult-responsive caregivers, free play, and positive social support. When these are not provided, it represents a broken continuum of support, and we should not be surprised that various psychopathologies result.

"Lack of nest provision means the evolved trajectory for the development of human nature is also broken. Instead, the child becomes insecure and unconfident in self, parents, and the world. Such a child will look like they need adult guidance to grow. They will look and be dysregulated, which again, adults will interpret as 'the way babies are' and use coercion to shape them differently. The child will forever after be ruled by external forces because the development of an internal compass was broken early on by the ignorance of the adult caregivers. The child will learn to seek hierarchy because it provides a scaffolding for living life with some feeling of security. Self-protective aggression or withdrawal will be at the ready if the script is challenged. The personal narrative the child develops is one of deep flaws and so will forever seek relief through cultural narratives that assure safety (and dominance).

"In contrast, species-typical human development is apparent in cultures that maintain our prehistory ways of living (small-band hunter-gatherers), in which the human genus existed for 99 percent of its presence on the earth. They provide the evolved nest and show egalitarian relational attunement with others (including other-than-humans) and use their imaginations for communal ends that include the welfare of the biocommunity (plants, animals, rivers, forests). They live contentedly and sustainably (many for thousands if not tens of thousands of years). This is our human heritage. The evolved nest is critical for restoring human nature to its earth-centric origins."

Henry Giroux, McMaster University Professor for Scholarship in the Public Interest and The Paulo Freire Distinguished Scholar in Critical Pedagogy says, "Critical pedagogy has long argued that teaching and learning support classroom relations in which students learn how to narrate themselves, engage in dialogue with other students, and learn how to hold power accountable. A critical pedagogy rejects treating students as consumers and believes that they should learn how to be cultural producers. In this instance such a pedagogy is committed to expanding their imagination, sense of agency, and capacity for civic courage. In short, pedagogy must start from the bottom up, from the experiences and voices that people inhabit, in order to make learning meaningful in order to make it critical and transformative."

Last but not least, when it comes to education, one of the worst ideas we've seen is the profoundly top-down "No Child Left Behind" approach which forces schools and teachers to implement centrally designed programs. Teaching should be a bottom-up process where teachers engage with students to help them learn how to learn and how to think. It is reasonable for a culture, at a more central level, to set some goals in terms of what citizens should learn and have knowledge in, but the process of education should be a local one.

Visions for the Future

POSITIVE BOTTOM-UP APPROACHES TO CULTURAL

CHALLENGES, DANGERS, AND THREATS

"Why the Only Future Worth Building Includes Everyone."
—POPE FRANCIS, TITLE OF HIS 2017 TED TALK

THE FUTURE OF BOTTOM-UP APPROACHES TO OUR LIVES

After a long rise in the stock market, there's inevitably an adjustment. There's a sell-off and stocks prices find a new balance. After civilization and Western industrial culture, is it time for an adjustment? I think so. Civilization and industrial culture brought many advances, but there was a price—slavery, hierarchy, patriarchy, domination, community-destroying centralization and globalization, and authoritarian governments and laws.

As the internet, smart phones, open source, and texting continue to reawaken humanity's bottom-up epigenetic potential, we're seeing a fractal increase in democratization at all levels of culture and government. We're seeing the new technologies enable new ways for people, companies, organizations, and nations to connect and collectively cooperate, as Clay Shirky and Anne Marie Slaughter have described. The new tools have shifted the power balance in the world, as Joseph Nye has described, so now, individuals and groups have much more power and they have greater chance for their voices to be heard.

But this is a battle. There are people, groups, and forces that want to keep things the top-down way they were. Old white men, the ultrawealthy, authoritarians in power, as dictators, military, government, and religious leaders, big corporations and the people and companies that work for them will fight to keep the existing system and sociocultural structures. They will use all the bottom-up resources and tools they can to keep their wealth and power. That will include killing net neutrality, throttling the internet, ending media consolidation regulations, ending all kinds of regulations that protect people, workers, nature, the environment, free speech, the press, journalists, and human rights. They will do it using bottom-up language, claiming they are protecting liberty and protecting traditions and values.

It will be very important for people to wake up to the bottom-up power that they have access to and for them to tap it to protect the new rights, powers, and freedoms. Or these will be taken away and lost. This is the battle that is going on right now. It is a battle that must be fought at all levels, but I believe that the bottom-up movement and revolution has its greatest power starting at the bottom, locally. It's important to have big picture goals and visions, but the bottom-up connection, revolution will be won by fighting locally, by becoming active and connected in many ways in your community.

If we are moving towards a more bottom-up world with a more bottom-up way of being, how will things look down the road? I've put together a list of some of the ways that the re-emergence of bottom-up epigenetic factors and our embrace of bottom-up will, hopefully, positively affect our culture, people, and relationships.

- Values: Absence of bottom-up connection consciousness will be considered as unattractive and offensive as bigotry, killing elephants, or other human and animal rights abuses.

- Externalities, good or bad, are included in economic assessments and cost analyses.

- Bottom-up economics is embraced for big-ticket funding, so money must be disbursed bottom-up through individuals and small businesses instead of top-down in one clump to big banks.

- SMALL is serious investment in research and building networks of small business as the desired alternative to big and bigger business. Funding is made available for research on keeping businesses small.

- BIG is legislatively discouraged or stopped, including estates, billionaires, and mergers and acquisitions. Legislation makes it more profitable to stay small and network.

- The economics profession is shamed into waking up to embracing economic models that include workers, families, externalities, and bottom-up values instead of the white tower academic model the field of economics currently embraces. In other words, no more counting the number of faeries on the heads of economic pins.

- Globalization is changed to make helping citizens, communities, and small businesses, instead of transnational corporations the priority.

- The profession of economics stops focusing on counting faeries on the head of a pin and starts dealing with real economics that include people, jobs, communities, workers, and nature.

- Arts and sciences start doing a lot more crowdsourcing and work more systematically.

- Platform cooperatives—user owned—begin to flourish and compete with the giant platforms (Facebook, Google, Amazon, Apple,

Microsoft, Uber, AirBNB, Yahoo) and help organize, coordinate, and empower the workers for the biggest corporations.

- Government at all levels is re-assessed and restructured to embrace bottom-up values and principles.

- All operations in government, business, and organizations are routinely evaluated to identify ways that more bottom-up approaches can be implemented to make them more democratic, fair, and balanced. Bottom-up scoring systems will be created so that big organizations and operations can be publicly evaluated to show how top-down versus bottom-up they are.

- Bottom-up will become its own academic and scientific field, with its own advanced degrees, fields of study, conferences, journals, stories, and heroes, just like psychology, history, sociology, economics, and political science.

- Collective cooperative work and approaches will develop a collection of language terms and framing that goes far beyond the top-down, negatively framed characterizations that are currently dominant, such as communism and socialism.

- New bottom-up ways to do business will continue to emerge—ways that produce trillions in new businesses.

- Anti-top-down values, regulations, and laws will continue to emerge and promulgate, gradually eroding and taking away excessive power from the ultra-wealthy and giant corporations, thus handing more power to the people. This will hopefully include making it illegal to be a billionaire, plus strong laws to end the existence of multigenerational billionaire dynasties that produce children born on third base.

THE BATTLE TO ACHIEVE BOTTOM-UP VALUES AND SYSTEMS

Some of these changes are already well under way. But there is a long way to go and the old ways of top-down, hierarchical powers and systems will expend incredible efforts to protect their power and old systems. When I say incredible efforts, I mean trillions of dollars and millions of lives. I believe the transition from top-down to bottom-up, from vertical to horizontal, is inevitable. But the process will not be easy. It will come at a great price.

Top-down power holders and their economic, political, and military mercenaries will kill millions of people and crush millions, even billions, of lives in their efforts to hold on to what they have and grab more. As this battle unfolds, tens of thousands of life forms will go extinct. The planet will be put at risk. But bottom-up humanity WILL prevail.

My hope is that this book has inspired you to embrace your bottom-up genetic heritage. I hope you'll use the ideas and apply them to business, work, organizations, relationships, diplomacy, and change so that you find deeper connections and meanings in your life and so that your work and your business contribute to making the world a better, more balanced place.

How do you, personally, do this? Start connecting more with people and nature. Call out unjust or wrong top-down practices, behaviors, or even rituals. Start living more locally and make extra efforts to build and support your local community. Share this book and the ideas it proposes. You don't have to be an evangelist, but start pointing out connections to other people to raise their bottom-up connection consciousness. If you have a business or a brand, brag about your bottom-up efforts and policies. People will be attracted to them.

Finally, have courage, have trust, and give love, compassion, and care, with a daring and creative imagination. These will not only be a gift to those who receive them, they will also nurture your inner self and make you a stronger, better person more able to be loved and to love. They are, perhaps, the most powerful of the soft powers.

Appendix

Most of the people quoted in this book were guests on my Rob Kall Bottom-Up Radio Show. It used to be broadcast on WNJC radio and more recently it has been syndicated on Pacifica Radio and Progressive Radio Network. Past shows are also available on iTunes, SoundCloud. com, stitcher.com and at my community blog site, OpEdNews.com/ podcasts. A few of the people quoted were interviewed with the intent of using the interview for the book. And a few quotes came from phone and email conversations—often a combination of both.

The interviews are available at OpEdNews.com/podcasts.

Introduction

Kucinich, Dennis, and Rob Kall. "Dennis Kucinich Interview Jan." 31 Jan. 2013.

Newmark, Craig, and Rob Kall. "Craig Newmark of Craigslist.com on Breaking Through Government, Secrecy, Building Trust, Transparency." 18 Mar. 2010.

Shirky, Clay, and Rob Kall. "Clay Shirky; Social Media Visionary." 17 June 2011.

Chapter 1

Narvaez, Darcia, and Rob Kall. "Darcia Narvaez; Morality's Evolutional, Neurobiological, Bottom up Underpinnings." 15 Apr. 2016.

Bolen, Jean Shinoda, and Rob Kall. "Archetypal, Mythic Strong Women and Patriarchy—A Conversation with Jean Shinoda Bolen." 22 Sept. 2014.

Joyce, Kathryn, and Rob Kall. "Kathryn Joyce—Covering the Extreme Right Christian World." 1 Jan. 2015.

Kimmel, Michael, and Rob Kall. "Why Are White Men Angry? Rob Kall Interviews Author Michael Kimmel." 31 May 2017.

Quinn, Daniel, and Rob Kall. "Daniel Quinn, Author of Ishmael, on Invisible Success and Memes We Live By." 11 Apr. 2013.

Jensen, Derrick, and Rob Kall. "Derek Jensen Debunks the Human Supremacy Myth." 12 Feb. 2010.

Greenwald, Glenn. "Glenn Greenwald; With Liberty and Justice for Some... and How the Occupy Movement Could Change Things." 1 Nov. 2011.

Goldbard, Arlene, and Rob Kall. "Arlene Goldbard: Art and Story as Activism, Awakener, and Change Catalyst." 17 Apr. 2014.

Scott, James, and Rob Kall. "James C. Scott Domination, Resistance, Anarchy and the Scientific Study of Underdogs." 16 May 2014.

Stryker, Deena, and Rob Kall. "Deena Stryker, on Her Conversations with Fidel, Che and More." 16 June 2016.

Zinn, Howard, and Rob Kall. "Howard Zinn and Dorothy Fadiman." 12 Feb. 2010.

Steele, Robert. "Former Spy Robert Steele—Critiquing US Intell Agencies and on Open Source Everything." 1 Aug. 2014.

Mele, Nicco, and Rob Kall. "Nicco Mele: The End of Big—How the Internet Makes David the New Goliath." 28 June 2013.

Burstow, Bonnie, and Rob Kall. "Bonnie Burstow—The Dangers of State Empowered Psychiatry and Psychiatric Drugs and Treatments." 3 Jan. 2016.

Flaccavento, Anthony, and Rob Kall. "Bottom Up, Local Economics with Anthon Flaccavento." 4 Aug. 2017.

Swanson, David, and Rob Kall. "David Swanson Anti-War Philosopher." 28 June 2017.

Miller, Ellen, and Rob Kall. "Ellen Miller; Transparency and OpenGovernment—Armaments Against Corporate and Plutocratic Powers." 6 Nov. 2013.

Thatcher, Robert, and Rob Kall. "Advances in Understanding the Brain, Z-Score Neurofeedback, Why EEG Is More Important than Ever." 9 July 2010.

Madrona, Lewis Mehl. "How To Use Stories to Re-Program Your Mind—Lewis Mehl Madrona and Barbara Mainguy." 27 Oct. 2016.

De Waal, Frans, and Rob Kall. "Frans De Waal; Primates, Fairness, The Evolution of Morals." 17 Sept. 2013.

Capra, Fritjof, and Rob Kall. "Fritjof Capra—The Systems View of Life—Replacing the Mechanistic View." 3 Jan. 2015.

Klein, Naomi, and Rob Kall. "Interview with Naomi Klein." 26 Oct. 2008.

Holman, Peggy, and Rob Kall. "Engaging Emergence, Moving from Chaos to Order." 21 Dec. 2011.

Schwartz, Gary, and Rob Kall. "Afterlife, Dream, Parapsychology Studies." 2 May 2010.

Joseph, Peter, and Rob Kall. "Zeitgest Movement Founder Peter Joseph, Interviewed by Rob Kall." 9 Oct. 2017.

Chapter 2

Jackson, Maggie, and Rob Kall. "Distracted: Coming of a New Dark Age." 18 July 2009.

Carr, Nicholas, and Rob Kall. "Nicholas Carr, Author, The Shallows; What the Internet Is Doing to Our Brains." 18 Aug. 2010.

Nye, Joseph, and Rob Kall. "Joseph Nye; Soft Power, Smart Power; The Future of Power." 30 Mar. 2011.

Binney, Bill, and Rob Kall. "NSA Whistleblower." 16 Jan. 2014.

Zuckerman, Ethan, and Rob Kall. "Ethan Zuckerman: Rewiring, Connection Expansion and How Unconnected We Are." 15 Aug. 2013.

Plastrik, Peter, and Rob Kall. "Connecting to Change the World." 9 Apr. 2015.

Taylor, Madeleine, and Rob Kall. "Connecting to Change the World." 9 Apr. 2015.

Trippi, Joe, and Rob Kall. "Unpublished Phone Interview." 17 June 2006.

C, Mihali, and Rob Kall. "Leading Positive Psychologist, Author, FLOW." 27 Oct. 2015.

Hodge, Helena Norberg, and Rob Kall. "Economics of Happiness." 15 Feb. 2011.

Shirky, Clay, and Rob Kall. "Clay Shirky; Social Media Visionary." 17 June 2011.

Pipher, Mary, and Rob Kall. "Mary Pipher; Being an Activist in Discouraging Times, in a Red State." 24 July 2014.

Levoy, Gregg, and Rob Kall. "Gregg Levoy; Opening the Window to a Science of Passion." 11 Feb. 2015.

Meade, Michael, and Rob Kall. "Michael Meade; Apocalypse, Living in the Shadow of Democracy, and Why the World Doesn't End." 2 May 2013.

Chapter 3

Lakoff, George, and Rob Kall. "George Lakoff—Language and Value Guru to The Left." 18 Mar. 2010.

Clark, Roy Peter, and Rob Kall. "Roy Peter Clark; The Glamour of Grammar." 29 Sept. 2010.

Smith, Pamela Jay, and Rob Kall. "Pamela Jaye Smith; Mythic, Archetypal & Symbolic Aspects of Evil, Bad Guys, Sociopaths and the Dark Side." 9 Sept. 2013.

Medrona, Lewis Mehl, and Rob Kall. "How To Use Stories to Re-Program Your Mind—Lewis Mehl Madrona and Barbara Mainguy." 27 Oct. 2016.

Medrona, Lewis Mehl, and Rob Kall. "Tapping the Power of Stories to Make Change Happen: Lewis Mehl-Madrona and Barbara Mainguy." 28 Oct. 2016.

Vogler, Chris, and Rob Kall. "Chris Vogler; Can There Be Blockbuster Movies and Stories Using an Occupy/Bottom Up/Horizontal 'Collective' Hero?" 31 May 2012.

Korten, David, and Rob Kall. "When Corporations Rule the World." 6 Oct. 2008.

Rushkoff, Douglas, and Rob Kall. "Douglas Rushkoff; Throwing Rocks at the Google Bus—Big Is Bad." 14 June 2016.

Chapter 4

Maher, Katherine, and Rob Kall. "Katherine Maher—Wikipedia And Counter-revolution, Dark Spaces, and Ways to Tap and Enable the Power of Wikipedia." 14 Jan. 2016.

Dorsey, Jack and Rob Kall, exclusive, previously unpublished interview, June, 2009 at Personal Democracy Forum

Breitbarth, Wayne, and Rob Kall. "Mastering LinkedIn with Wayne Breitbarth." 13 Apr. 2011.

Newmark, Craig, and Rob Kall. "Craig Newmark of Craigslist.com on Breaking Through Government Secrecy, Building Trust, Transparency." 18 Mar. 2010.

Boyce, David, and Rob Kall. "David Boyce CEO Fundly and Crowd Funding." 28 June 2012.

Lee, Ryan, and Rob Kall. "Ryan Lee: Continuity Income and Membership Sites." 6 July 2011.

Chapter 5

Medavoy, Mike, and Rob Kall. "Mega Hit Producer Mike Medavoy on How Movies & Media Affect USA's Relationship with the World." 12 Feb. 2010.

Nye, Joseph, and Rob Kall. "Joseph Nye; Soft Power, Smart Power; The Future of Power." 30 Mar. 2011.

Slaughter, Ann Marie, and Rob Kall. "Bottom-up Diplomacy and Statecraft." 21 June 2011.

Ross, Carne, and Rob Kall. "Carne Ross; The Leaderless Revolution." 14 Nov. 2012.

Wilson, Ward, and Rob Kall. "Ward Wilson—Rejecting Long Held Assumptions about Nuclear Weapons—They Don't Work and Never Did What They Were Supposed to Do." 15 June 2012.

Wilson, Ward, and Rob Kall. "Ward Wilson—Fighting Lies Supporting Nuclear Weapons." 12 July 2014.

Swanson, David, and Rob Kall. "David Swanson—We Debate and Discuss How to Handle Psychopaths, Sociopaths and Predators." 16 Apr. 2014.

Heimans, Jeremy, and Rob Kall. "Jeremy Heimans; What New Power Looks Like." 25 Apr. 2015.

Shirky, Clay, and Rob Kall. "Clay Shirky; Social Media Visionary." 17 June 2011.

Foran, John, and Rob Kall. "The Future of Revolutions; John Foran." 6 Apr. 2011.

Miller, Ellen, and Rob Kall. "Ellen Miller; Transparency and OpenGovernment—Armaments Against Corporate and Plutocratic Powers." 6 Nov. 2013.

Lesar, Jim, and Rob Kall. "Jim Lesar—A FOIA—Freedom of Information Act Request Master—Tips and History." 11 Nov. 2013.

Whistleblowers, and Rob Kall. "Peter Ludlow—On Systemic Evil, Whistleblowers and Hacktivism." 1 Oct. 2013.

McKibben, Bill, and Rob Kall. "Bill McKibben Ecology Activist, Organizer of the World's Biggest Demonstration." 16 June 2010.

Klein, Naomi, and Rob Kall. "Interview with Naomi Klein." 26 Oct. 2008.

Benjamin, Medea, and Rob Kall. "Medea Benjamin, Co-Founder Code Pink, on Israel's Flotilla Attack, BP Gulf Catastrophe and Code Pink." 3 June 2010.

Sitrin, Marina, and Rob Kall. "Marina Sitrin: Hope for Activists: A World of Successful Protest and Change—NOW—New Ideas, While Rejecting Democracy." 6 Nov. 2014.

Bar-yam, Yaneer, and Rob Kall. "Yaneer Bar-Yam: Applying Complexity Theory to the World's Hardest Problems." 6 Aug. 2017.

Trippi, Joe, and Rob Kall. "Unpublished Phone Interview." 17 June 2006.

Sifry, Micah, and Rob Kall. "Micah Sifry; The Big Disconnect, Why the Internet Hasn't Transformed Politics (Yet)." 7 Sept. 2015.

Flaccavento, Anthony, and Rob Kall. "Bottom Up, Local Economics with Anthon Flaccavento." 4 Aug. 2017.

Greenwald, Glenn, and Rob Kall. "Glenn Greenwald; With Liberty and Justice for Some... and How the Occupy Movement Could Change Things ." 1 Nov. 2011.

Clute , Sylvia, and Rob Kall. "Sylvia Clute: Calling for a Revolution in Justice and Prison Policy." 18 Aug. 2010.

Weaver, Jeff, and Rob Kall. "How Bernie Won." 24 May 2018.

Chapter 6

Lopez, Antonio, and Rob Kall. "The Media Ecosystem." 1 Aug. 2012.

Atkins, Larry, and Rob Kall. "Discussing Skewed News with Larry Atkins." 24 Aug. 2016.

O'Connor, Rory, and Rob Kall. "Rory O'Connor—The Future Of Media Is Social." 30 Apr. 2012.

Goldbard, Arlene, and Rob Kall. "Arlene Goldbard: Art and Story as Activism, Awakener, and Change Catalyst." 17 Apr. 2014.

Borwick, Doug, and Rob Kall. "The Bottom Up Arts Revolution—An Interview with Doug Borwick, Author, Building Communities, Not Audiences." 26 July 2012.

Whitacre, Eric, and Rob Kall. "Eric Whitacre; Conductor, Composer, Developer of the Virtual Choir, TED Speaker." 4 May 2011.

Chapter 7

Bhide, Amar, and Rob Kall. "Amar Bhide Top How the Top Down Economy and Financial Systems Caused Our Eco-Meltdown." 6 Oct. 2010.

Bakan, Joel, and Rob Kall. "11 Years After THE CORPORATION—In Depth with Author/Producer Joel Bakan." 31 Mar. 2014.

Hodge, Helena Norberg, and Rob Kall. "Economics of Happiness." 15 Feb. 2011.

Grayson, Alan, and Rob Kall. "Alan Grayson, Progressive Hell-Raiser." 25 June 2011.

Kunnie, Julian, and Rob Kall. "Globalization's Dangers to Earth and Its People: Interview with Julian Kunnie Part 2." 15 Jan. 2016.

Kelly, Marjorie, and Rob Kall. "Marjorie Kelly: Ownership Revolution: Transitioning from Extractive to Generative Economics." 15 June 2015.

Korten, David, and Rob Kall. "When Corporations Rule the World." 6 Oct. 2008.

Wolff, Richard, and Rob Kall. "Richard Wolff; Corporations Are Threatening and Bullying America." 11 May 2011.

Alperovitz, Gar, and Rob Kall. "Gar Alperovitz; America Beyond Capitalism." 21 Dec. 2011.

Collins, Chuck, and Rob Kall. "Chuck Collins; Answers to Tax Dodging, Ayn Rand Loving Teapartiers." 20 July 2011.

Chapter 8

Lafferty, Don, and Rob Kall. "Don Lafferty New Media for Writers, Authors, Publishers and Everyone Else." 12 Feb. 2010.

Trippi, Joe, and Rob Kall. "Unpublished Phone Interview." 17 June 2006.

Chase, Robin, and Rob Kall. "Zipcar Founder Robin Chase on Bottom up Approaches to Business." 26 Oct. 2013.

Trebor, Scholtz, and Rob Kall. "What to Do About the Monster Internet Platforms: Trebor Scholz on Platform Cooperativism." 1 Sept. 2017.

Brown, Ellen, and Rob Kall. "Ellen Brown—Detroit BankruptcyBrings 'Bail-Ins' To The USA." 9 Dec. 2013.

Brown, Ellen, and Rob Kall. "Ellen Brown; Public Banking, Bail-Outs and Bail-Ins." 1 May 2013.

Brown, Ellen, and Rob Kall. "Ellen Brown Author Web of Debt." 20 May 2010.

McCree, Walt, and Rob Kall. "Walt McRee How Public Banking Can Rescue Cities, Counties and States." 14 July 2017.

Robertson, Brian, and Rob Kall. "Holacracy—the Non-Hierarchical, Bottom-up alternative to Management—Discussing it with Creator Brian Robertson." 11 Nov. 2015

Tinari, Paul, and Rob Kall. "The Mind Boggling Implications of the 3D Printing Bottom-up Revolution: Intvw w. Dr. Future—Paul Tinari." 7 May, 2015

Chapter 9

John McKnight, Peter Block, and Rob Kall. "The Abundant Community; John McKnight & Peter Block; Awakening the Power of Families and Neighborhoods." 25 Aug. 2010

Russell, Cormac, and Rob Kall. "Cormac Russell: Community is not a noun It's a verb." 25 Nov, 2017

Giroux, Henry, and Rob Kall. "Henry Giroux on Trump Authoritarianism, Neoliberalism & Rabid Individualism." 22 Nov. 2017

Narvaez, Darcia, and Rob Kall. "Darcia Narvaez; Morality's Evolutional, Neurobiological, Bottom up Underpinnings." 15 Apr, 2016

Narvaez, Darcia, and Rob Kall. "Darcia Narvaez on the Neurobioogy of Narcissism, Psychopaths, Sociopaths, Empathy, Connection." 26 Apr. 2016

About the Author

Photo by Noah Kall

Rob Kall is an award-winning journalist, inventor, software architect, connector, and visionary. Articles by and about him have been featured in the *New York Times*, the *Wall Street Journal*, CNN, ABC, the *HuffPost, Success, Discover,* and other media. He has given talks and workshops to Fortune 500 execs and national medical and psychological organizations, and he has pioneered first-of-their-kind conferences in Positive Psychology, Brain Science, and Story. He hosts some of the world's smartest, most interesting and powerful people on his Bottom-Up Radio Show. Rob founded and publishes one of the top Google-ranked progressive news and opinion sites, OpEdNews.com, which has seen over 23 million visitors. He started using the internet in 1993 and created his first website in 1995.

Rob is a recipient of the Pillar award for supporting whistleblowers. He is co-author of *Bioprovleniya*, a Russian/English book on biofeedback.

He graduated from Pennsylvania State University with a PA in Psychology and from Temple University with and M.Ed. in Counseling Psychology. He was elected to be a board member of the Association for Applied Psychophysiology and Biofeedback and served two terms as a board member of Tzedek v Shalom synagogue. Rob has published over 130 articles with *The Huffington Post* and over 2200 with OpEdNews.com. He has also had articles published in *Omni Magazine*, *Success*, *Family Health Magazine*, The Drummer, *Writer's Digest*, Commondreams, Truthout, and CounterPunch.

Rob developed/architected software for biofeedback in the 1980s and has been architect for the populum content management system used by OpEdNews and a number of other websites. He has presented his Anatomy of Positive Experience model at the US and Canadian Positive Psychology national meetings and has presented on various subjects at AAPB, AABT, ASPM, NRBS, and other venues.

In addition to OpEdNews.com, Rob's websites include Robkall.com Bottomupmind.com Storycon.org positivepsychology.net smallacts.com Futurehealth.org and brainmeeting.com. Sign up for Rob's mailing list at RobKall.com

Contact Rob at rob@robkall.com

INDEX